I0799848

IMAGES
of America

NESHANIC AND NESHANIC STATION

On the Cover: The bridge over the south branch of the Raritan at Neshanic was ordered from a catalogue from the Berlin Bridge Company of Connecticut. The bridge was erected in 1896, and it is pictured here about 1906. Only 50 of these bridges still remain of the more than 1,000 constructed. The bridge is listed on the National Register of Historic Places as part of Hillsborough's Neshanic Mills Historical District. (Photograph courtesy of Harry Smith.)

IMAGES
of America

NESHANIC AND NESHANIC STATION

Neshanic Station Historical Society

ARCADIA
PUBLISHING

Copyright © 1999 by Neshanic Station Historical Society
ISBN 978-0-7385-0140-6

Published by Arcadia Publishing
Charleston, South Carolina

Printed in the United States of America

Library of Congress Catalog Card Number: Applied For.

For all general information contact Arcadia Publishing at:
Telephone 843-853-2070
Fax 843-853-0044
E-mail sales@arcadiapublishing.com
For customer service and orders:
Toll-Free 1-888-313-2665

Visit us on the Internet at www.arcadiapublishing.com

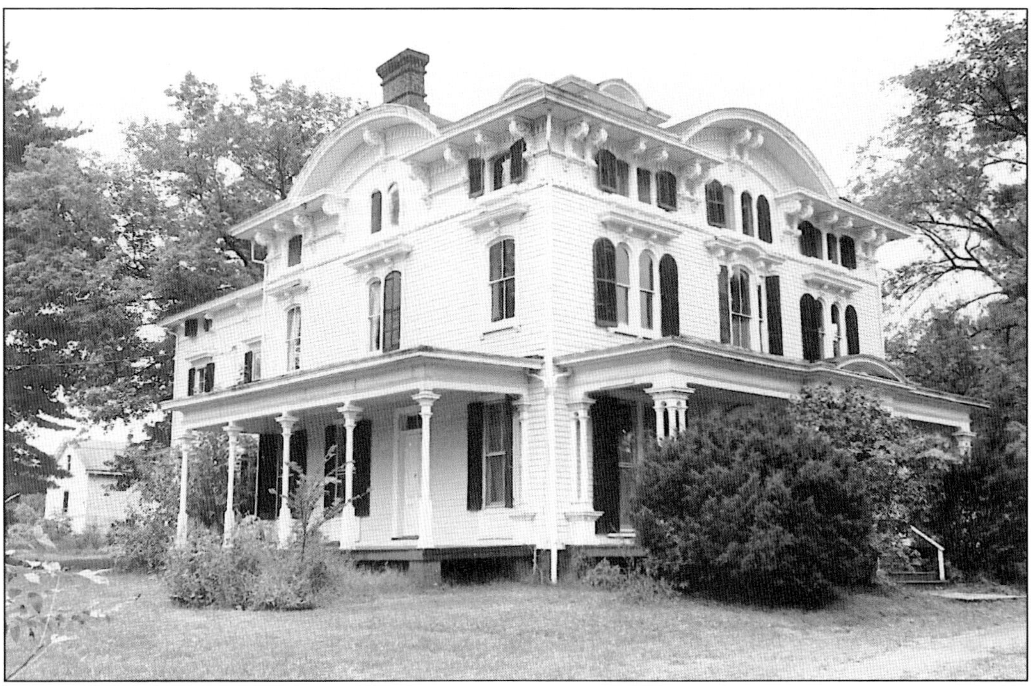

This view of Shadowlawn shows the front porch and south-side entrance facing the Central Railroad of New Jersey. Mr. John G. Schenck, the original resident of Shadowlawn, helped to bring the railroad to the area. The home, started in 1858, had its frame blown down in a storm during the Civil War and was completed at the end of the war. (Photograph courtesy of Branchburg Township Historical Society.)

CONTENTS

Acknowledgments

We thank everyone who offered pictures, stories, ideas, and information. Each and every contribution has added to the quality of this book. A heartfelt thanks to Laurence B. Lane for sharing a large portion of the Lane family glass negatives, and to Paul Kurzenberger for sharing postcards of our area and for putting us in touch with Robert Yuell, who also shared his postcard collection. Thanks to William Schleicher and to Robert Bouwman for their advice.

This project was funded in part by a grant from the Somerset County Cultural & Heritage Commission and Forbes, Inc.

Regarding errors and omissions, we admit to not being perfect and we were limited to the number of pages seen within.

The Neshanic Station Historical Society: Joe Hoff, president; G.W. "Bill" Amerman; Alma Quick Deak; Amy Fenwick Frank; Jim Grill; Robert Guterl; Eric and Traci Gorky; Karen Hoff; Frieda Miller; Ted and Heidi Schlatter Saunders; and Bob and Kathie Schwarz.

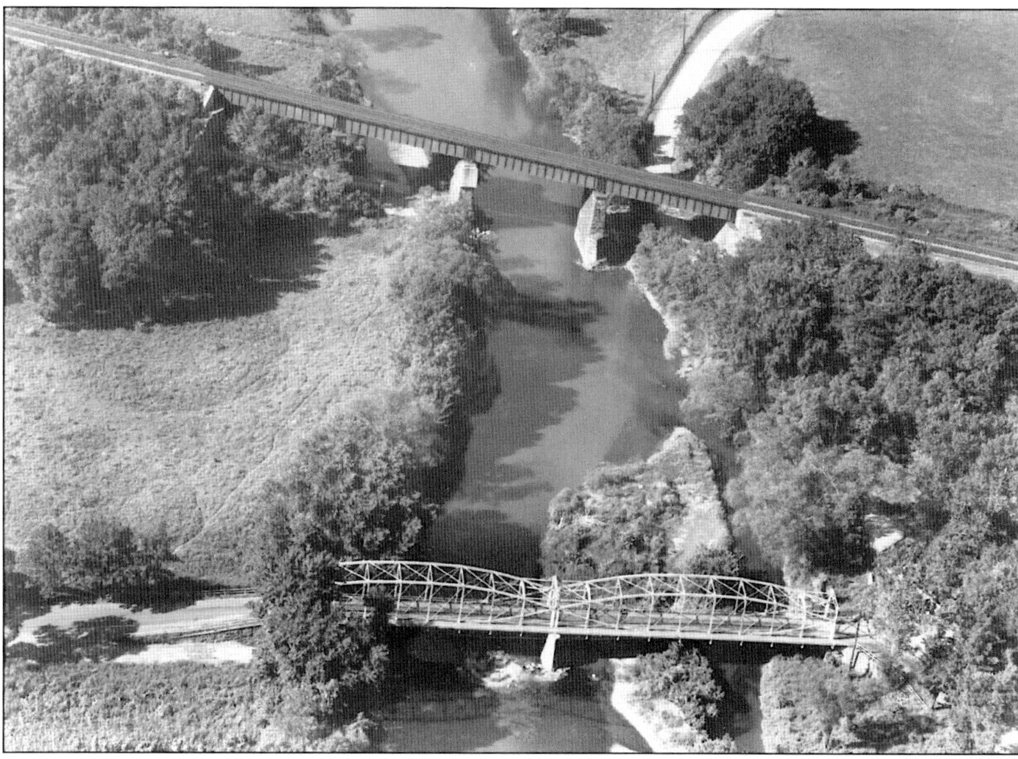

This aerial view of the historic Elm Street Bridge and the Lehigh Valley Railroad Dual Track Bridge was taken by A. Schenck Bergen. (Unpublished work, c. 1998; courtesy of Olivia Cutler.)

Introduction

After the land grants of the late 17th century, the areas that would become Branchburg and Hillsborough Townships gradually became settled. While Hillsborough was organized in 1745, Branchburg (originally a part of Bridgewater Township) was not organized until 1845. Many of those coming to the area after the Revolutionary War were veterans. Amwell Road was a main thoroughfare from the earliest days, and the village of Neshanic was formed around the traffic that passed through. The name is said to have originated from the name for the area, which was based on the curved South Branch of the Raritan River that was seen to resemble the neck of a goose. During this period, the population in the area grew sufficiently to merit the organization of the Reformed Dutch Church of Neshanic in 1752. One of the founders of the Reformed Church was Reverend John Frelinghuysen, ancestor of Rodney Frelinghuysen, a current member of Congress. The first mill in the area was built at about 1770, at or near the end of Mill Lane. A second mill replaced it in 1810, not far away from the first, toward the village of Neshanic. A final replacement built on the site is now a private residence. While crossings over the South Branch of the Raritan River were originally made at a ford, a listing of the bridges in existence in Somerset County in 1797 includes a bridge at New Shannick (Snell's History of Hunterdon and Somerset Counties).

In 1860, much of the present village of Neshanic Station was still a part of one of the area's larger farms, belonging to John Schenck. His home, Shadowlawn (which still stands), was under construction in 1860 when the frame apparently was blown down in a storm. It was completed during the Civil War. Local folklore says that the large trees in front of the house were being planted on the day that President Lincoln was shot. Schenck was a New Jersey assemblyman (1861–1865 and 1872–1874), a state senator (1879–1881), and a state railroad commissioner. He is credited with bringing at least one of the two railroads to Neshanic Station. The South Branch Railroad, a part of the Central Railroad of New Jersey that extended from Flemington to Somerville, was chartered in 1870, and completed soon after. According to Snell, it had stations at "Somerville (connecting with the main line, east and west), Ricefield, Flaggtown, Neshanic, Three Bridges, and Flemington." It was the two railroads that gave the village of Neshanic Station its identity. Previously, the village of Neshanic was known as "Upper Neshanic," while the village of Neshanic Station was known as "Lower Neshanic." The two villages were linked by a road, named "Main Street."

One interesting story about the construction of the Lehigh Valley Railroad embankment has emerged more than once. Apparently, the railroad was originally erected on a wooden trestle, which was replaced with the present earth embankment. A landslide during the course of construction was blamed for the death of a worker who allegedly perished with his mules and wagon. Since it was clear that he had died, his body was left and the work continued with a minimum of delay. The story is consistent with the reputation of the railroads as cruel spoilers during that period. Other stories about Union soldiers during the Civil War bivouacking on the field down from Orville Shurts's feed mill (now the Neshanic Garden Center) and being fed from produce purchased locally are also believable.

A map on file at the Somerset County Clerk's office shows Neshanic Station, in 1873, with the tracks of the Central Railroad, the Easton and Amboy Railroad (later leased and operated by the Lehigh Valley Railroad), the Central Railroad station, and a cluster of homes at the intersection of Main Street and Elm Street. Snell's History of Hunterdon and Somerset Counties describes the village of Neshanic in 1881, as containing "one Reformed (Dutch) church, a hotel (temperance), a district school, two stores and some 25 dwellings. About ten more are at Neshanic Station."

At the end of the 19th century, Neshanic Station reached its commercial high point, and the village of Neshanic gradually lost its commercial identity. The area had become an established fruit growing region, and older lifetime residents recall being told of the long lines of wagons laden with fruit waiting to be loaded onto freight cars bound for the cities. As commerce in the area grew, these railroads came to support two passenger stations, two freight stations, two creameries, two lumber yards, as many as four general stores, a blacksmith's shop, a hotel, a butcher shop, a silver shop, saddlery, and a fruit evaporating company founded by John Schenck.

The fruit trees, which for a time provided the major source of income for the farmers in the area, died early in this century after contracting a mysterious blight. This apparently brought about the failure of the fruit evaporating business operated by John Schenck. After his bankruptcy, the residential nature of the village was enlarged by the construction of homes on the county's first recorded subdivision, "Villa Sites," filed in 1875. Many of the homes on those lots were built in the first ten years of the 20th century, with the sale of lots by the trustees of John G. Schenck continuing after his death in 1905. It was apparently a matter of family honor that the investors in the failed fruit evaporating business were to be paid in full, and tradition has it that they were.

A major fire in 1910 destroyed the lumber yard, the hotel, and a number of other buildings and stores. Only the hotel and lumber yard were rebuilt. Stories about Presidents Theodore Roosevelt, Woodrow Wilson, and others giving short speeches from the rear of a train or from the front porch of the Methodist church are likely to be true since campaigning by railroad was common during this period. Also during this period, there was an icehouse by the river, and the millpond produced a regular supply of ice for local residents and neighboring farms. Electricity came to the village in 1922, and a volunteer fire company was started in 1928. There were plenty of summer baseball games and even some local theatrical productions in the fire company hall, which was built with a stage.

As the 20th century progressed, Neshanic Station's commerce started to decline as the four general stores gradually dwindled to one. Passenger service to and from Neshanic Station on the Central Jersey Railroad ended in 1953. Freight service continued for a few years on the Central Jersey line, but finally ended on this line with the bankruptcy of the Central Jersey Railroad in the 1970s, the ultimate sale of its properties, and even its right of way. By the 1960s, the J.S. Amerman lumber yard, Orville Shurts's feed store, the J.S. Covert John Deere dealership, Hoff's Electric, the post office (since relocated to a larger modern facility), a bar and restaurant in the old hotel, the volunteer fire company, and one general store remained.

Many current residents have lifelong links to the villages. Orville Shurts operated the feed mill that his father founded. When his grandfather, Garrett Stryker Shurts, died suddenly in 1910 on his farm, his widow, Mary Lavina Shurts, sold the family farm and built her home in Neshanic Station so that she could be near her son, Lester Shurts. In 1898, he had started the feed store business that his son Orville eventually took over in 1898. Another resident, Robert May, came here with his father, the first pastor of the Neshanic Methodist Church. It was his father who successfully approached tobacco magnate James B. Duke for funds to aid in the building of that church. G.W. "Bill" Amerman, a descendant of the earliest settlers of the area, operated the local lumber yard until recently and was the major contributor to this book. Laurence B. Lane's father operated the general store in the village of Neshanic until it was destroyed by fire.

Today, Neshanic and Neshanic Station are almost entirely residential communities, but the pictures in this book will give a glimpse of a very different time for these villages. Conrail still makes regular freight runs on the Lehigh tracks, and the hills still ring with the sounds of train whistles. While much of the commerce is gone, the sense of community remains.

One

Neshanic of Hillsborough

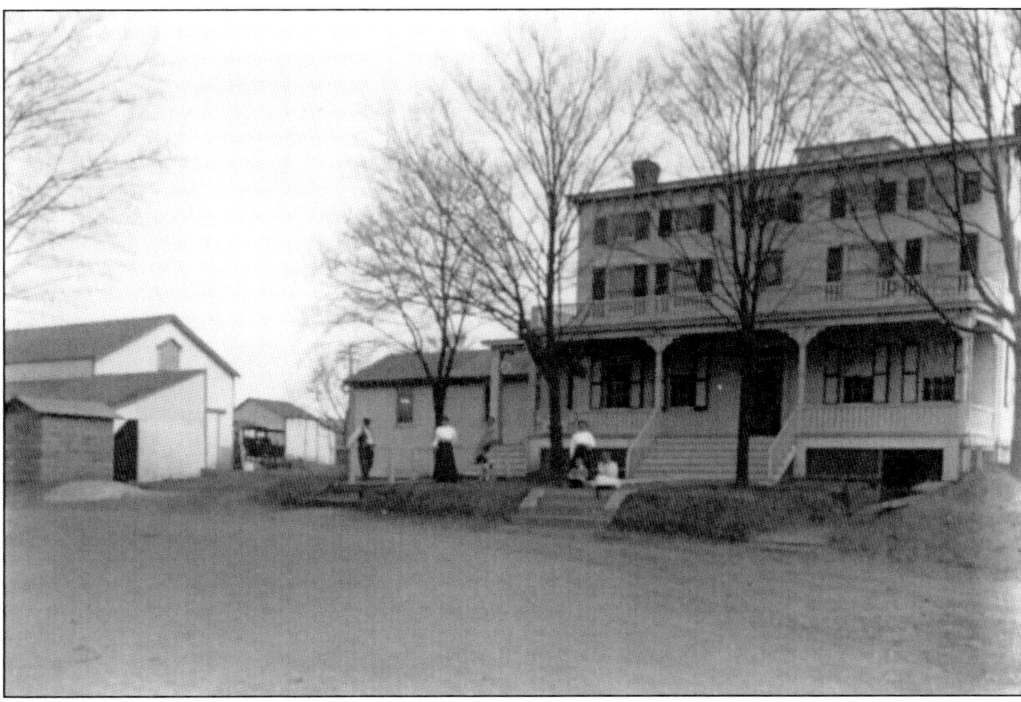

The Neshanic Hotel (724 Amwell Road) appears on the Hillsborough Registry directly after the Reformed Church, built in 1752. The inn and tavern seem to have co-existed, since the inn was listed as a temperance inn in 1873. The post road from New Brunswick to Flemington was established by Congress in early 1838, and the Amwell Stage Line started in that year. The line made trips three times a week between Johines Hotel, in New Brunswick, and Mahlon C. Harts, in Flemington, via Millstone, Flagtown, Shannock (Neshanic), Clover Hill, and Reaville. (Photograph courtesy of L.B. Lane.)

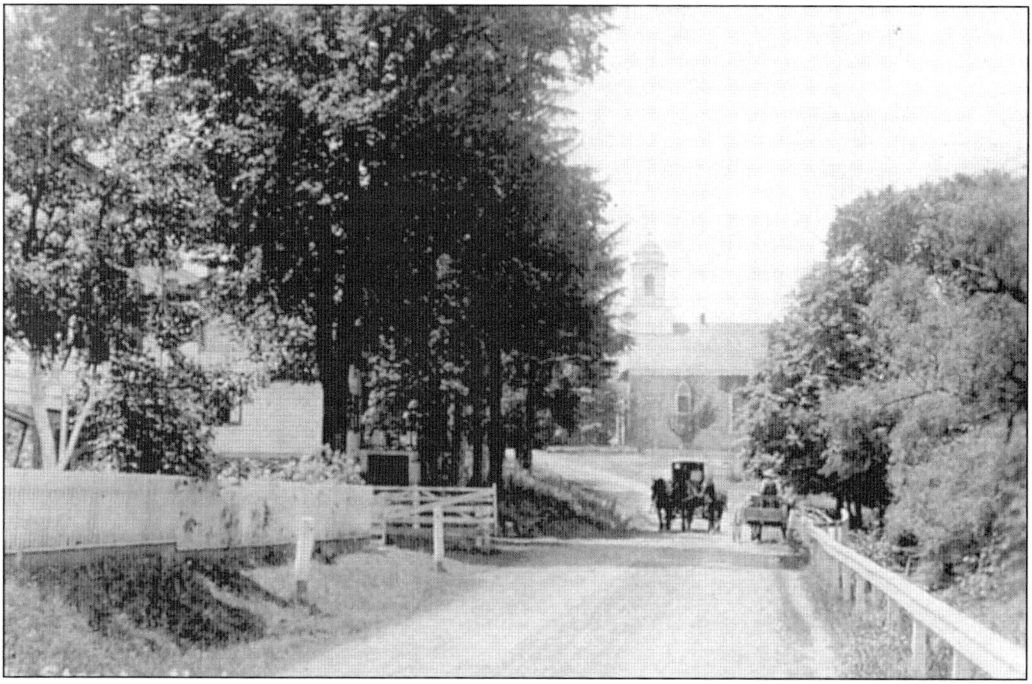

A triple horse team hitch is shown, in this 1908 postcard, meeting another wagon east of Neshanic Reformed Church on Amwell Road. Note the stovepipe on the church roof. Stoves served in all four corners of the church prior to the furnace installation. (Photograph courtesy of Paul Kurzenberger.)

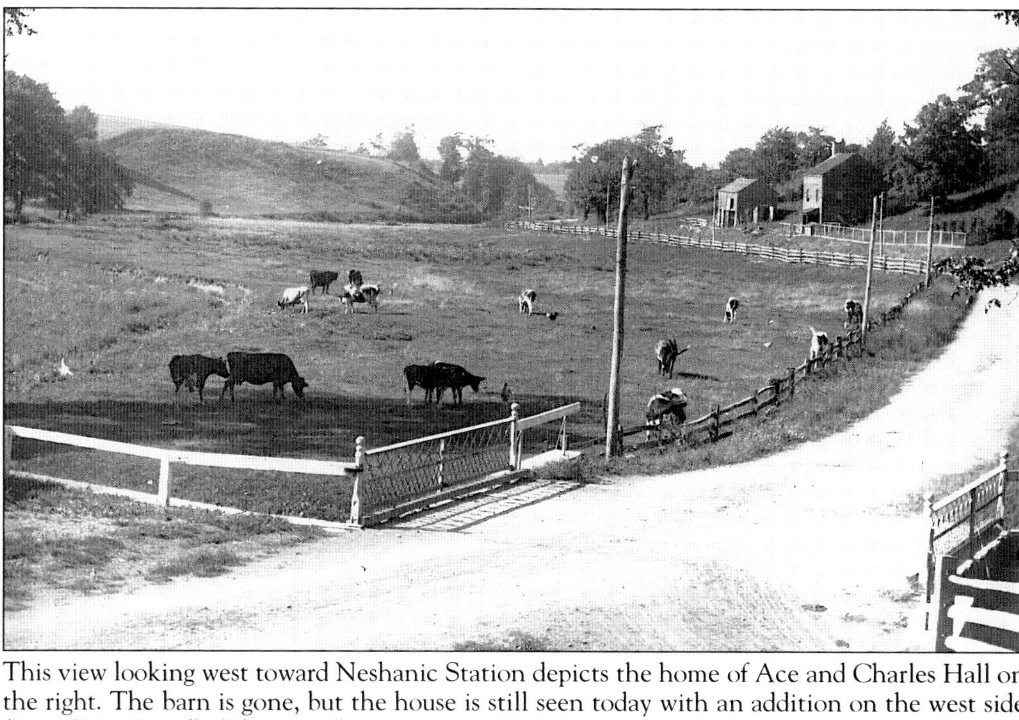

This view looking west toward Neshanic Station depicts the home of Ace and Charles Hall on the right. The barn is gone, but the house is still seen today with an addition on the west side (1144 River Road). (Photograph courtesy of L.B. Lane.)

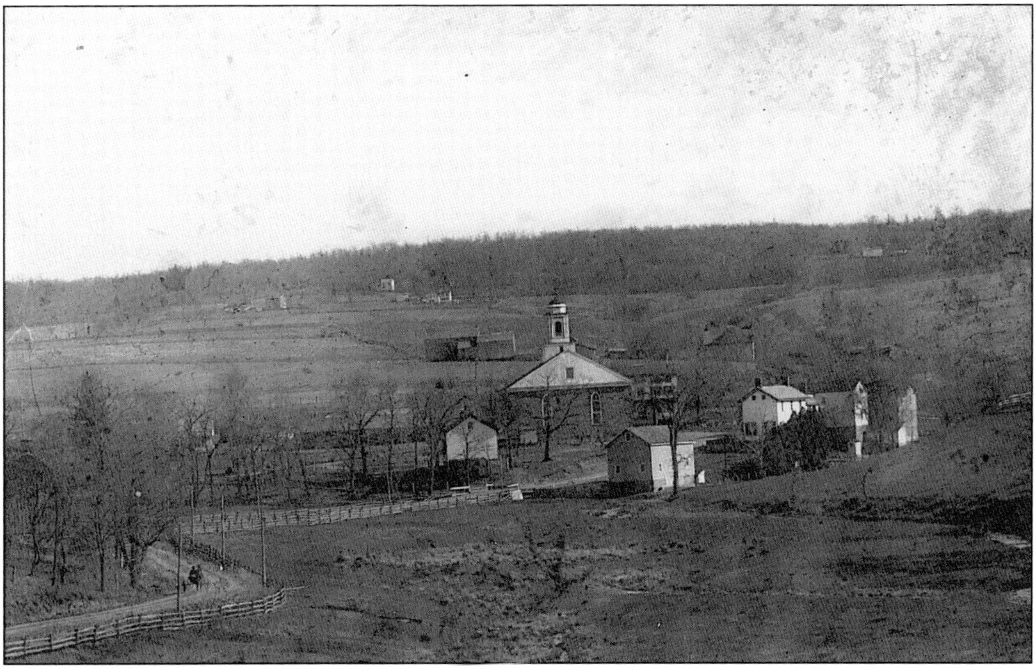

This c. 1900 image presents a view of Neshanic, along Amwell Road, as seen from the McGill Farm (721 Amwell Road), also known as DuBois or Sebring Farm. Note the buggy on the road. (Photograph courtesy of L.B. Lane.)

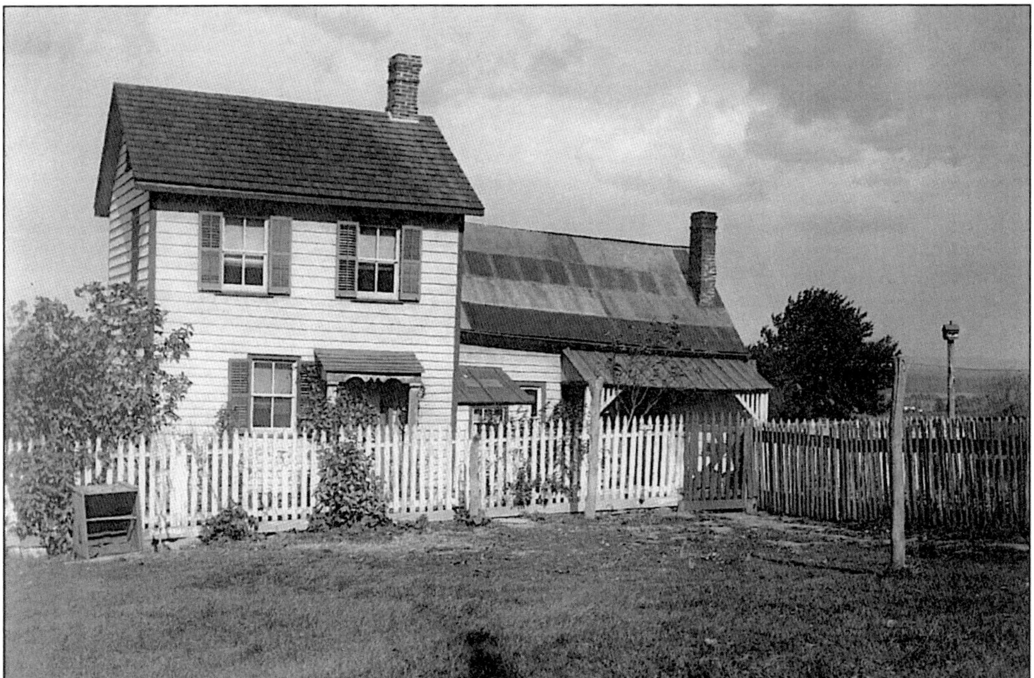

On the right can be seen the original home of Esther Karsner (deceased) off of Zion Road, overlooking the village of Neshanic. (Photograph courtesy of L.B. Lane.)

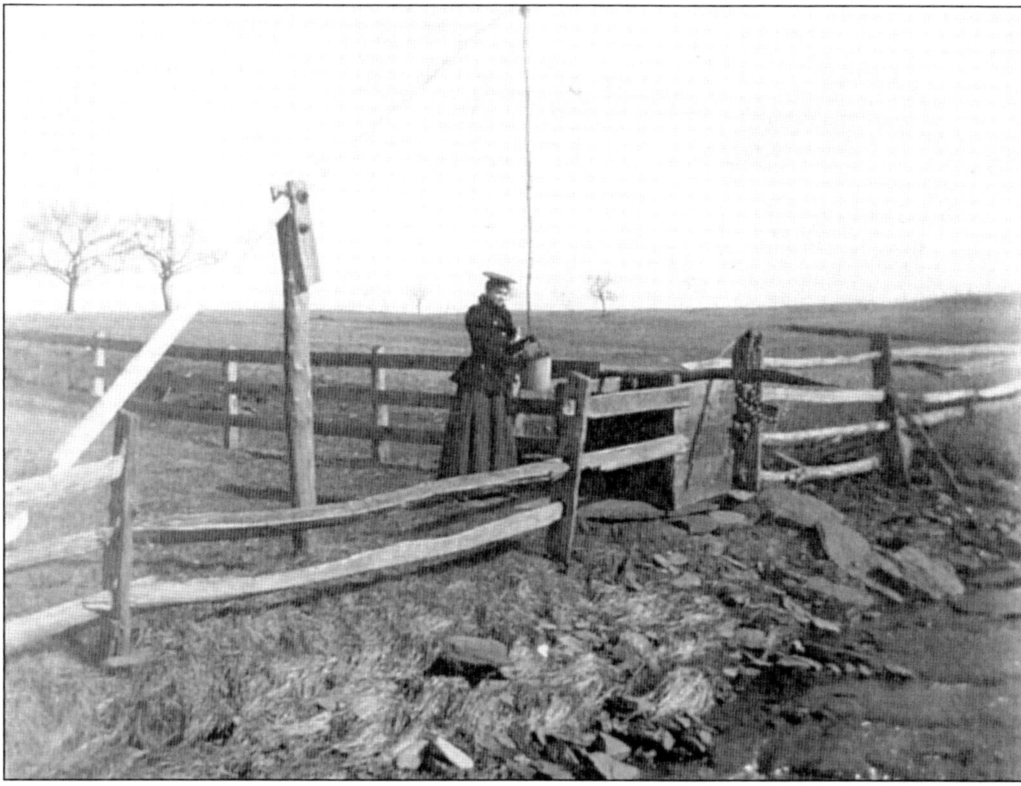

This unknown person is standing next to an artesian well with a dipping pail beam *c.* 1900, located near the foot of Zion Road. (Photograph courtesy of L.B. Lane.)

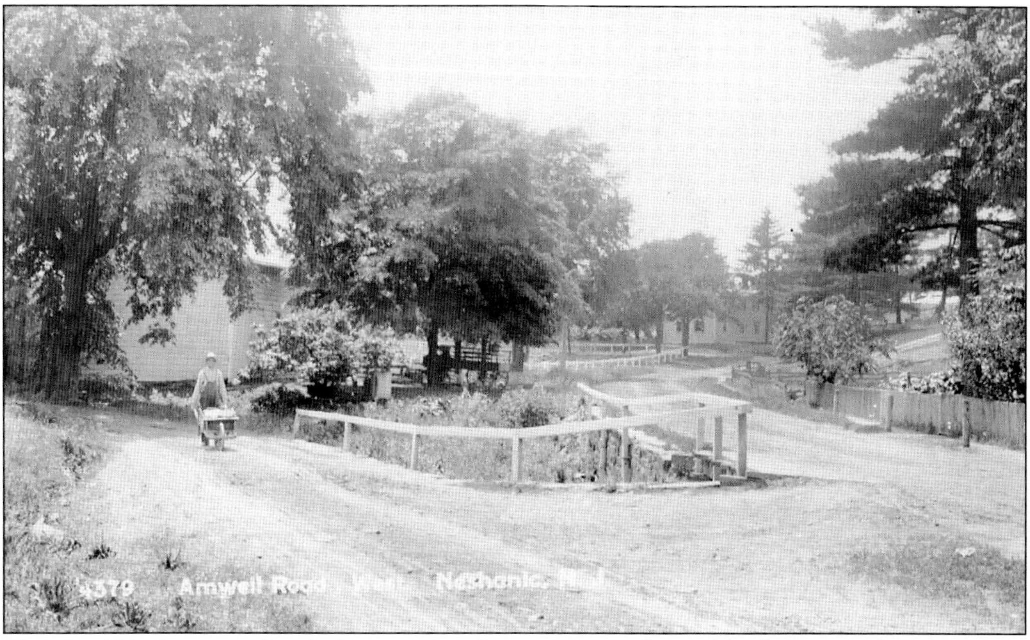

This *c.* 1900 Garroway Reed photo postcard shows Amwell Road looking west (on the right) and Zion Road (on the left). (Photograph courtesy of L.B. Lane.)

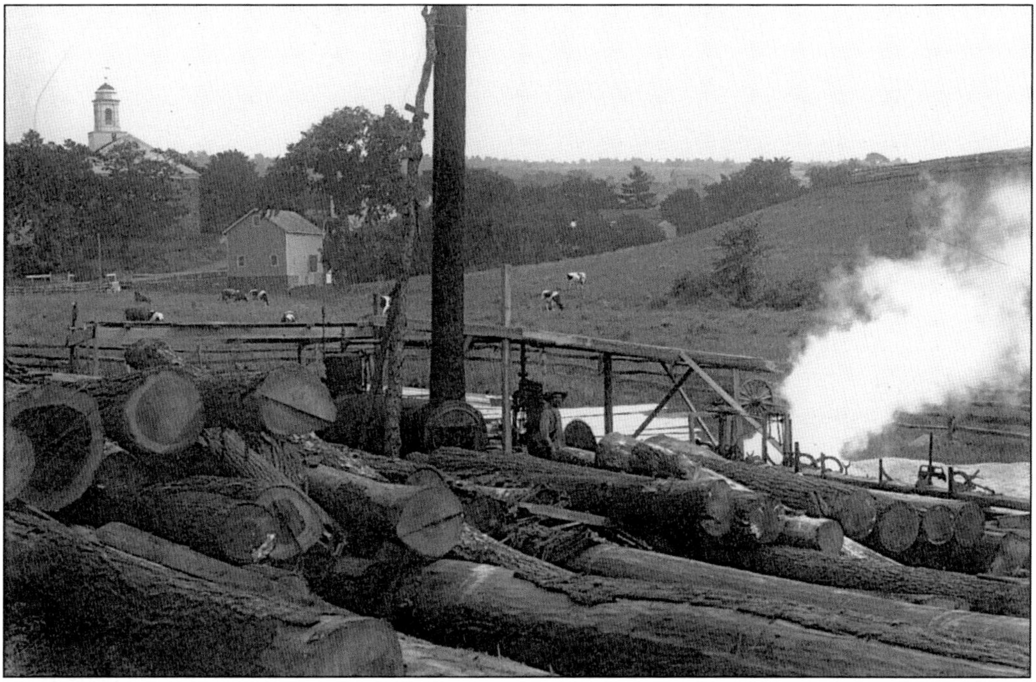

A wood-fired, steam-powered sawmill is shown in this pre-1900 photograph sawing oak logs from the Sourland Mountains. Horse-drawn wagons and sleds brought the logs down to the roadside below the Neshanic Church, seen in the background. (Photograph courtesy of L.B. Lane.)

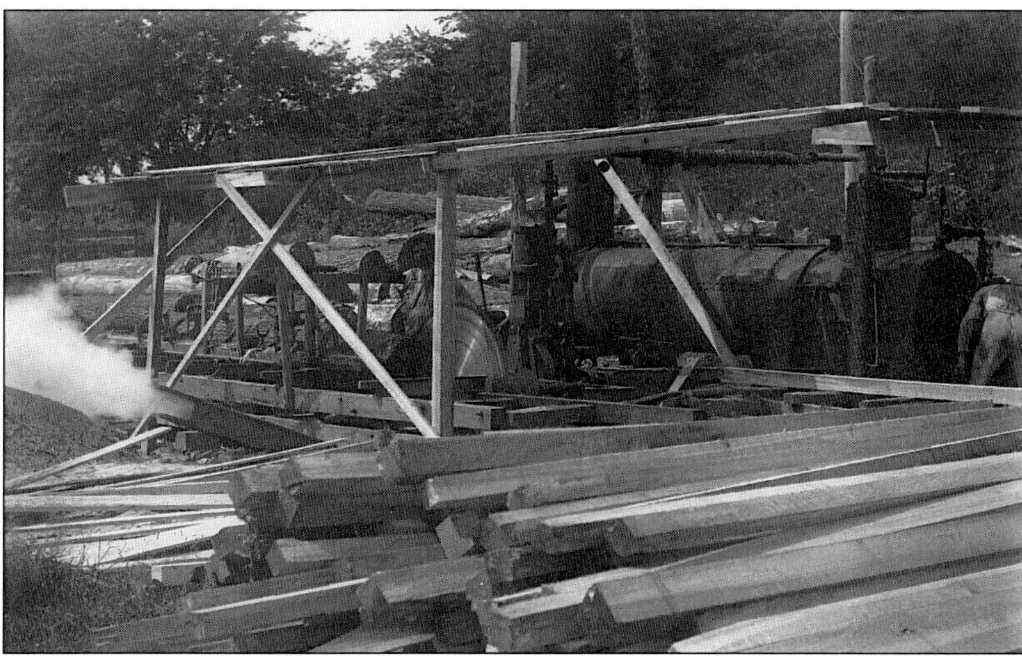

A sawyer is shown in this photograph standing by the running blade. Railroad ties are waiting to be cut to length, possibly for the Central Railroad of New Jersey South Branch Line, which ran through Neshanic Station. (Photograph courtesy of L.B. Lane.)

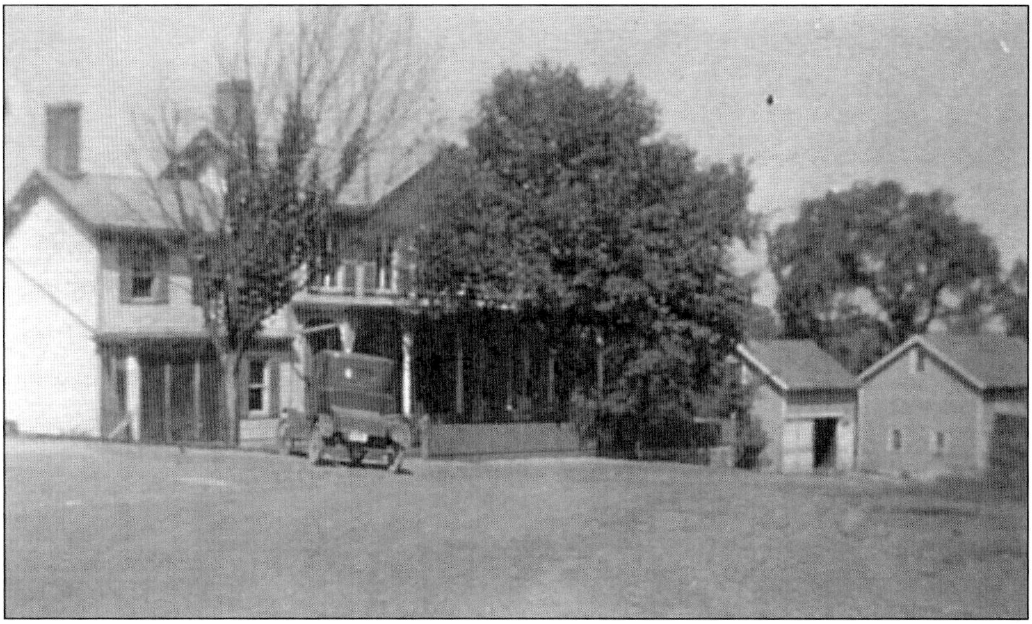

This photograph, taken in 1919, illustrates the home of Dr. John E. Andersen (1143 River Road), alongside the Neshanic Reformed Church, with his Model T parked in front. Dr. Andersen started his practice here in 1874, and he served the community for half a century. (Photograph courtesy of L.B. Lane.)

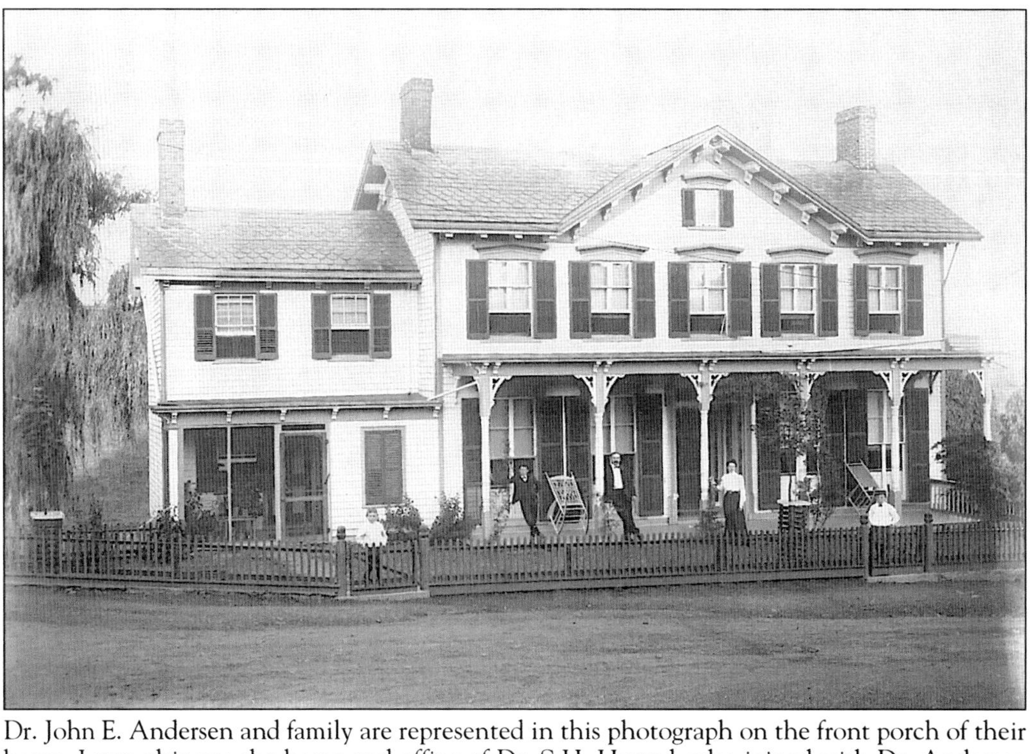

Dr. John E. Andersen and family are represented in this photograph on the front porch of their home. Later, this was the home and office of Dr. S.H. Husted, who joined with Dr. Andersen just prior to his retirement. (Photograph courtesy of Dan Bassuk.)

Dr. Andersen is shown here on Amwell Road with his pet hunting dog in 1919. (Photograph courtesy of L.B. Lane.)

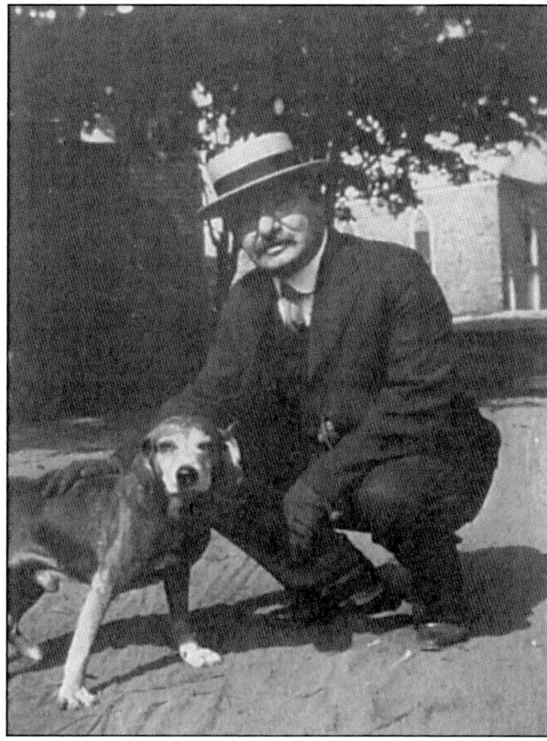

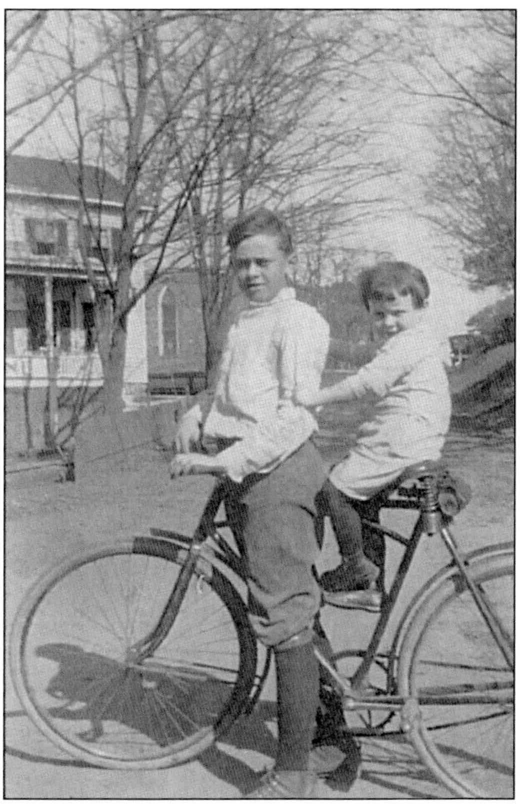

J.C. Lane Jr. is shown here with L.B. Lane (on bicycle seat) on Amwell Road in 1919. (Photograph courtesy of L.B. Lane.)

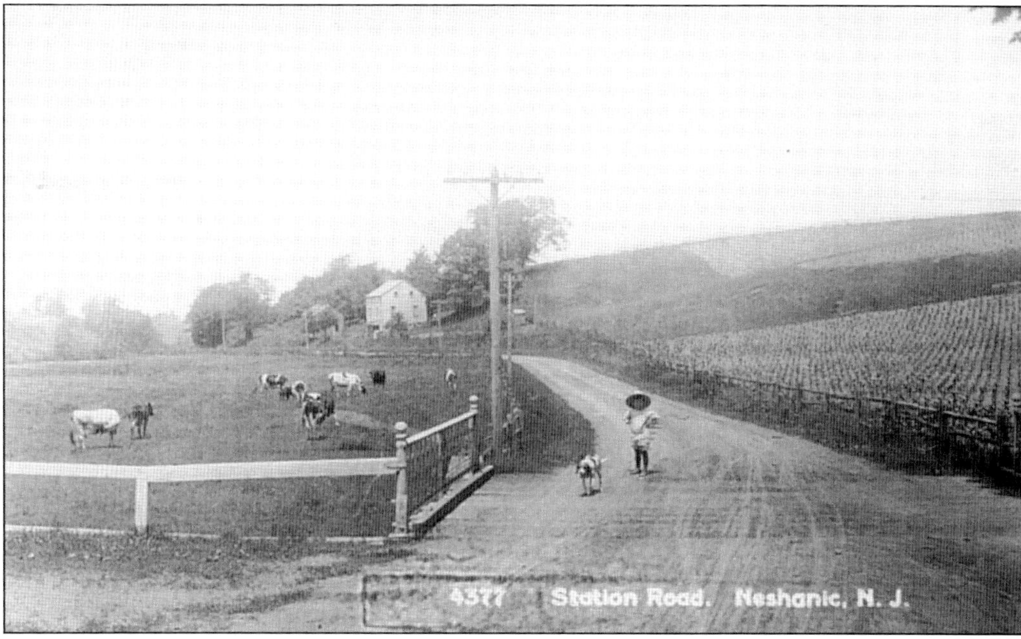

Station Road is shown in this *c.* 1912 photo postcard looking from "Old Neshanic" toward Neshanic Station. Dr. Andersen's dog and daughter are in the foreground by the bridge. (Courtesy of Robert Yuell.)

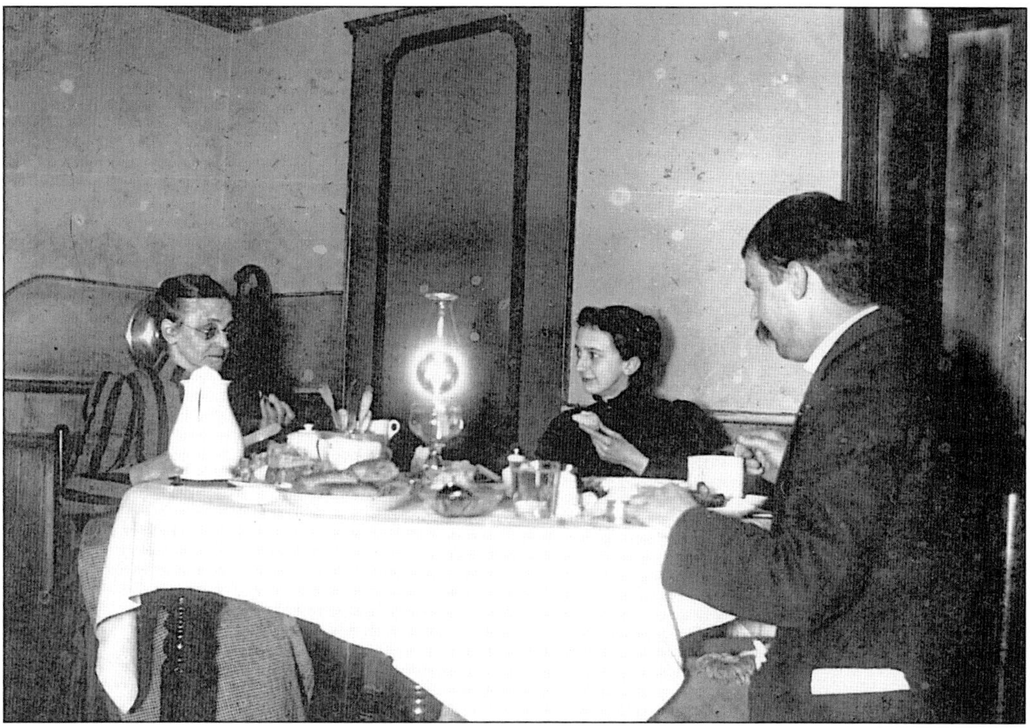
Elizabeth Lane, Laura Lane, and John C. Lane are seen here enjoying Sunday dinner at home prior to electricity in 1919. Mr. Lane operated the country corner store next to the Andersens' home. (Photograph courtesy of L.B. Lane.)

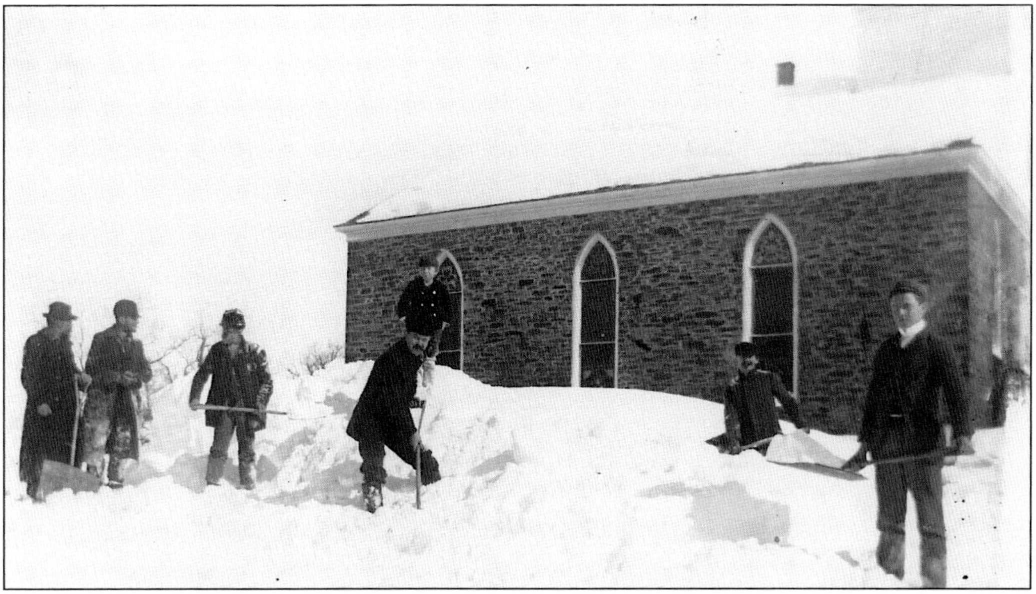

In this *c.* 1900 winter scene, John Lane (in the center with a shovel) is trying to clear the road in front of his store with the help of some neighbors. (Photograph courtesy of L.B. Lane.)

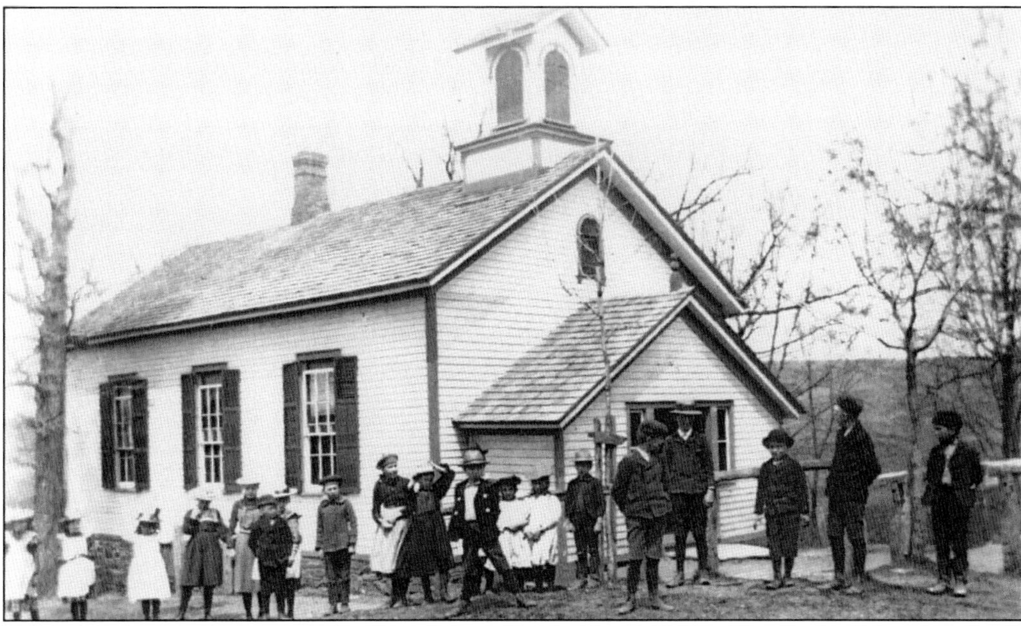

This *c.* 1900 photograph shows the Neshanic School. This one-room school was later used by the Neshanic Reformed Church for Sunday school and now forms the central part of Brookside Hall. Snell's History of Somerset County records that the Neshanic School "probably dates back to 1750." In 1880, it was one of 14 schools in Hillsborough Township. The following statistics are recorded for the year ending August 31, 1879: total received from all sources for public school purposes, $1,183.08; present value of the school property, $25; children of school age residing in the district, 111; average number of months the school was kept open, 9; children enrolled in school register during the year, 65; seating capacity, 20. (Photograph courtesy of L.B. Lane.)

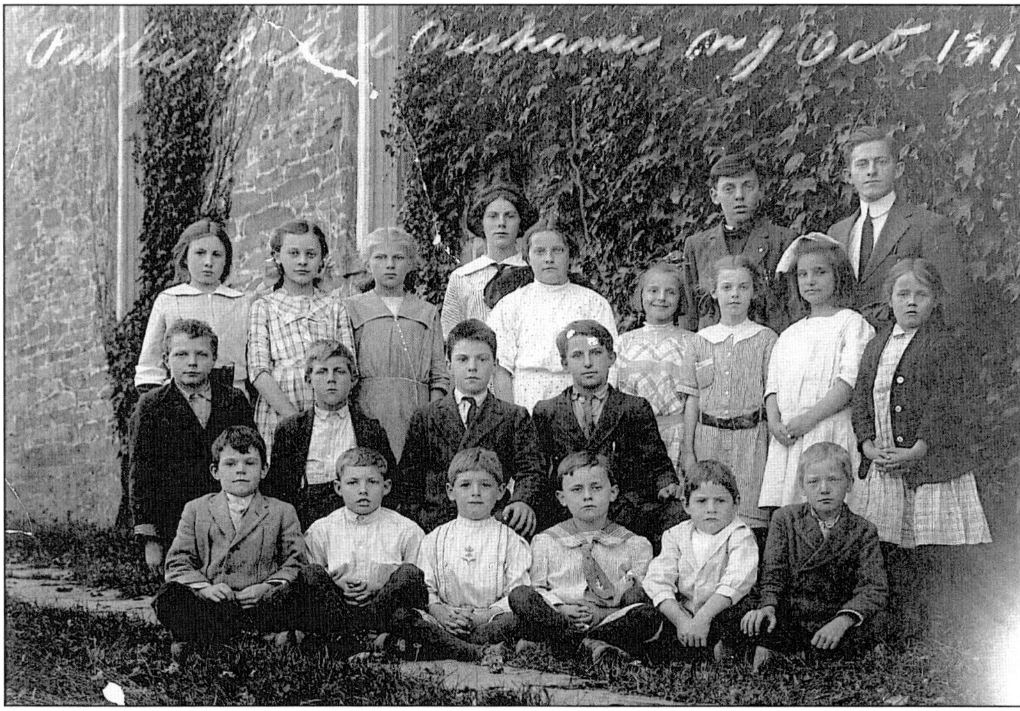

This photograph represents the class of 1913 at the Neshanic School. (Photograph courtesy of L.B. Lane.)

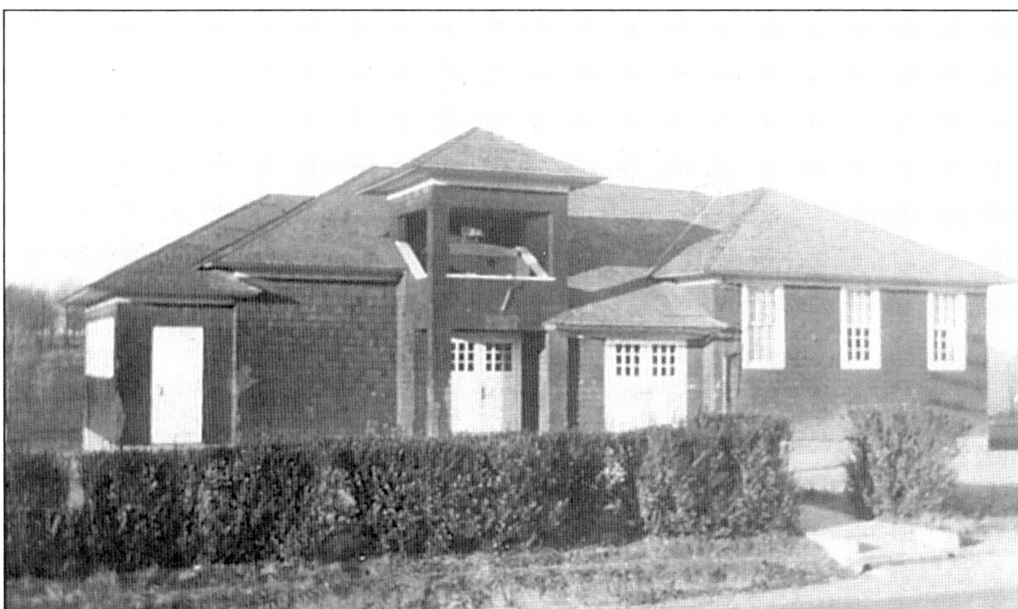

Neshanic School is shown here on Amwell Road around 1935. The replacement of the old one-room school was a period of new design with windows across one side of a building that contained two or four classrooms. This two-room school on Amwell Road in Hillsborough was built in 1913. After its use as a school was discontinued, it housed the Neshanic Printing Co. Today, it is home to the Somerset Valley Players. (Photograph courtesy of the Quick Family.)

Two

NESHANIC STATION OF BRANCHBURG

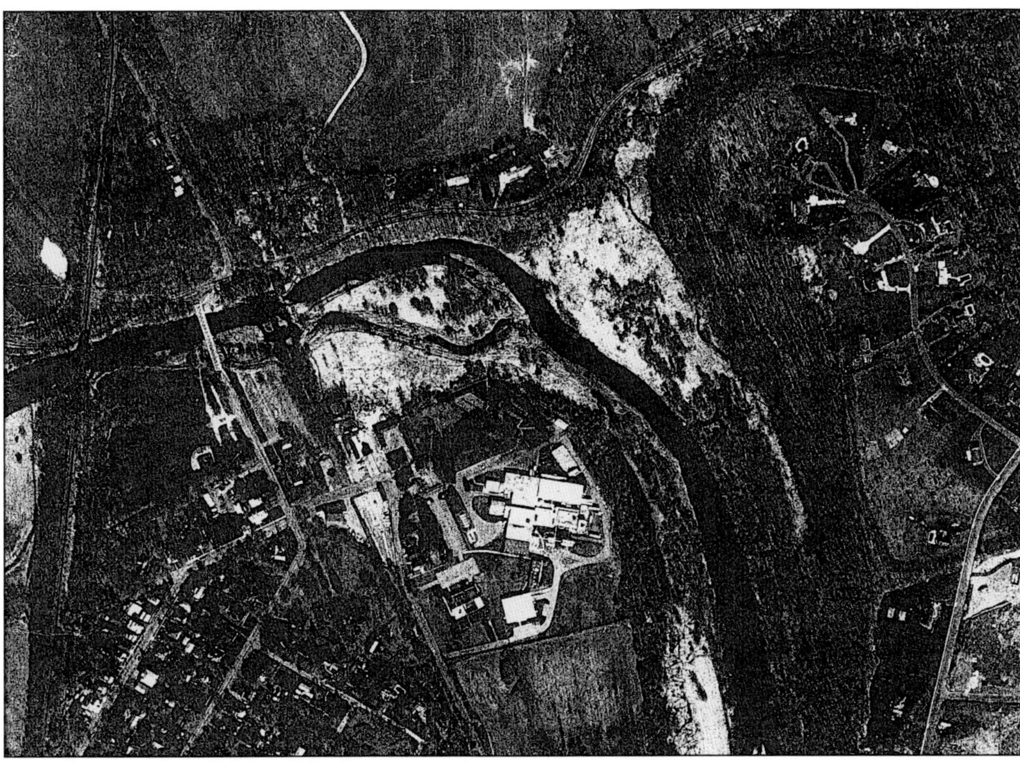

Neshanic was named by the Lenni Lenape Indians for "goose neck," as can be seen in this photograph of the south branch of the Raritan River as it winds through the Neshanic Station area. (Photograph from Somerset County 1995 Aerial Survey.)

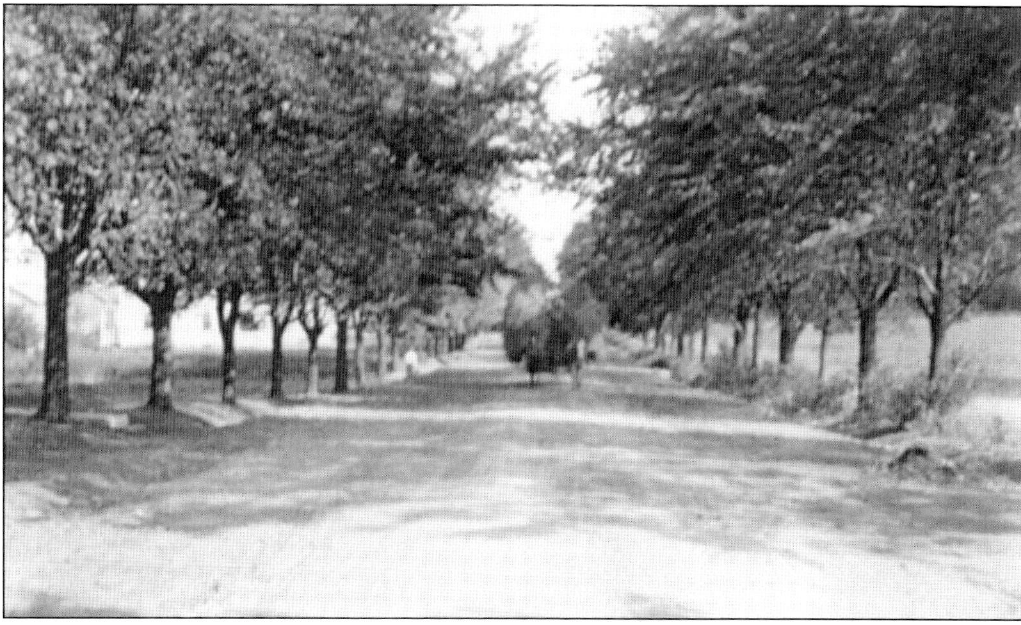

The main street of Neshanic Station is shown here as it appeared around 1900. A full load of hay is making its way to the hay press at J.S. Amerman Co. on this tree-lined street, now known as Maple Avenue. (Photograph courtesy of Paul Kurzenberger.)

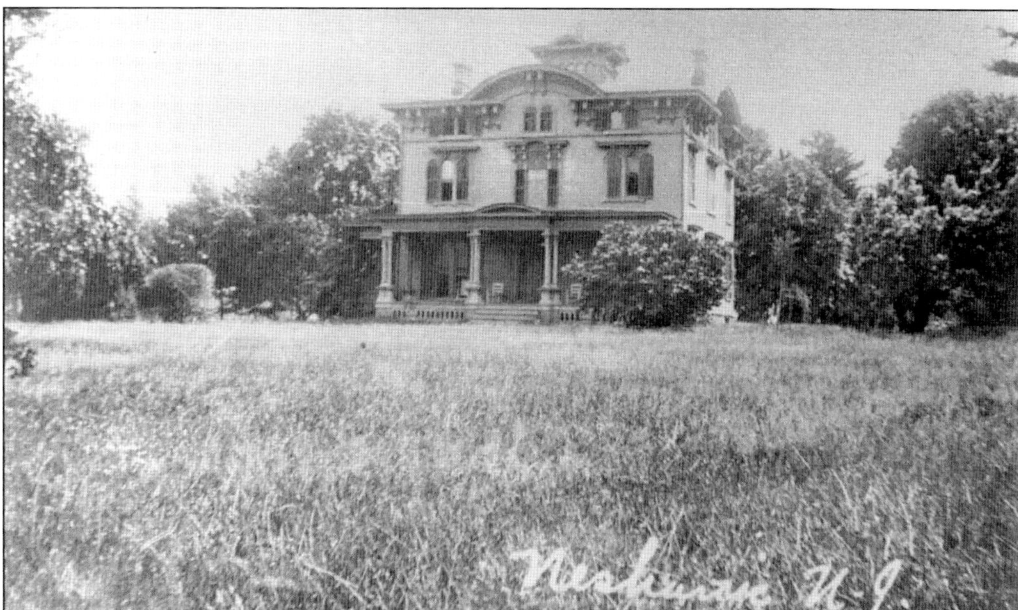

Shadowlawn (304 Maple Avenue) was built in the 1860s and is an excellent example of Italianate residential architecture. John G. Schenck, who served in the New Jersey State Senate and Assembly during the 1860s and 1870s, built the residence as a home for his family and a centerpiece for his peach farm, which encompassed most of the present-day village of Neshanic Station. He landscaped the area around the home with many trees and shrubs, the most notable being a lovely willow oak which provides a beautiful canopy shadowing much of the large front lawn. (Photograph courtesy of Neshanic Station Historical Society.)

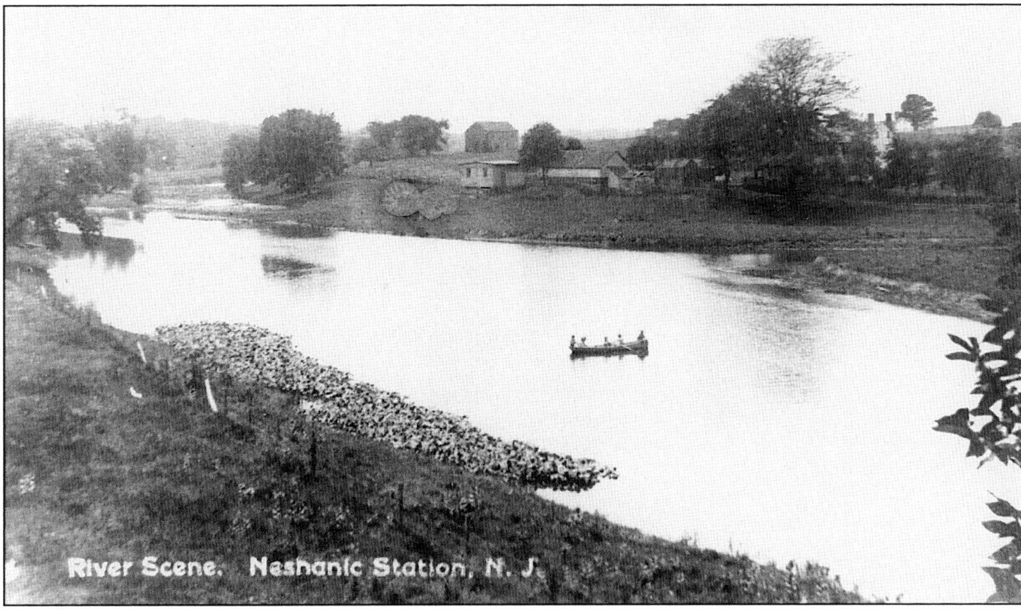

Here, a group of people enjoy the pleasure of a peaceful mid-summer boat trip. In the past, as well as the present, the village has provided relaxation for a variety of people who have come to fish and canoe along the south branch of the Raritan River. (Photograph courtesy of M. Jane [Nevius] Brown.)

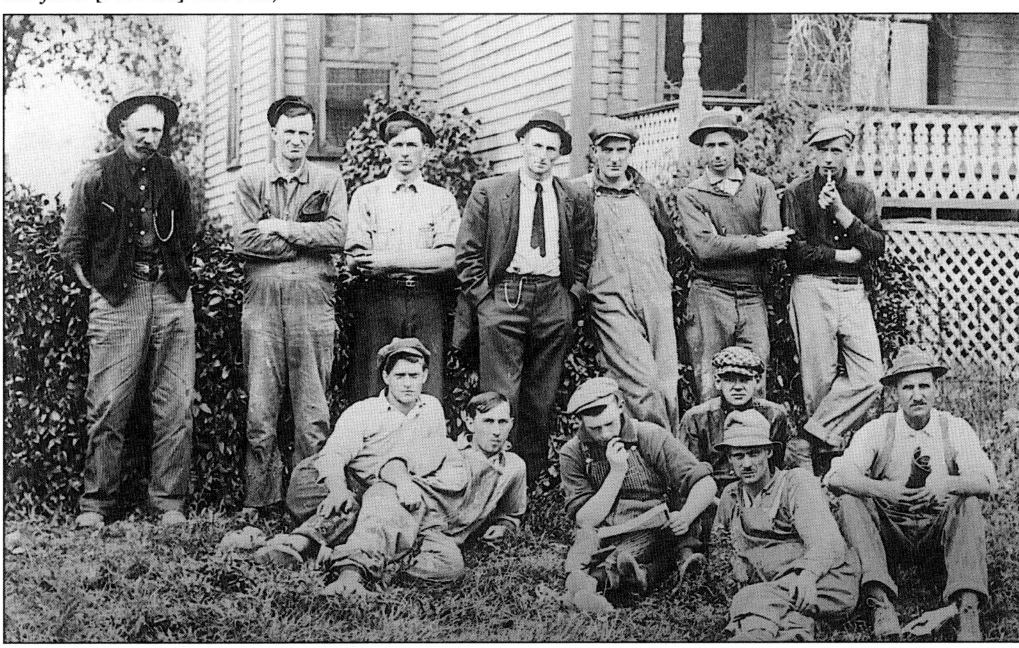

In order to provide protection for this farming community, the Neshanic Station Vigilant Society was formed in 1920, and it included many prominent citizens of the time. The members paid dues for the protection of the society. Once a theft was reported, the society was responsible for the recovery of the stolen animal or article. If not found, the society promised to reimburse the member for the theft. The society quickly went bankrupt. (Photograph courtesy of M. Jane [Nevius] Brown.)

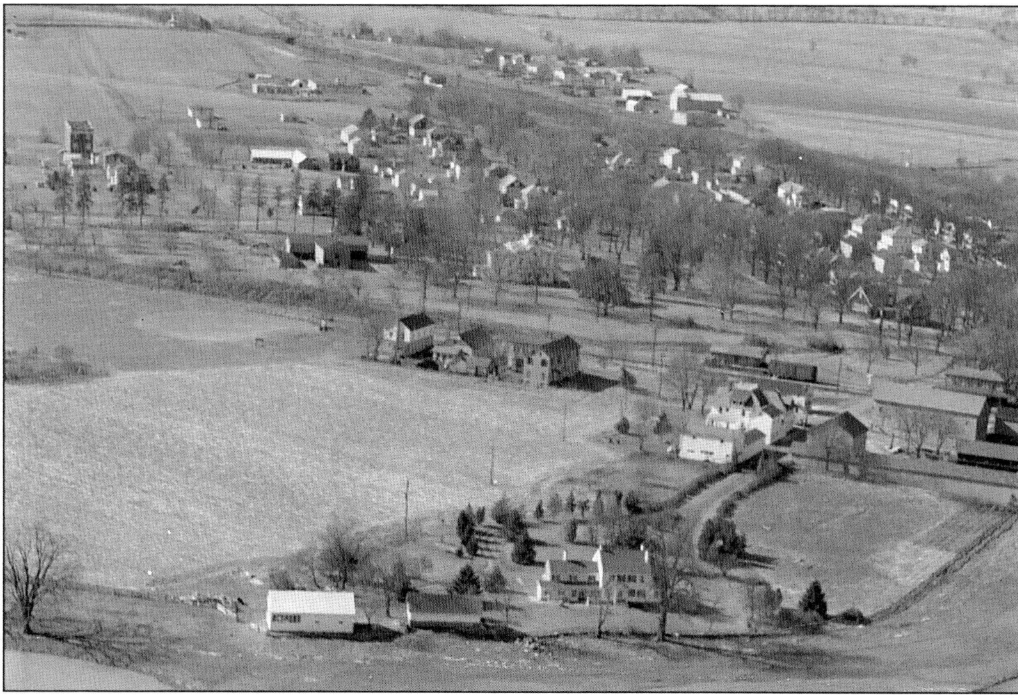

This aerial photograph, taken in 1952, shows the complete subdivision of John Schenck's former peach farm stretching into the village of Neshanic Station. (Photograph by Walter Kostro.)

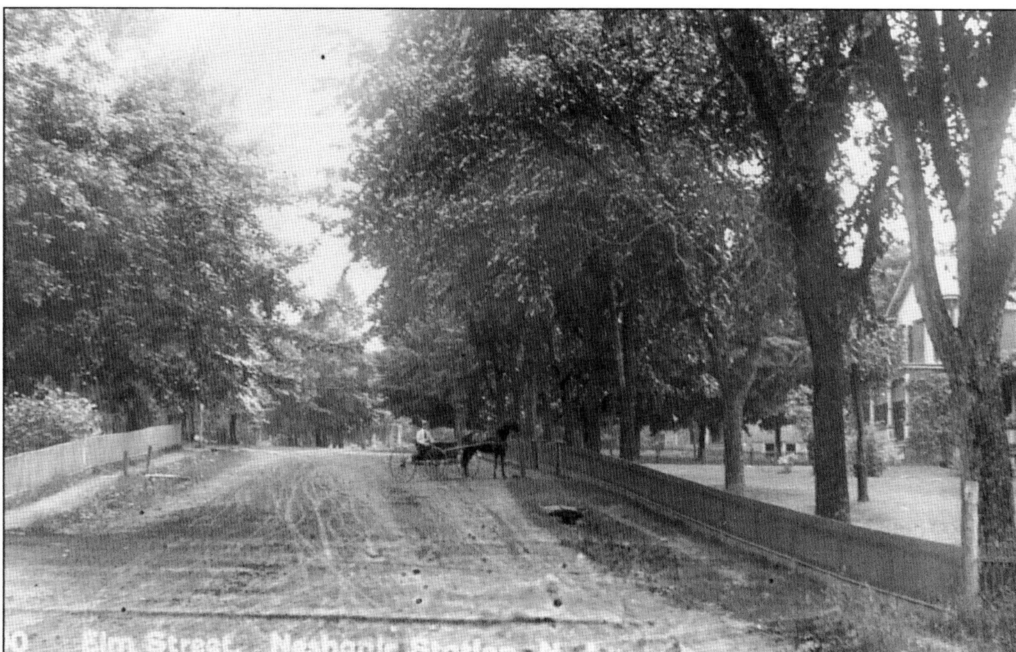

This c. 1910 photograph shows a morning carriage ride along Elm Street, looking southwest from the river. The Covert and Opie homes can be seen on the far right. (Photograph courtesy of Paul Kurzenberger.)

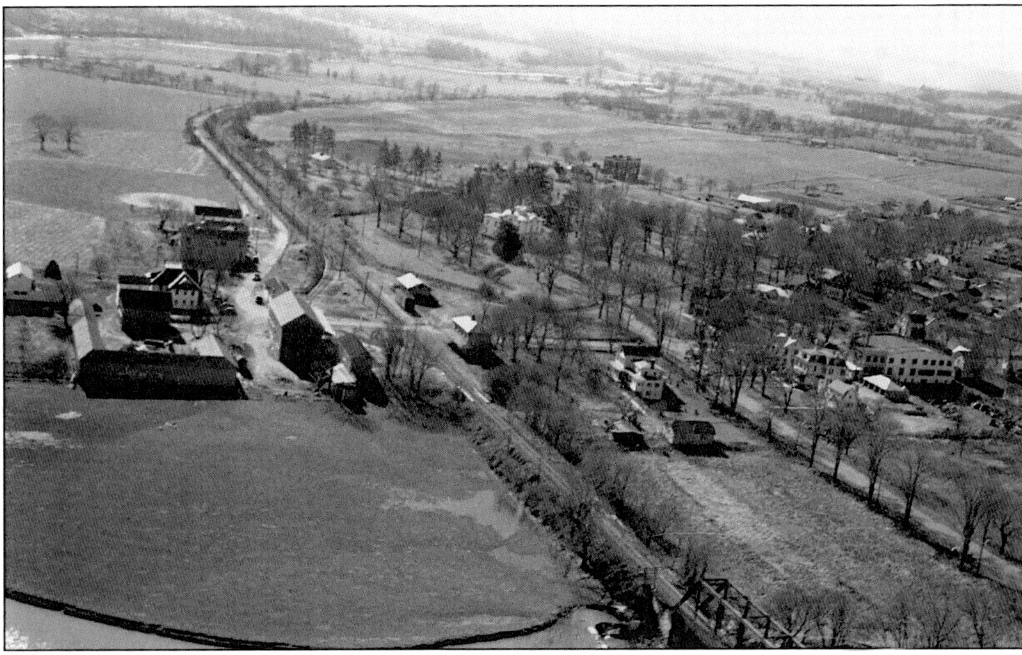

This view is of Neshanic Station and the surrounding farmlands in the winter of 1952-1953. The flea market grounds can be seen to the right of the Central New Jersey Railroad Station. Fairview School, the two-story brick building, which can be seen well in the upper center portion of the image, was later demolished. (Photograph taken by Walter J. Kostro, courtesy of John Vermeulen & Son.)

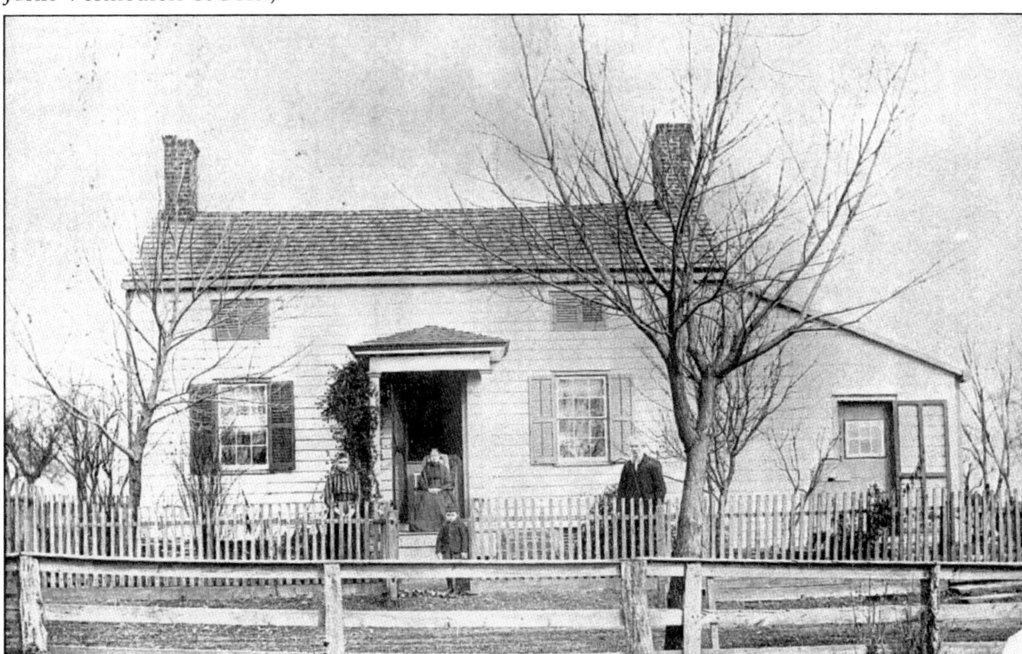

Homewood Acres (322 Blackpoint Road) still stands on Blackpoint Road. Here the original home can be seen as it appeared in 1887. (Photograph courtesy of Richard Hammel.)

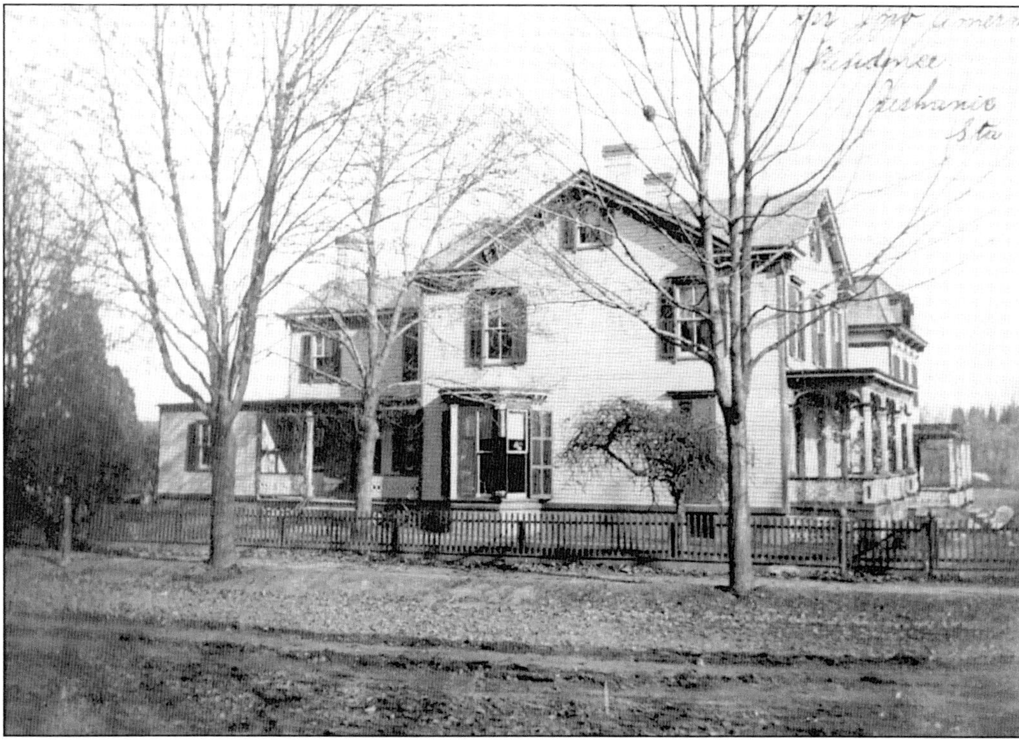

The John Amerman residence, located at 101 Elm Street, is seen here in 1910 and was later the home of J.S.Covert. (Photograph courtesy of Paul Kurzenberger.)

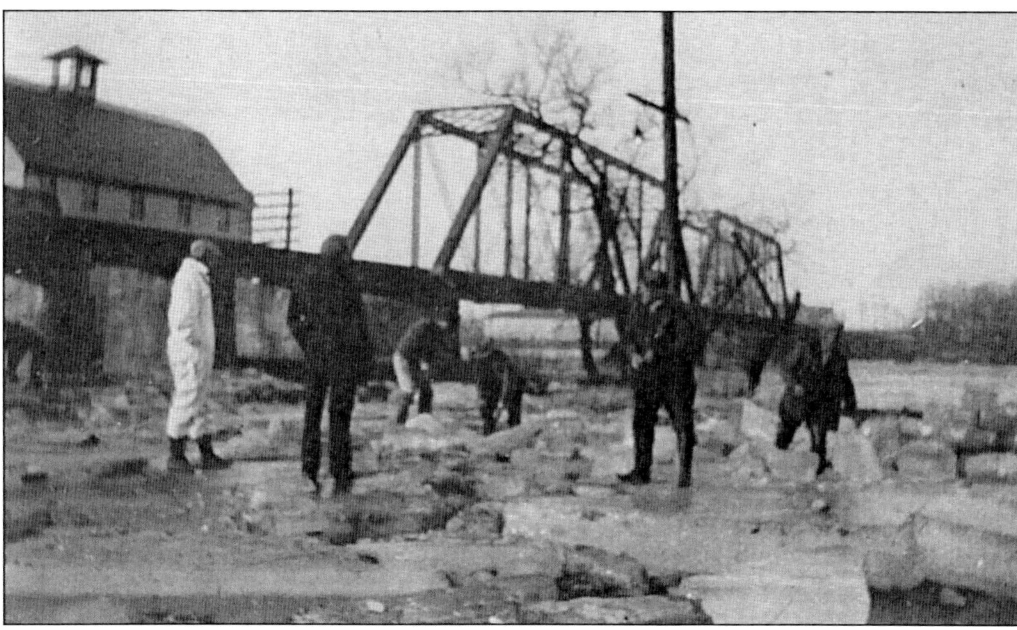

Here, in the shadow of the Amerman Mill, residents can be seen harvesting the ice that formed along the south branch of the Raritan River in March 1934. (Photograph courtesy of Mary Hausch Sixt.)

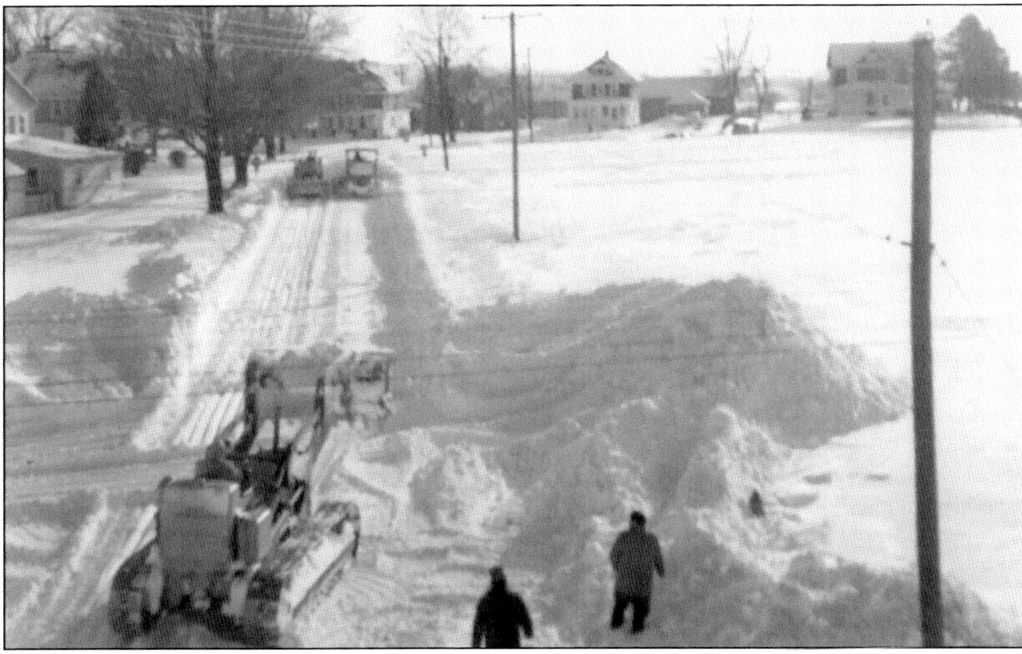

Winters along the south branch of the Raritan River often challenged residents. A view from atop the Conrail freight line overpass, looking south along Pleasant Run Road, shows the heavy equipment that was needed to dig out of a major storm during the winter of 1966. (Photograph courtesy of G.W. Amerman.)

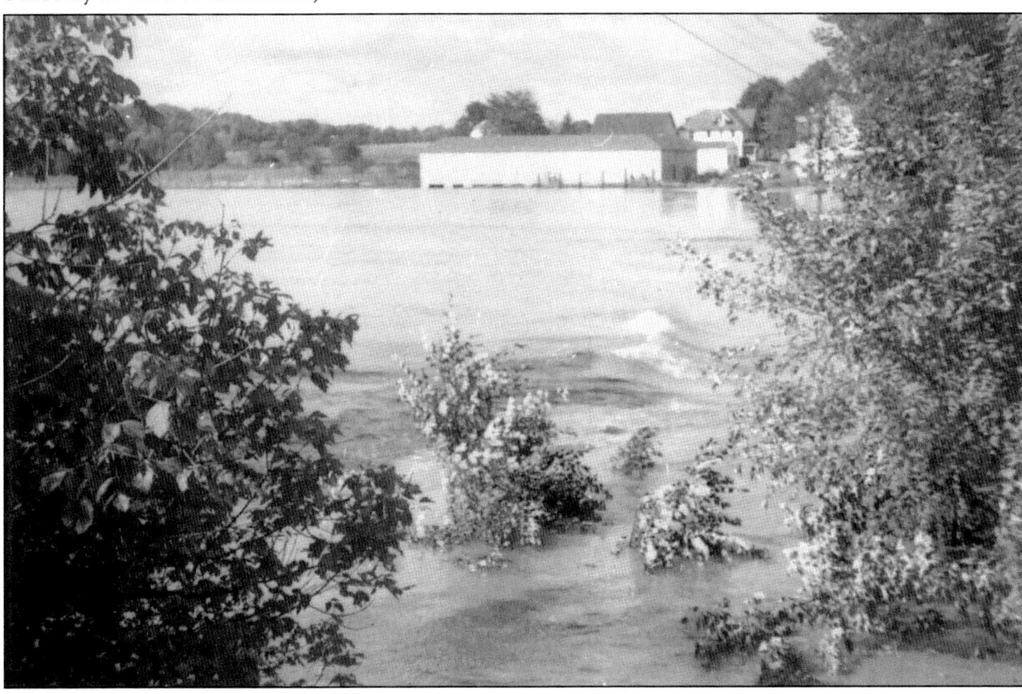

On August 28, 1971, Hurricane Doria struck the village of Neshanic Station, leaving a flood in her wake. The swollen banks of the south branch can be seen cresting. (Photograph courtesy of G.W. Amerman.)

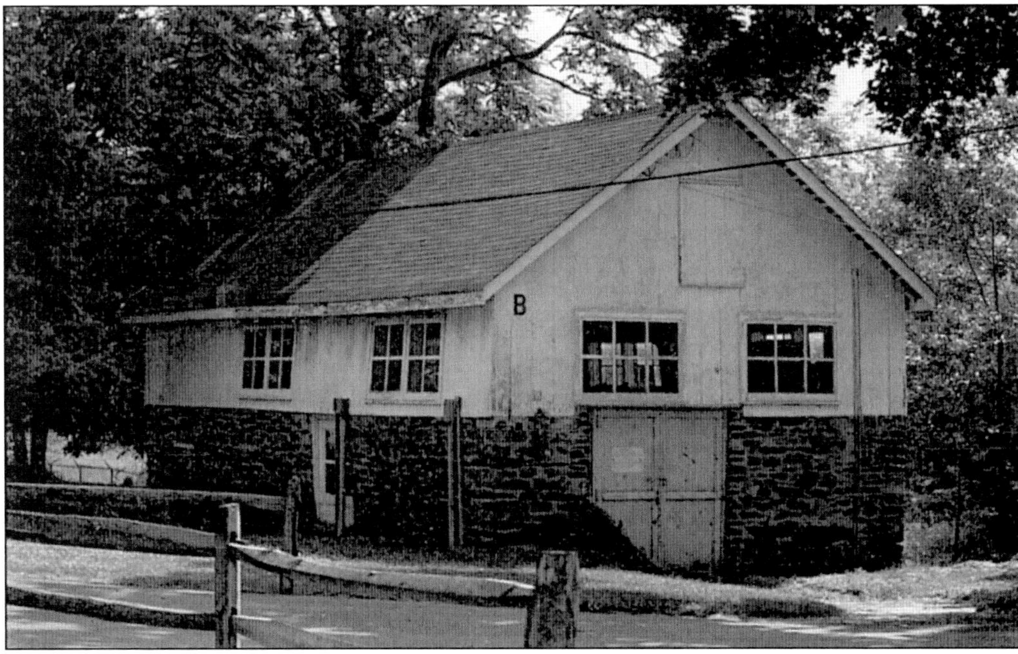

The Brokaw Ice House, shown here, still stands behind the Neshanic Inn (now Murphy's Crocodile Inn). (Photograph courtesy of G.W. Amerman.)

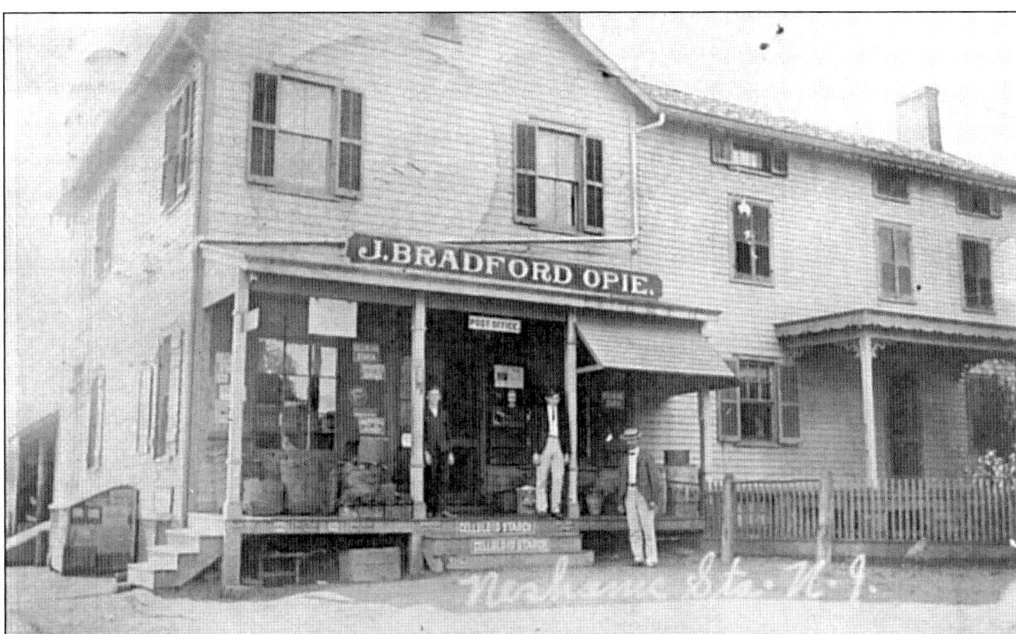

When J. Bradford Opie was appointed postmaster in 1899, his general store on Woodfern Road became home for the Neshanic Station Post Office. In those days, the post office was often combined with a general store and the site of the post office moved with the appointment of a new postmaster. (Photograph courtesy of Neshanic Station Historical Society.)

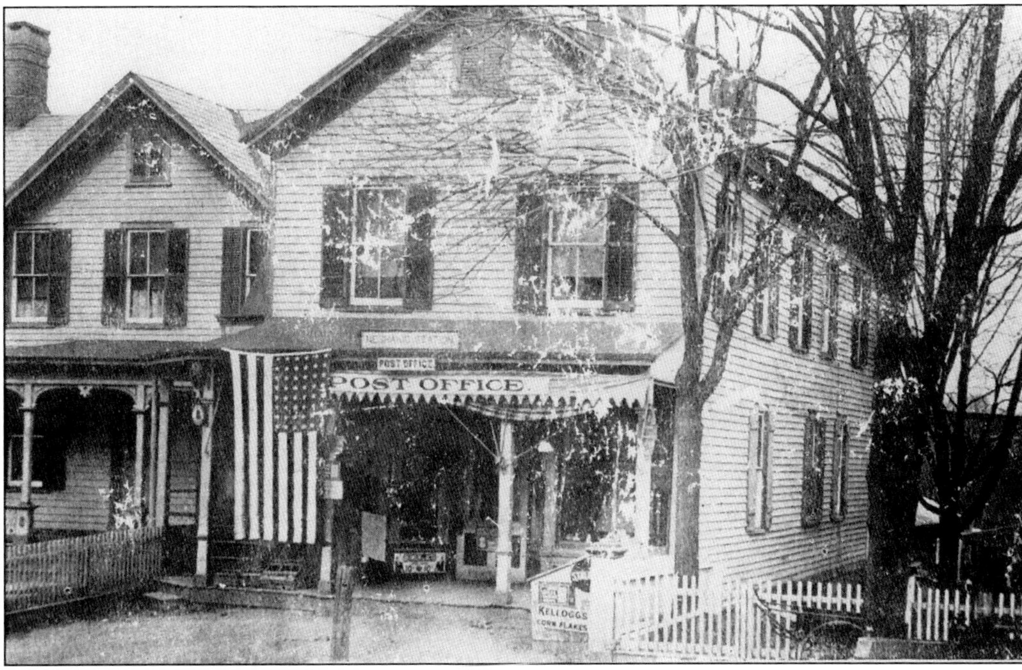

In 1914, when Walter R. Huff became postmaster, the post office was moved to his general store at 211 Pearl Street, at the bend of Olive Street. (Photograph courtesy of Neshanic Station Historical Society.)

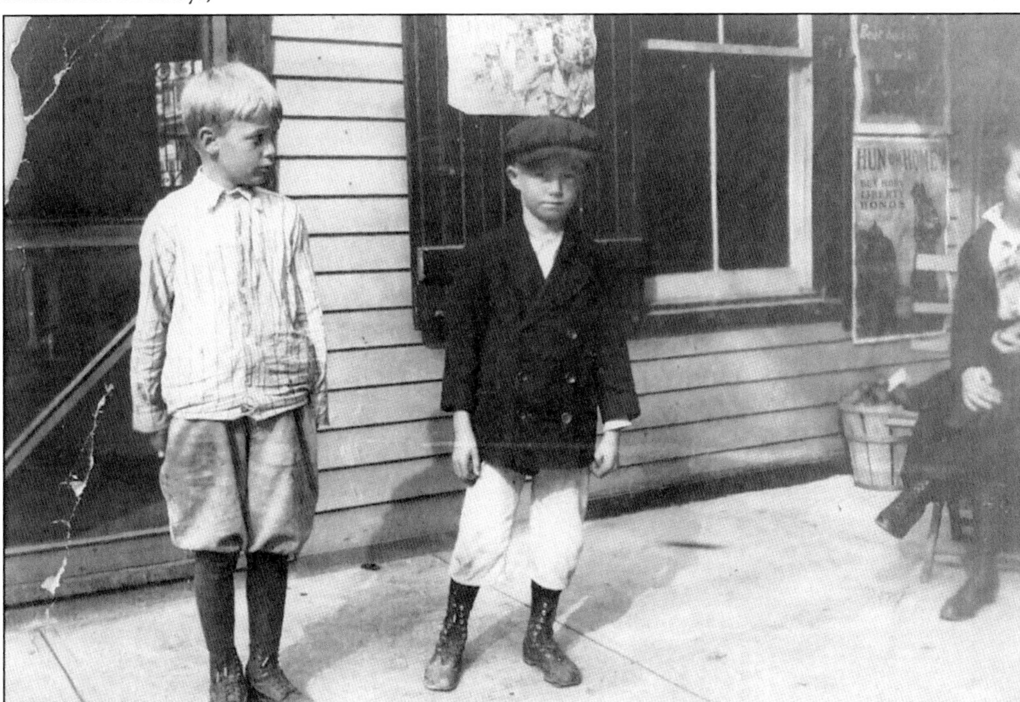

In 1917, the post office was in a separate building on the side of the general store. Note the poster urging people to buy Liberty Bonds. (Photograph courtesy of Alma Quick Deak.)

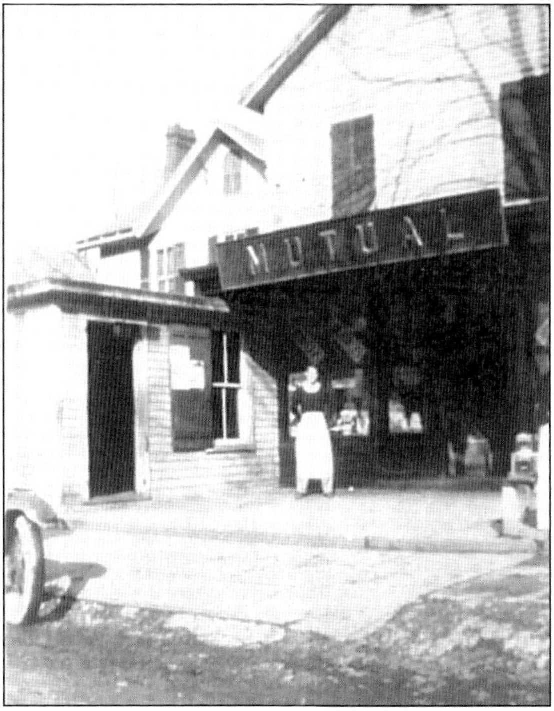

Postmistress Ruth E. Amerman is shown here in 1923. (Photograph courtesy of the Quick Family.)

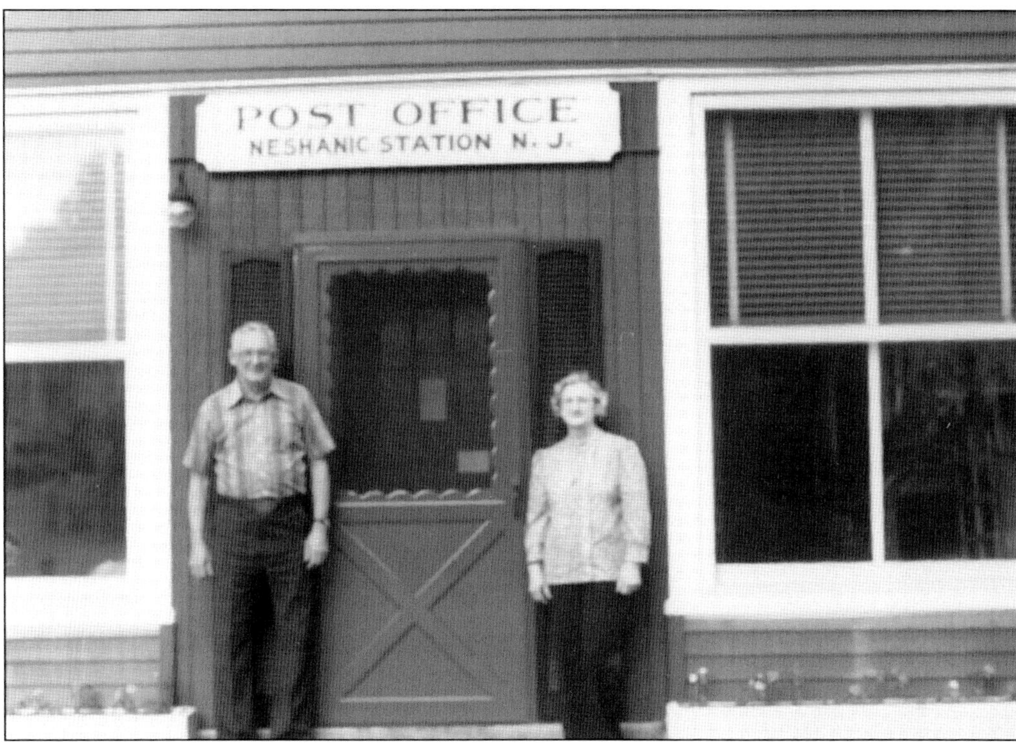

In the 1950s, the post office returned to the 211 Pearl Street location after the grocery store closed. Mrs. Alma Deak, shown here with her husband, Andrew, worked in the postal service for many years. (Photograph courtesy of Alma Quick Deak.)

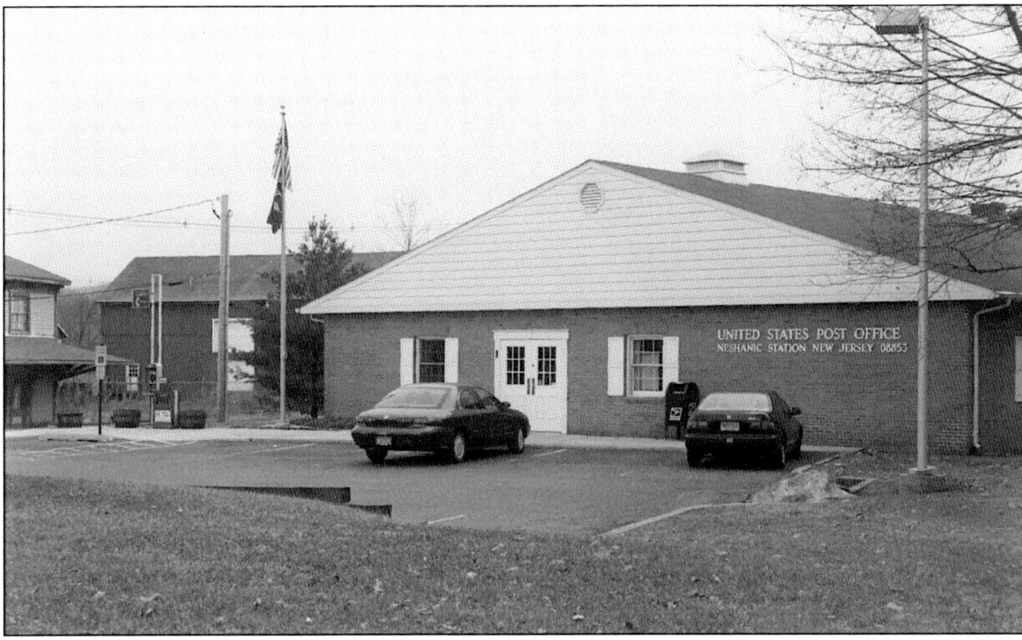

With the residential growth in the 1970s and 1980s, the need for a larger post office became obvious. A new post office was built on the former site of the Central Railroad of New Jersey's freight station on Main Street, across from the old passenger station and the Neshanic Methodist Church. (Photograph courtesy of G.W. Amerman.)

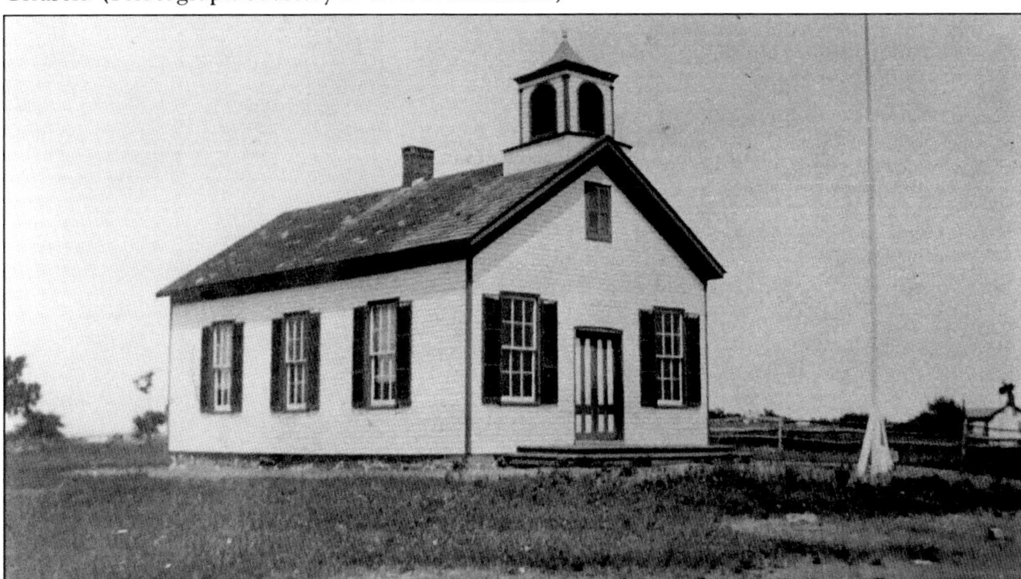

The Fairview School, on Fairview Drive, was one of four schools in Branchburg Township in 1880. At that time, according to Snell's History of Somerset County, the school district served by Fairview School had 74 children between five and 18 years of age. The school was supported by a total budget of $300, and the valuation of school property was listed as $1,000. Snell further recorded that Branchburg employed "one female and three male teachers at an average salary of $35 per month." (Photograph courtesy of Neshanic Station Historical Society.)

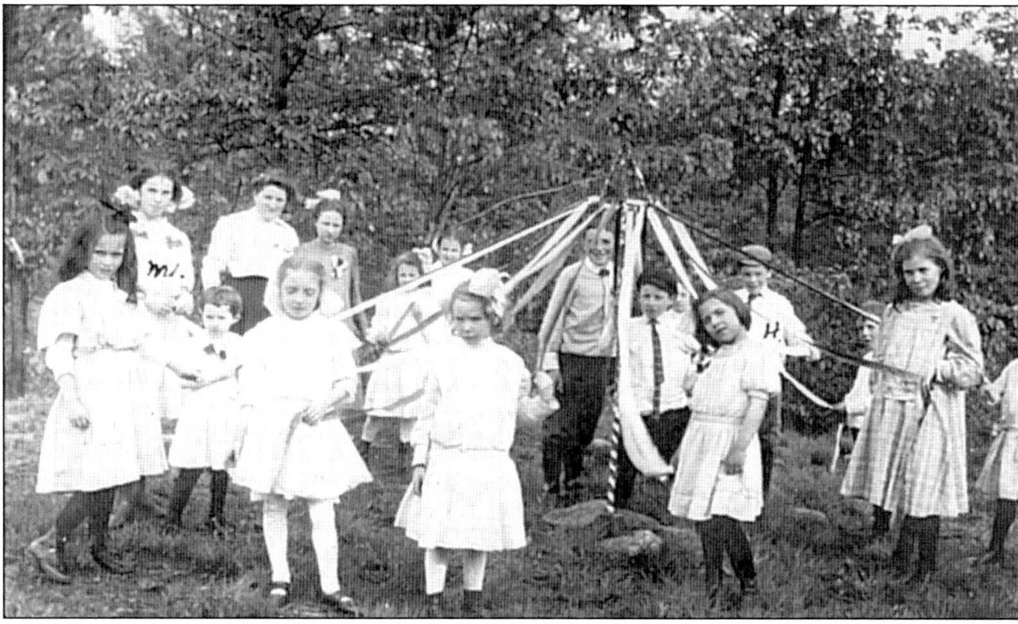

This *c.* 1910 photograph shows children at the Fairview Road School participating in a May pole dance. (Photograph courtesy of E. Saums.)

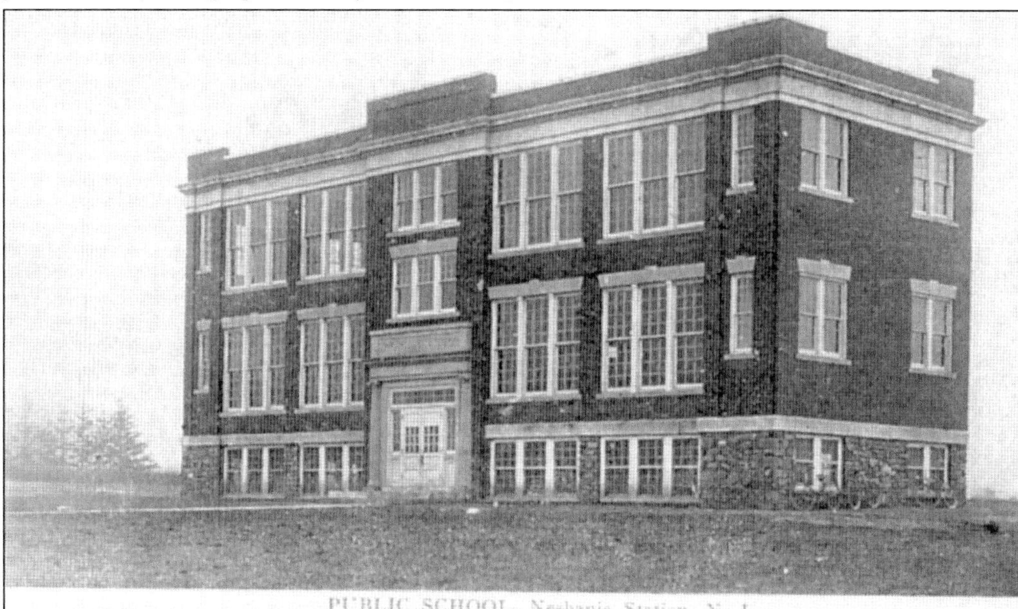

The one-room Fairview School was replaced by a two-story, four-room brick structure at the intersection of Marshall Street and Chester Avenue in Neshanic Station. Built in 1914, this school was also known as Fairview School. Because the state rejected the school's construction, wood floor beams with only a center hall stairway, only the two rooms on the first floor were used as classrooms. This building was phased out after Old York School was built in 1950. Even in the 1950s, when both Branchburg and Hillsborough students attended the school, it had no indoor plumbing and separate outhouses for boys and girls were used. (Photograph courtesy of Ralph Manners.)

During WW II, children from Fairview School participated in collecting salvage materials, as documented by this photograph of the "scrappers" that appeared in the *Courier News*. The children are listed as Ralph Manners (holding the flag), two sons of Mr. and Mrs. Alfred Lehman of Centerville, the two children of Mr. and Mrs. Richard Stryker of Neshanic, Lois Amerman, Jean Bergen, and Harold Van Fleet. (Photograph courtesy of A.S. Bergen, *Somerset Messenger-Gazette*.)

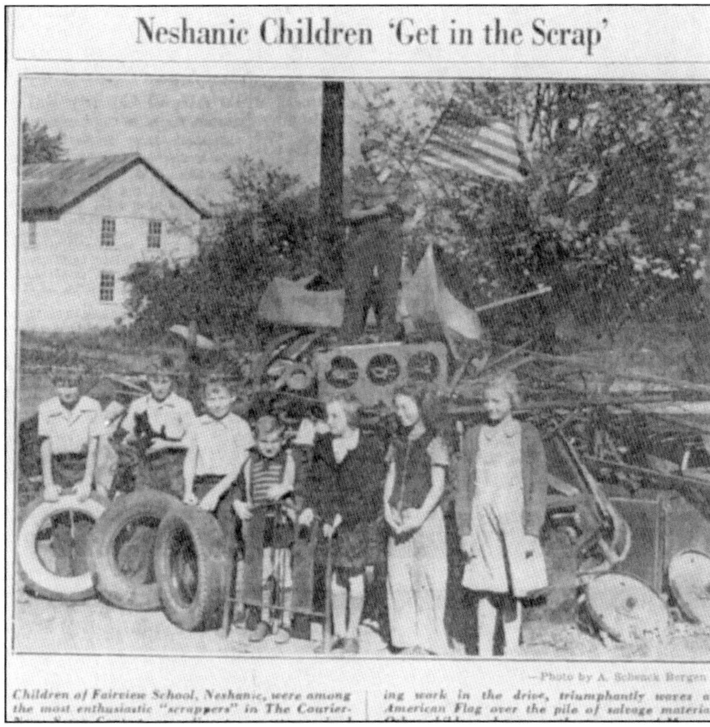

Neshanic Children 'Get in the Scrap'

—Photo by A. Schenck Bergen

Children of Fairview School, Neshanic, were among the most enthusiastic "scrappers" in The Courier-

ing work in the drive, triumphantly waves an American Flag over the pile of salvage material.

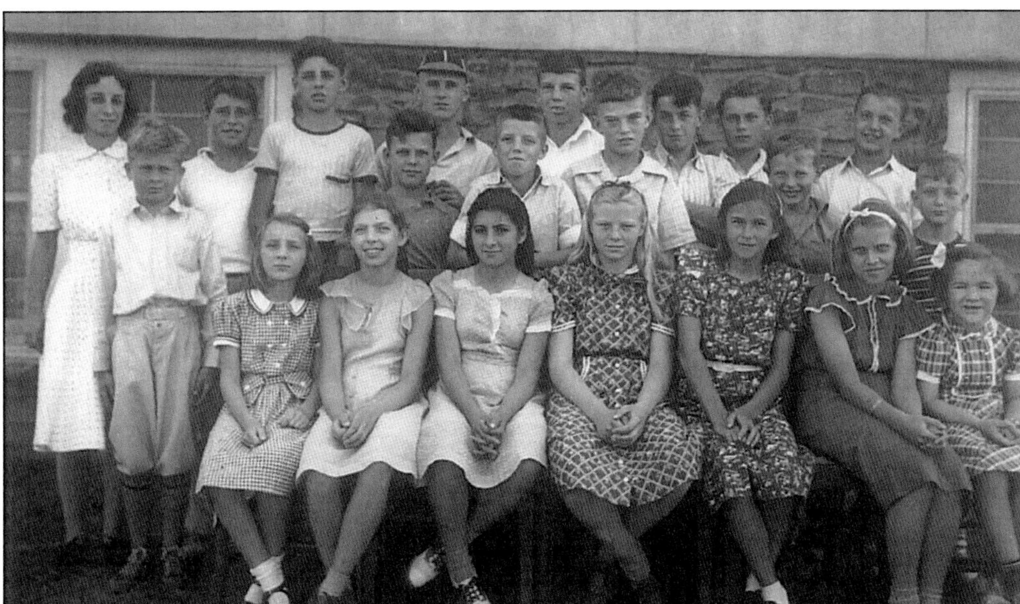

Fairview School class of 1940 is shown, from left to right, as follows: (front row) Joan Ogden, Ann Totten, Anna LaMarco, Betty MacQuaide, Georgianna Grenther, Gilberta Schenck, and Jean Hall; (middle row) Raymond Brokaw, Larry Totten, Ted Dilts, William Emmons, Harold Van Fleet, and Donald Henry; (back row) Eva Cromwell (teacher), Richard Krautwald, Bill Colbert, Elmer Saums, Claude Dilts, Harry Bryan, Henry Smithana, and Ed Foltin. (Photograph courtesy of Harold Van Fleet.)

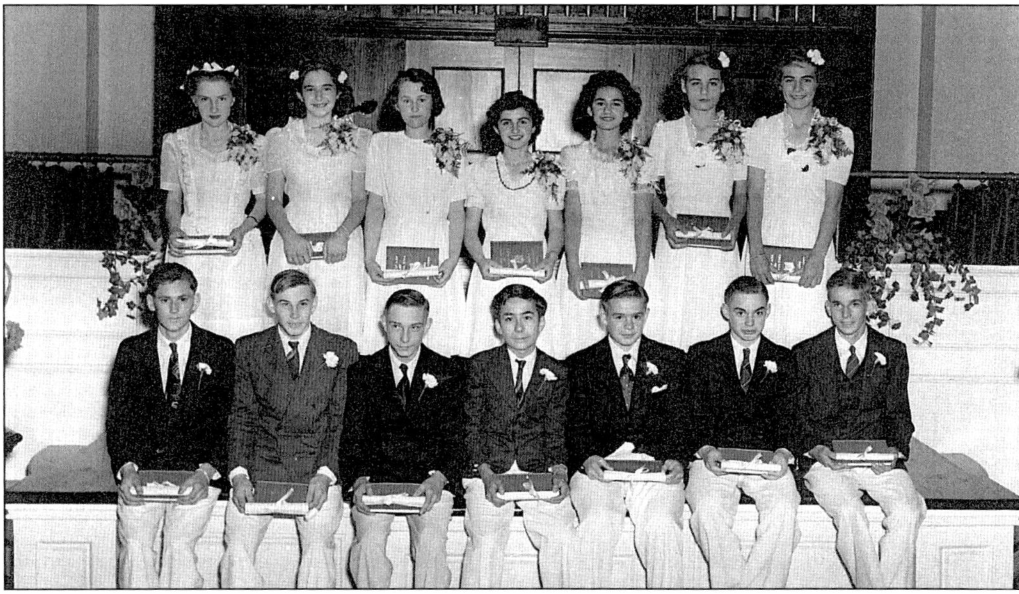

Branchburg Township eighth grade graduation in 1945 was held at the Neshanic Methodist Church. Prior to 1950, the eighth grade graduation for students from all of Branchburg's schools alternated between the North Branch Reformed Church and the Neshanic Methodist Church. Graduates are shown here, from left to right, as follows: (front row) Joe Stala, Richard Melick, Kenneth Snyder, Genero Deroda, Rudolph Krautwald, Jacob Emmons, and Gerald McCray; (back row) Evelyn Breitenberger, June Stryker (Amerman), Lois Winegardner, Rosalind Fineman, Eleanor Perfumo, Frances Shimanowitz, and Doris Shimanowitz. (Photograph courtesy of June Stryker Amerman.)

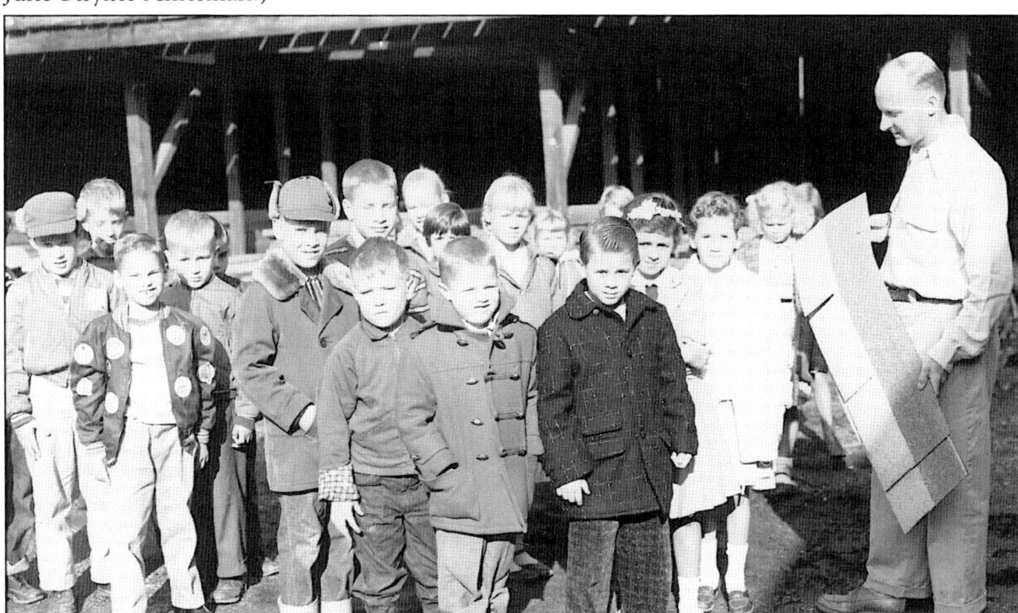

Second and third grade students from Branchburg Township's Old York School are seen here visiting the J.S. Amerman Lumberyard on a class trip. Pictured here are G.W. "Bill" Amerman and the students in October 1958. (Photograph courtesy of Overbrook Studio.)

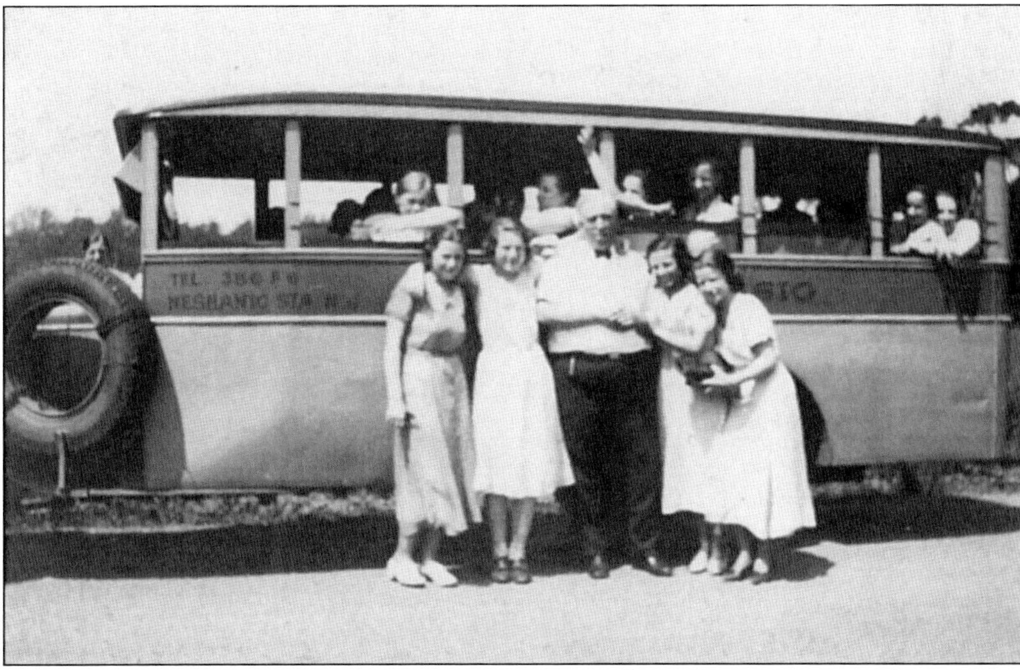

Mr. Albert F. Messig, a school bus owner-operator, is shown here in 1933, with a Fairview School class. Mr. Messig operated the first school buses from Neshanic to the local school and to Somerville High School. (Photograph courtesy of the Quick Family. Current residents Don and Jim Quick are Mr. Messig's great-grandsons.)

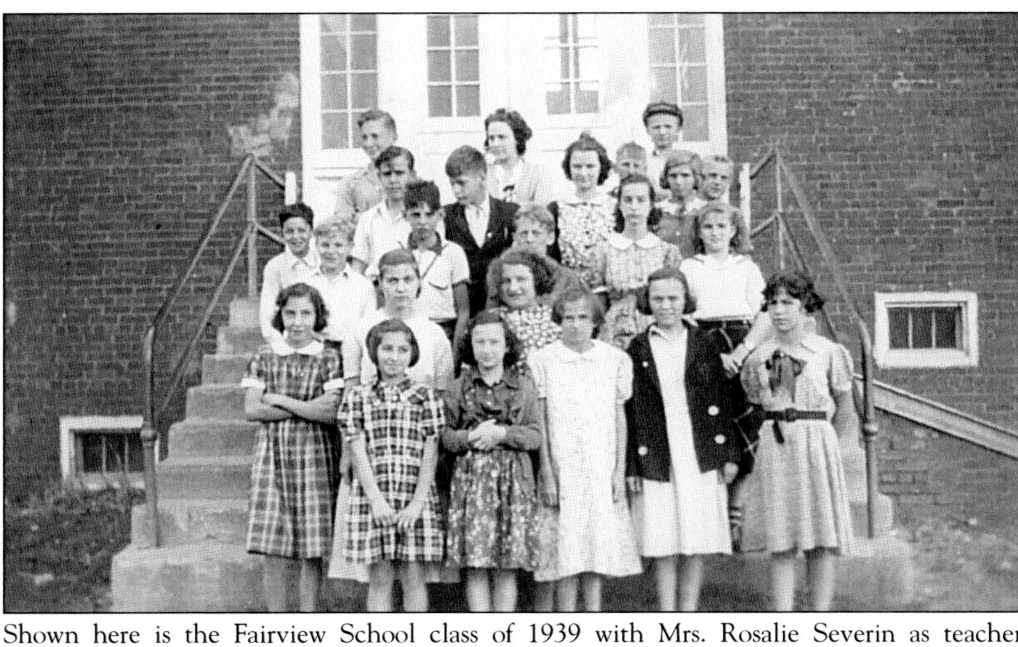

Shown here is the Fairview School class of 1939 with Mrs. Rosalie Severin as teacher. (Photograph courtesy of Dorothy Stryker Sipler.)

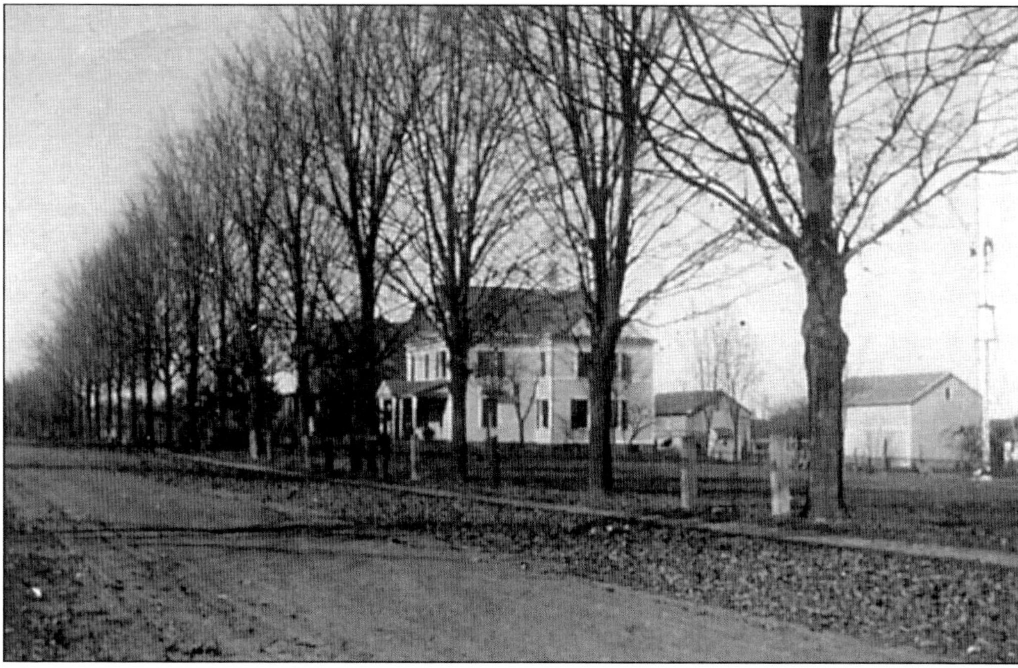

This c. 1912 photo postcard view was taken on Maple Avenue looking west showing the Quick residence with its carriage house and windmill (307 Maple Avenue). (Photo postcard courtesy of Paul Kurzenberger.)

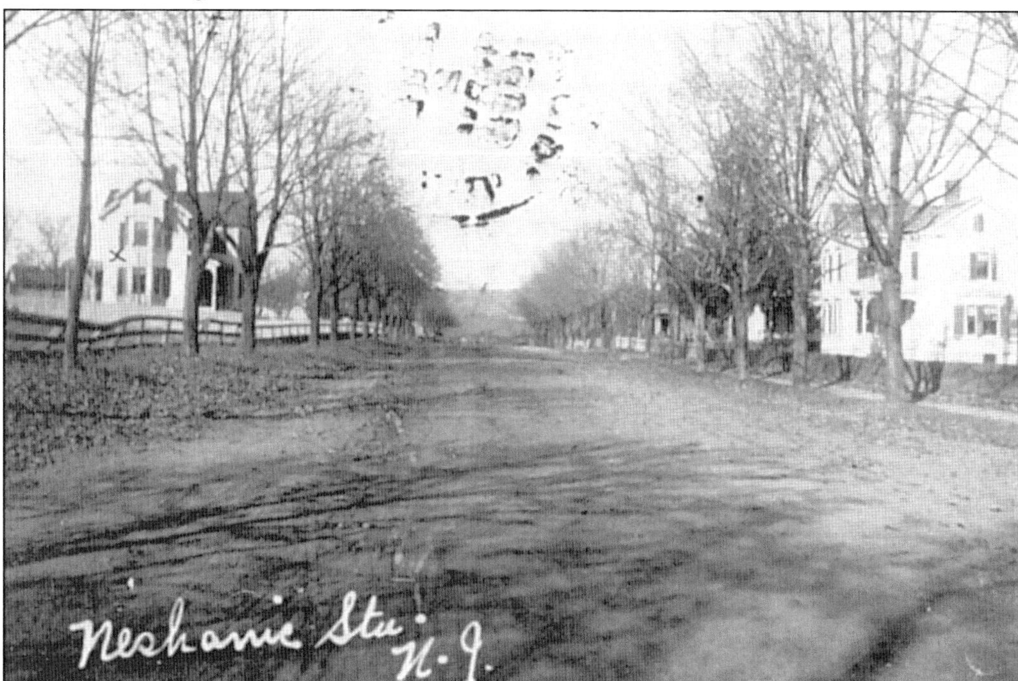

This c. 1912 photo postcard view shows Olive Street looking west toward the Frederic Hall residence (208 Pearl Street), on the left, and the Harry Huff home (207 Pearl Street), on the right. (Photo postcard courtesy of Paul Kurzenberger.)

Mary Lavina Shurts and her husband, Garrett Stryker Shurts, were grandparents of Orville Shurts. When her husband died suddenly in 1910, the widow sold their farm in Hillsborough and had a home built on 422 Olive Street so she could be near her son, Lester Shurts. Lester Shurts had started the feed business in the old creamery on Fairview Drive in 1898 (current location of Neshanic Farm, Home & Garden Center). (Photograph courtesy of Orville Shurts.)

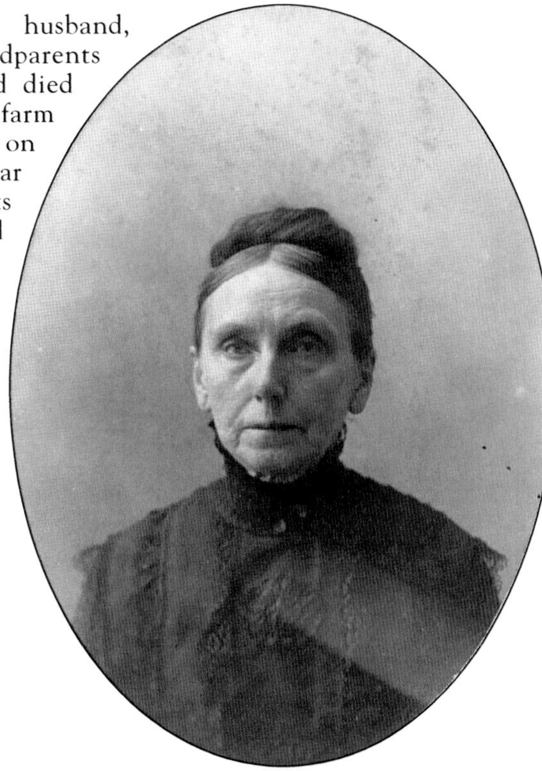

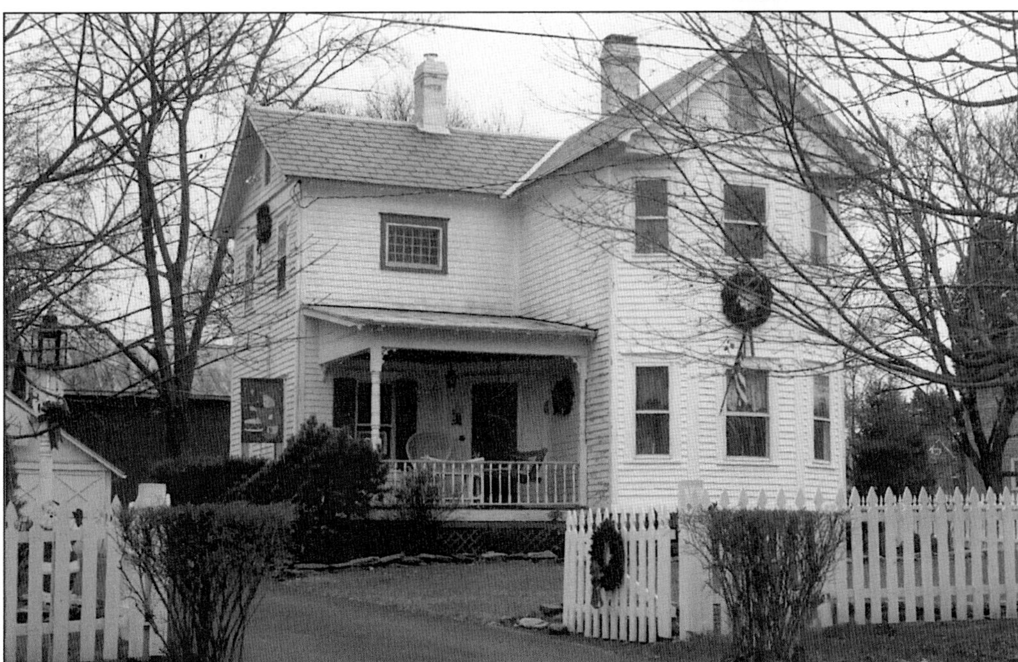

The residence at 422 Olive Street, built by Mary Lavina Shurts, was recently the home of our fourth justice from the area, the Honorable Robert Guterl. (Photograph courtesy of Robert Guterl.)

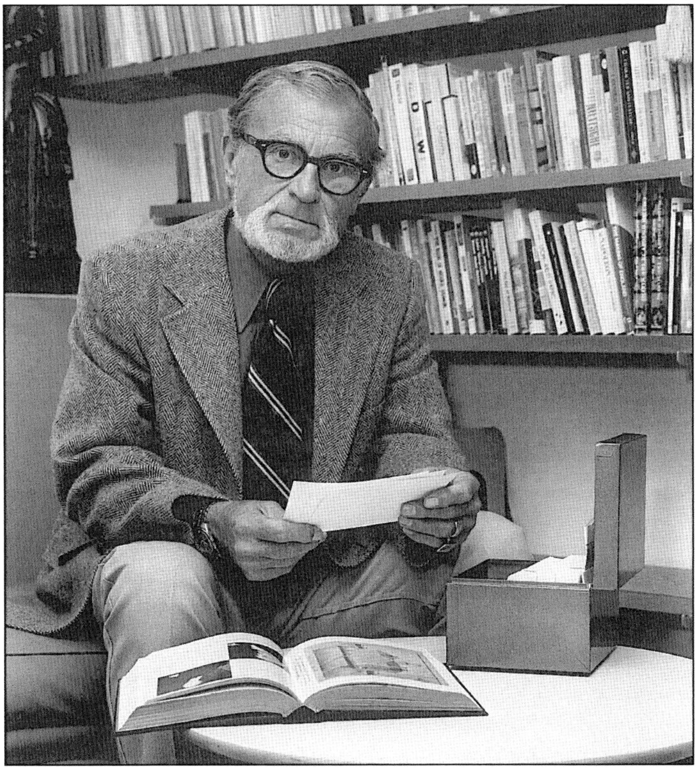

Dr. Richard Schlatter, one of the most prominent of the 20th-century residents of Neshanic Station, is represented here. Holder of degrees from Harvard and Oxford; recipient of multiple fellowships; and professor, provost, and vice president of Rutgers University between 1946 and 1982; Dr. Schlatter lived in the village for over 40 years. (Photograph courtesy of Heidi Schlatter Saunders.)

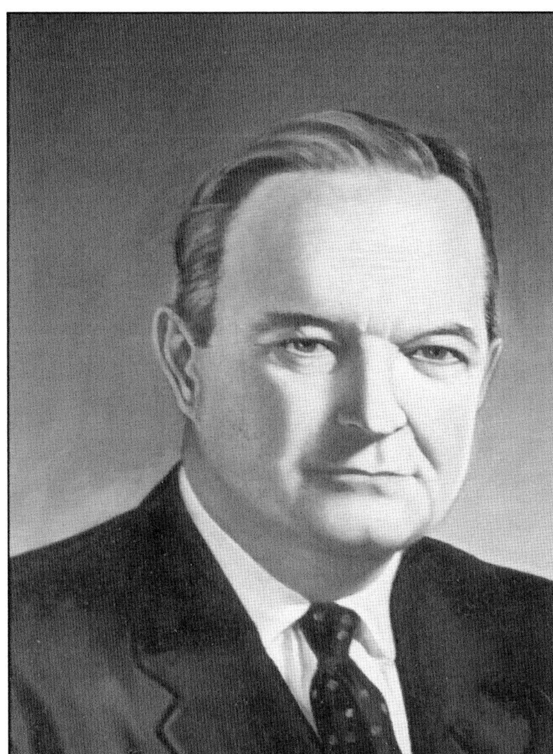

This image portrays Melville Wilson. Mr. Wilson purchased the Woodfern Road farm from Gordon Saunders and started Wilson Products Corp. with 10 to 12 employees in 1950. The company produced color concentrates for the plastics industry, first supplying the product for "hula hoops." Later, it served Dart Industries that produced Tupperware, as well as supplying Ford Motor Co. and Western Electric colored wire coatings. The firm grew to 120 employees and also operated a plant on Maple Avenue, opposite the Lehigh Railroad Station site. Most recently, it was operated by Dart Industries and the AKZO Corp. (See page 19 for an aerial view of the plant.) (Photograph and information courtesy of Jack Weiss.)

This portrait is of John G. Schenck. Mr. Schenck was the original owner of the Shadowlawn farm. As a railroad commissioner, he brought the south branch of the Central Railroad of New Jersey to Neshanic Station, and developed much of the commerce associated with the village. His Villa Sites, filed in 1875, became the first registered residential area in Somerset County. (See map of the subdivision on page 57.) (Portrait courtesy of John L. Schenck Jr.)

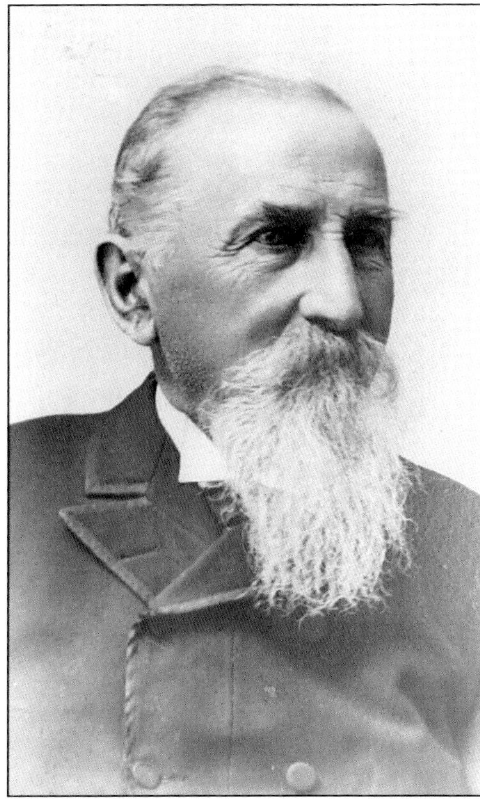

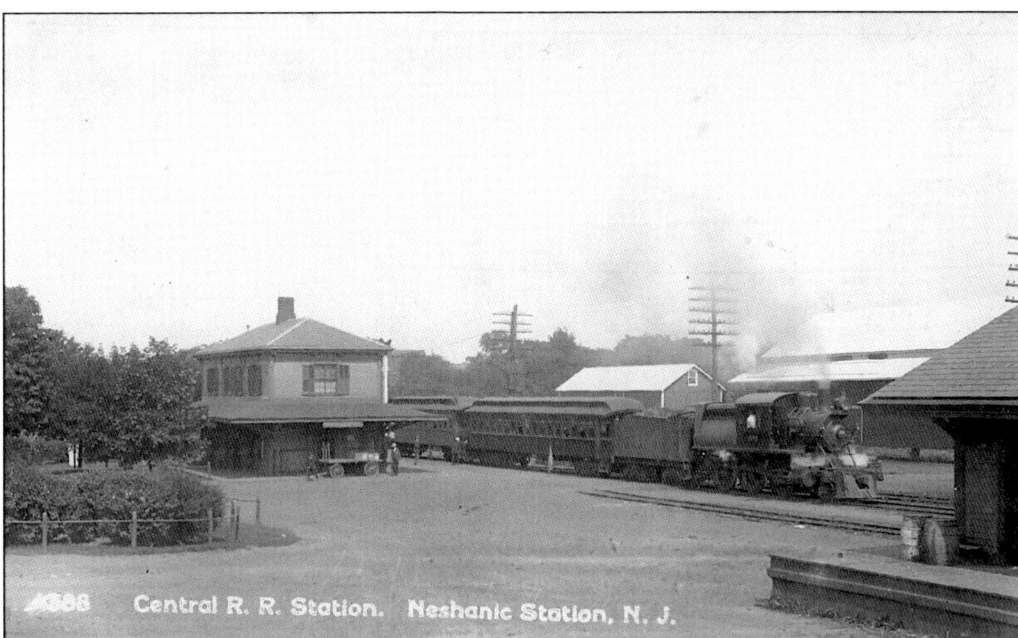

This *c.* 1912 Garroway studio photo postcard illustrates the Central Railroad Station in Neshanic Station. This scene shows the rebuilt J.S. Amerman Lumberyard and hay press building in background. (Courtesy of Robert Yuell.)

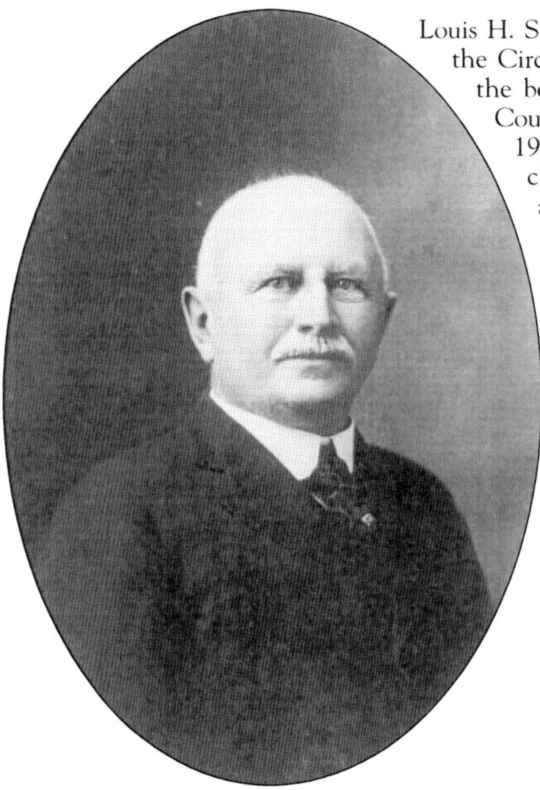

Louis H. Schenck was a lawyer and became a judge of the Circuit Court from 1900 to 1910. He occupied the bench at the first trial in the new Somerset County Court House, which was completed in 1909. He graduated from Rutgers University, class of 1874, and served for five years as an alumnus member of the Board of Trustees of the University, beginning in 1905. He was also president of the Branchburg Township Board of Education for 19 years. (Courtesy of John L. Schenck Jr.)

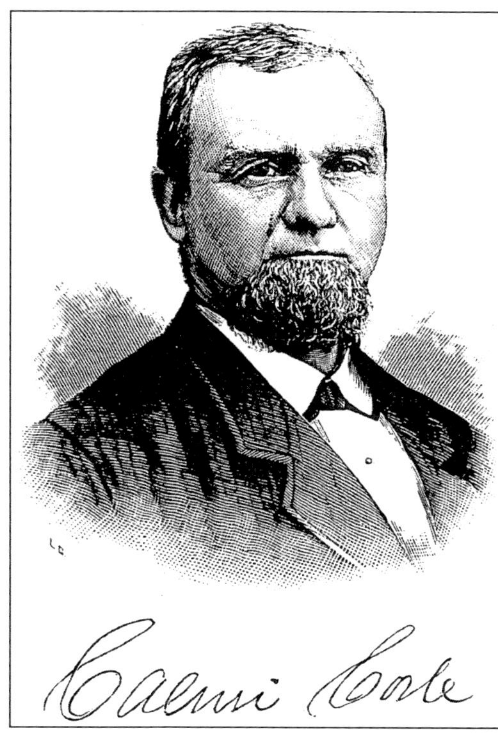

Calvin Corle, who was a state senator in the 1870s and president of the Somerset County Bank in Somerville, is shown in this photograph. He lived at the Field Crest Farm, later known as Four Pillar Farm, on South Branch Road. (See picture of farm, page 75.) (Courtesy of Robert Guterl.)

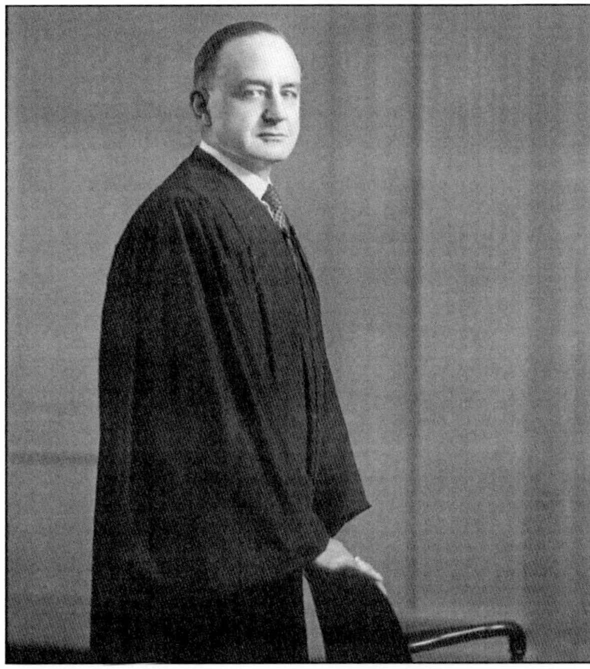

Justice Frederick W. Hall was the best known of Neshanic Station's judges. Although born without a left hand, he started school in third grade in Neshanic Station at the age of five and went on to high school at the age of ten. He graduated Phi Beta Kappa from Rutgers in 1927, and he graduated cum laude from Harvard Law School in 1931. After an exemplary legal career, he served as a justice of the New Jersey Supreme Court where he authored many noteworthy decisions, including the first *Mt. Laurel* decision. He died in 1984. (Photograph courtesy of Peter Hall.)

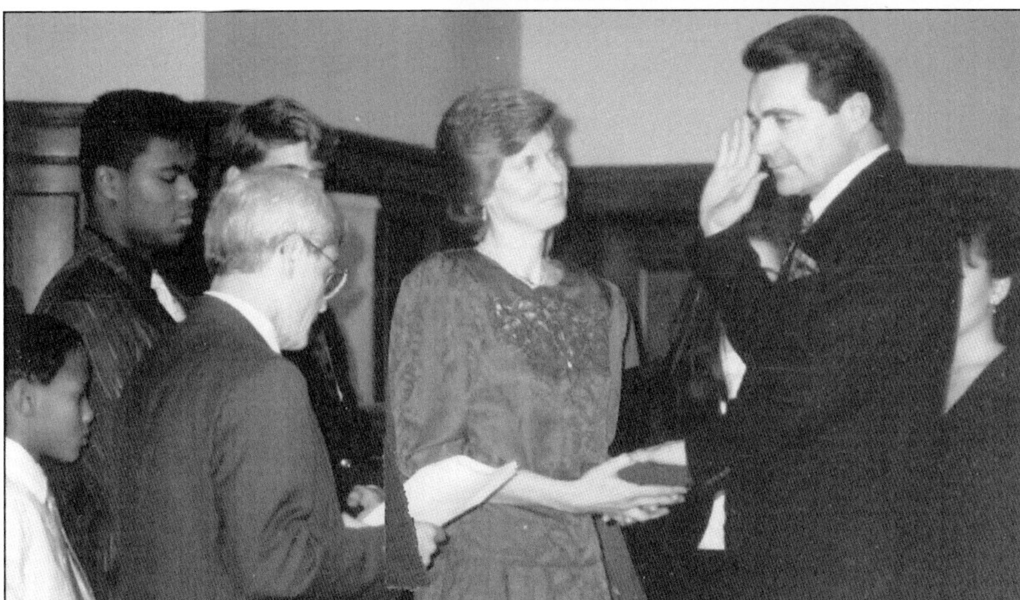

Justice Robert Guterl is shown here being sworn in by Judge Wilfred P. Diana, with wife, Sheryl Guterl, holding the Bible. A Neshanic resident for many years, Justice Guterl was appointed as a judge of the Superior Court of New Jersey by Governor Thomas Kean in 1989. Originally from Jersey City, he is a graduate of St. Peter's College, receiving his Juris Doctor from Rutgers Law School, in Newark, in 1964. He also did graduate work at the New York University School of Law. Justice Guterl and his family were recently the owners of the Shurts home at 422 Olive Street and among the founders of the Peanut Butter Playhouse, a children's theater group that operated in Neshanic for several years. (Photograph courtesy of the Guterl Family.)

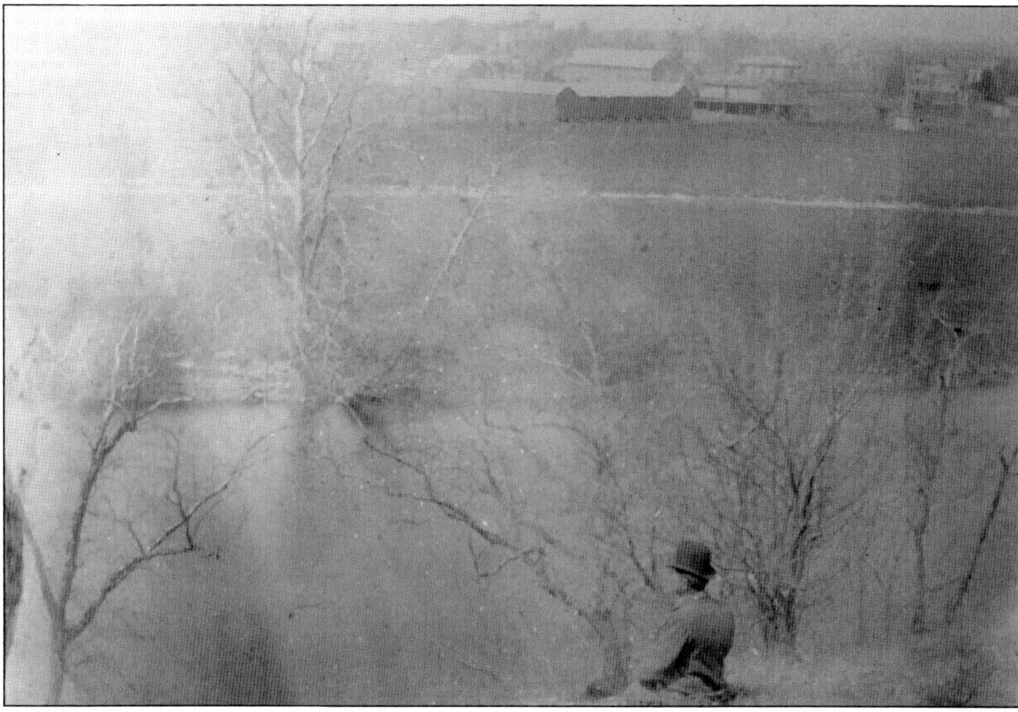

In this *c.* 1900 photograph, John G. Schenck is surveying Neshanic Station from the riverside in Hillsborough Township. His Shadowlawn home is shown in the top center of the photograph. The lumberyard and coal yard, built by A.A. Cortelyou and the Central Jersey Railroad Station, are also visible. (Photograph courtesy of John L. Schenck Jr.)

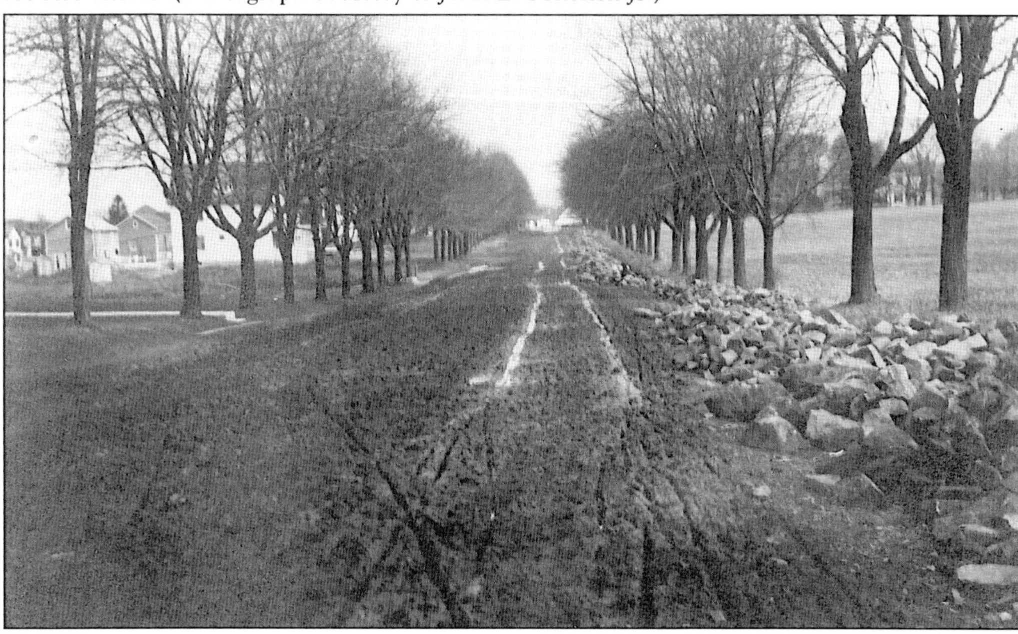

This *c.* 1914 view down Maple Avenue shows the rock ballast from Zion Mountain, which was used below the paving done by Richards & Gaston Contracting of Somerville, New Jersey. (Photograph courtesy of L.B. Lane.)

Three

VILLAGE CHURCHES

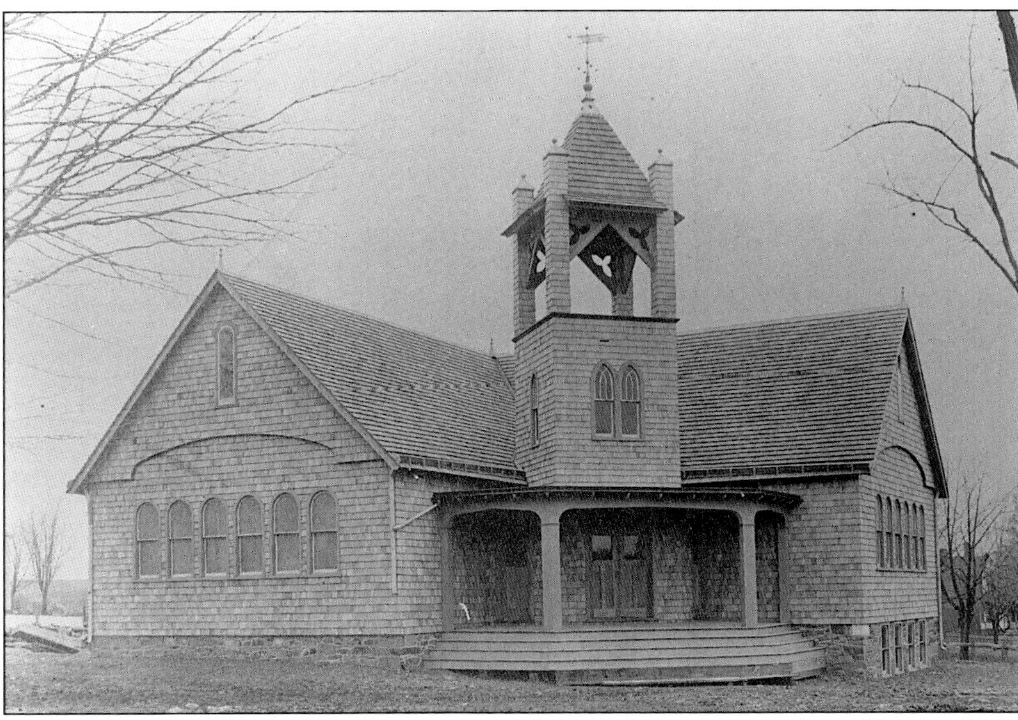

Neshanic Methodist Church, built in 1907 and dedicated in 1908, cost about $6,800 to build. In 1906, local Neshanic Methodists, weary of the buggy ride to Centerville, decided to build a church and bought the lot for $350 from Senator Schenck. The first minister, John May, was given the task of raising the building funds. He met James B. Duke, the tobacco millionaire who had a home in Hillsborough Township, and Mr. Duke agreed to give $3,500 if the church could raise an equal amount. Rev. May raised $500 from the Methodist denomination. Then, while in Philadelphia for a Bible study group, he met John Wanamaker, who agreed to match with any necessary funds to have Mr. Duke pay his offer. (Photograph courtesy of the Neshanic Station Historical Society.)

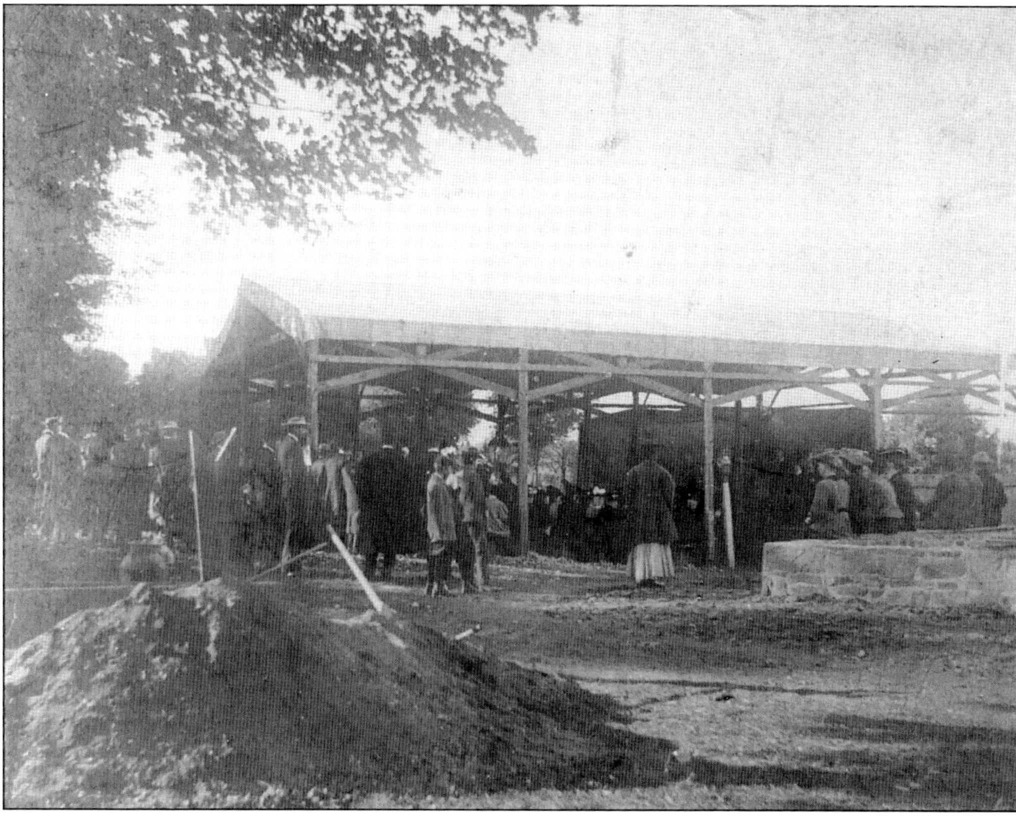

This image depicts a Methodist Church Tent Meeting in 1907. Services were held here as soon as the building was started with a stone foundation. (Photograph courtesy of Robert May.)

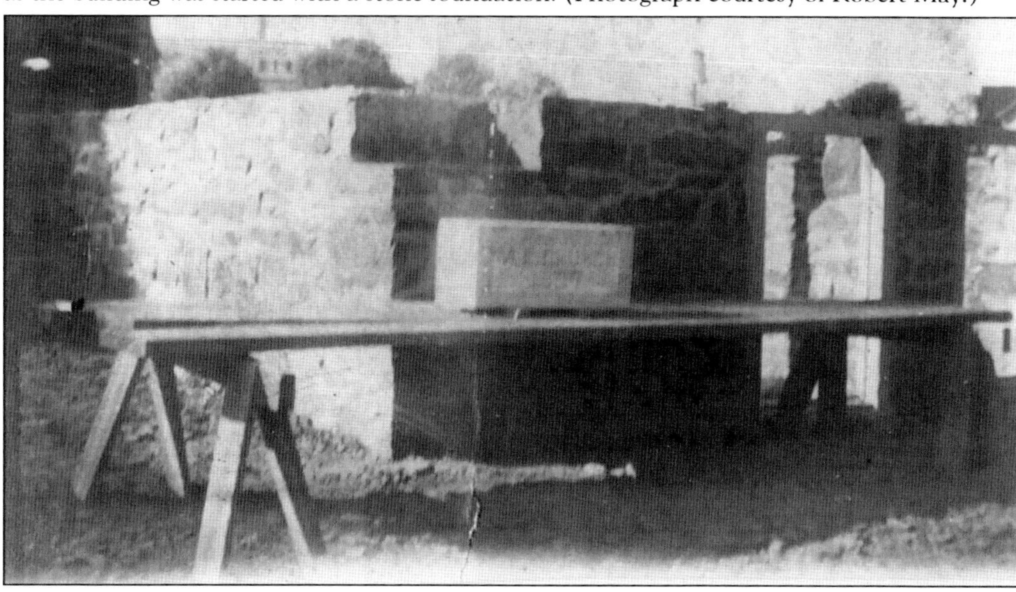

The Methodist Church cornerstone laying ceremony is represented here in 1907. Note Senator Schenck's home, as well as the windmill tower of the adjacent Maple Street residence, in the background. (Photograph courtesy of Robert May.)

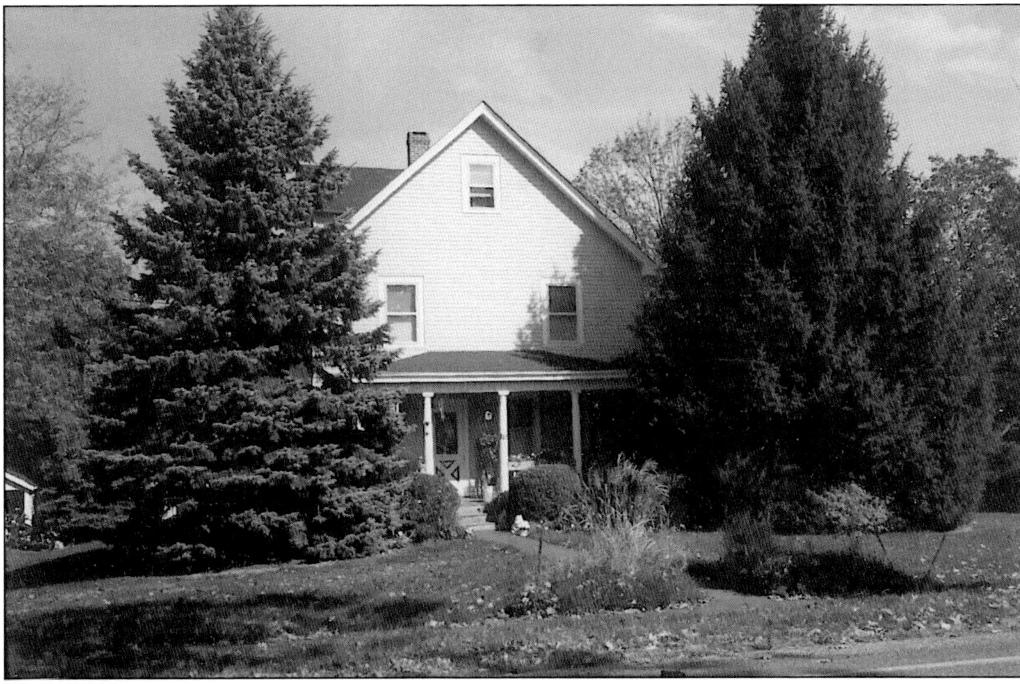

Neshanic Methodist Parsonage, with its Victorian gable front, is seen here at 315 Maple Avenue c. 1910. (Photograph courtesy of Robert Guterl.)

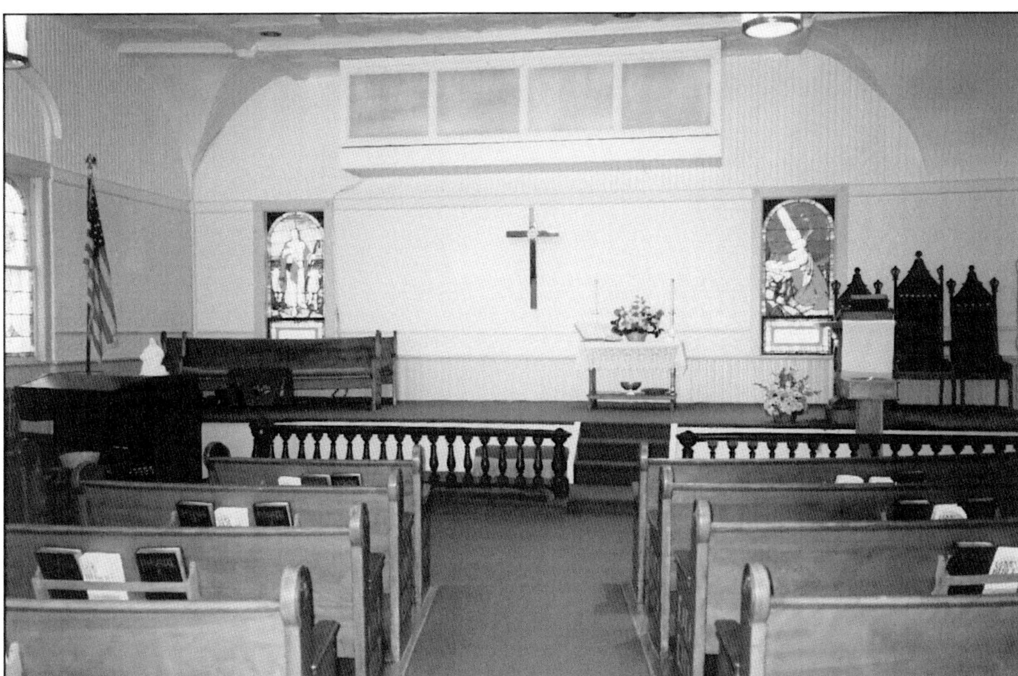

The interior of Neshanic Methodist Church is represented in this 1999 photograph. (Photograph by G.W. Amerman.)

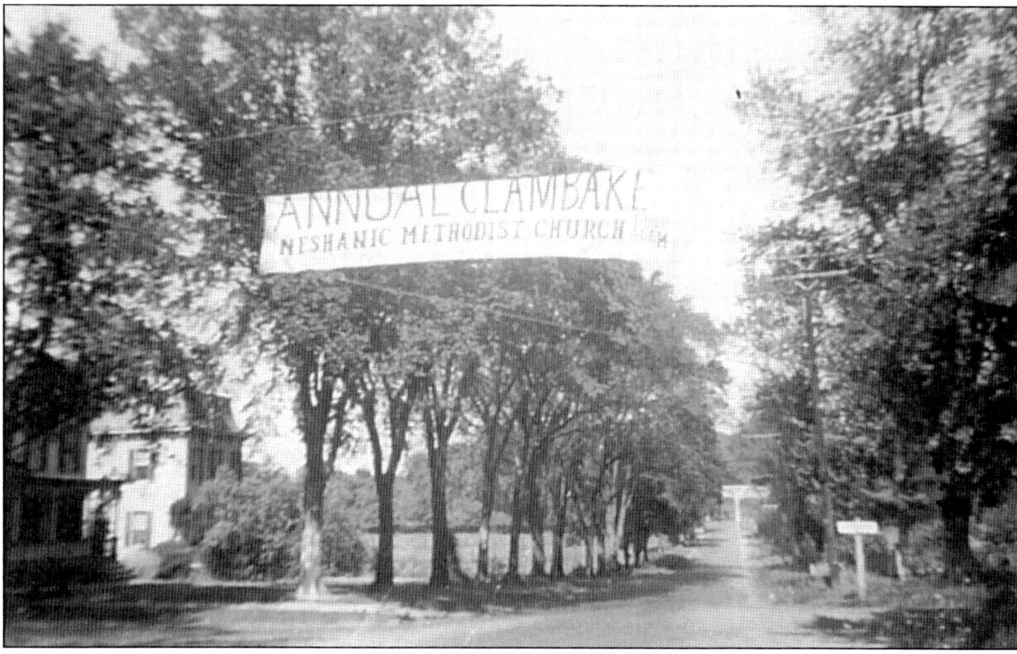

Prior to the Neshanic Fire Co., the Methodist Church began the traditional clambakes. Clams were steamed on a bed of hot rocks heated by a day-long bon fire and covered with sea weed. This picture, taken in 1941, looks down Elm Street. (Photograph courtesy of the Toles Family.)

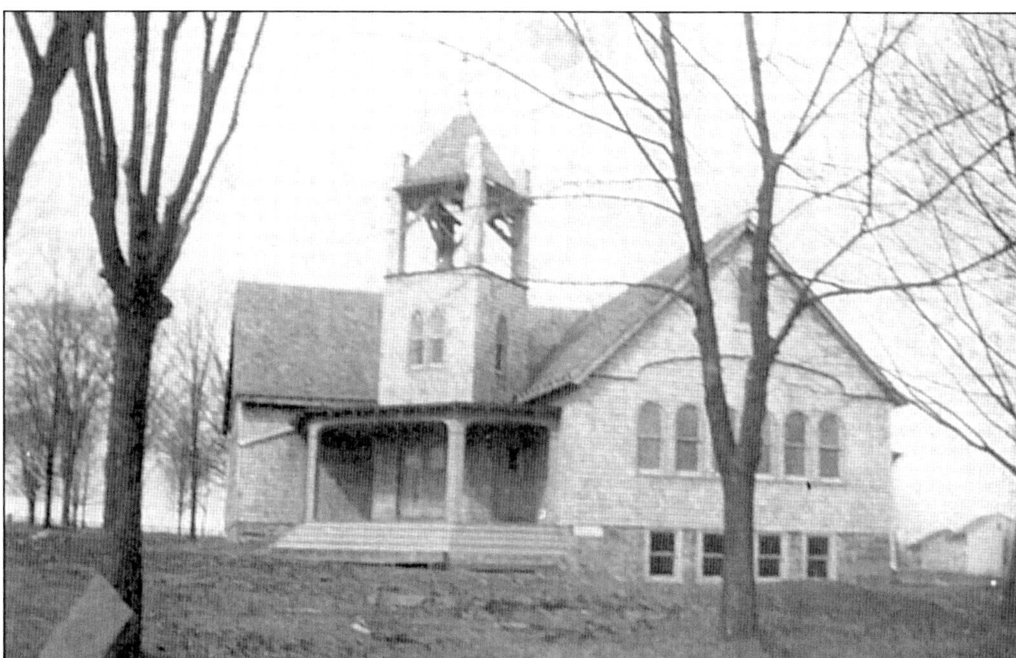
At the time of this view of the Neshanic Methodist Church in 1908, the church had been completed and services were being held, but note that the bell had not yet been placed in the belfry. (Photograph courtesy of Robert May.)

Robert May was the son of the Reverend John May, the first pastor of Neshanic Methodist Church. Bob has been a lifelong active member of this church and has been the faithful, ever-present bell ringer for nearly 50 years. (Photograph courtesy of Robert May.)

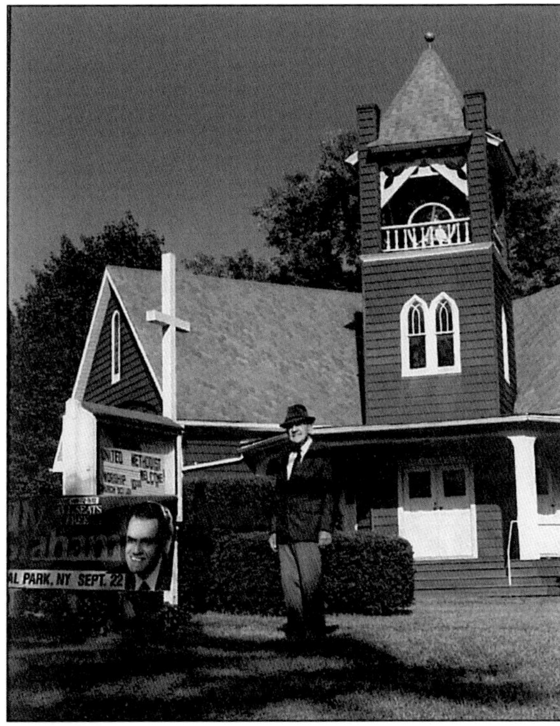

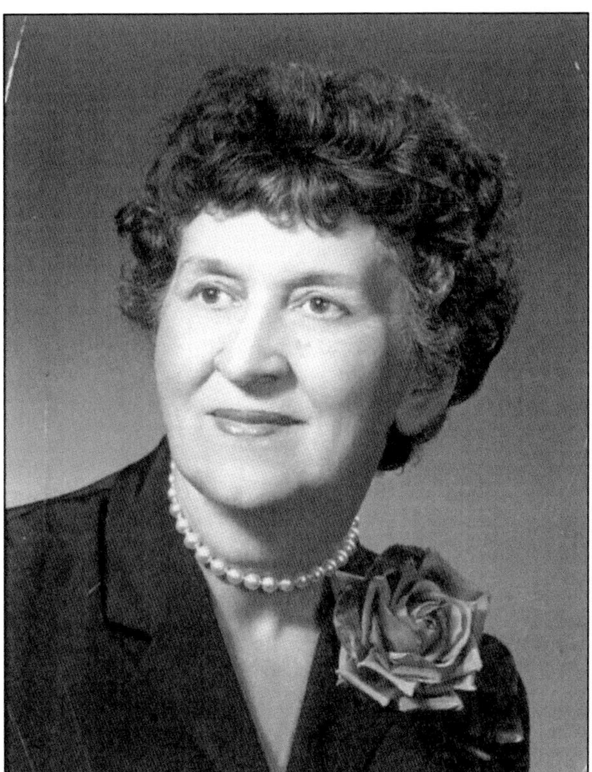

Mary Boughton touched all that knew her with her strong presence at the Neshanic Methodist Church and in the community. Drawing her strength from her Christian faith, she was always sharing her unconditional love with an encouraging word, a warm hug, or an understanding smile. Mrs. Boughton was born in September 1905, married here in 1931, and left with her husband to serve in the ministry. She taught music for many years and returned to Neshanic in 1973. Mrs. Boughton passed away in January 1999. (Photograph courtesy of Ann Boughton.)

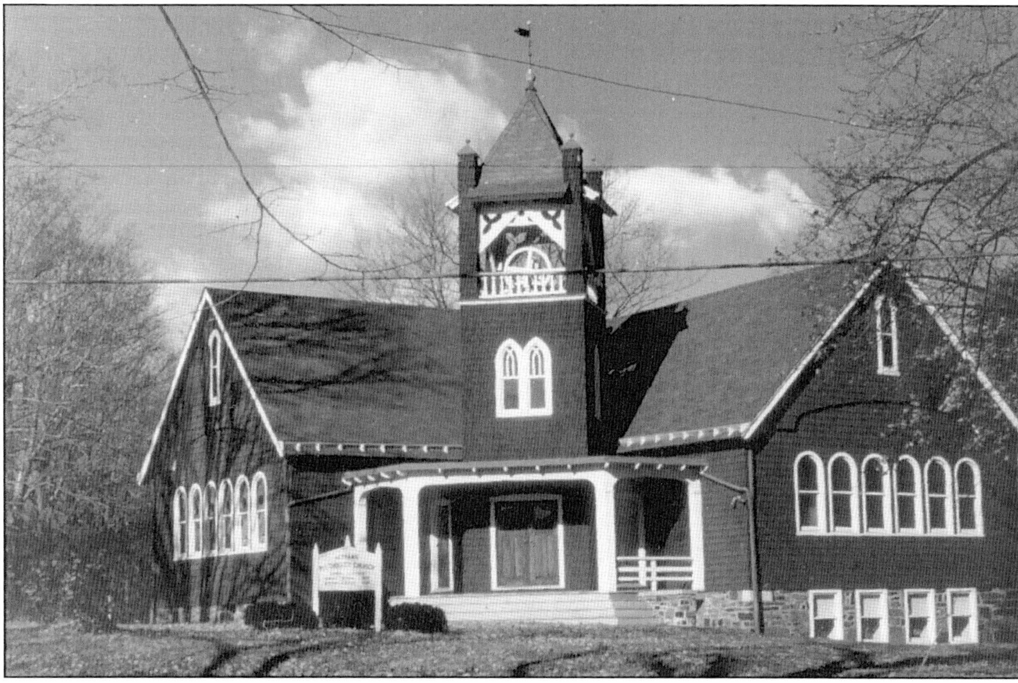

Now over 90 years old, the Neshanic Methodist Church has a young, active membership, carrying on many of the church's traditions in the village. Every November, on Election Day, there is a traditional turkey dinner, and, during Christmas week, there is caroling at night in the streets. (Photograph courtesy of Neshanic Station Historical Society.)

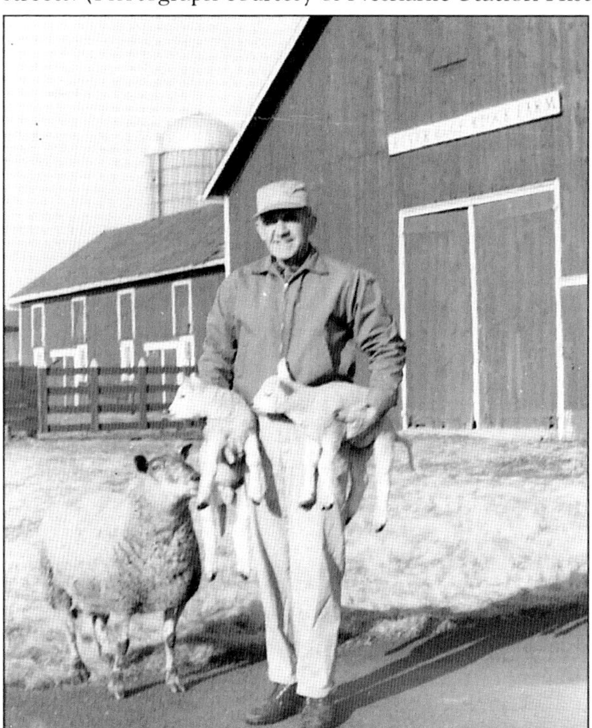

Robert May, the last shepherd at the River Edge Stock Farm, is shown here in 1968. (Photograph courtesy of Robert May.)

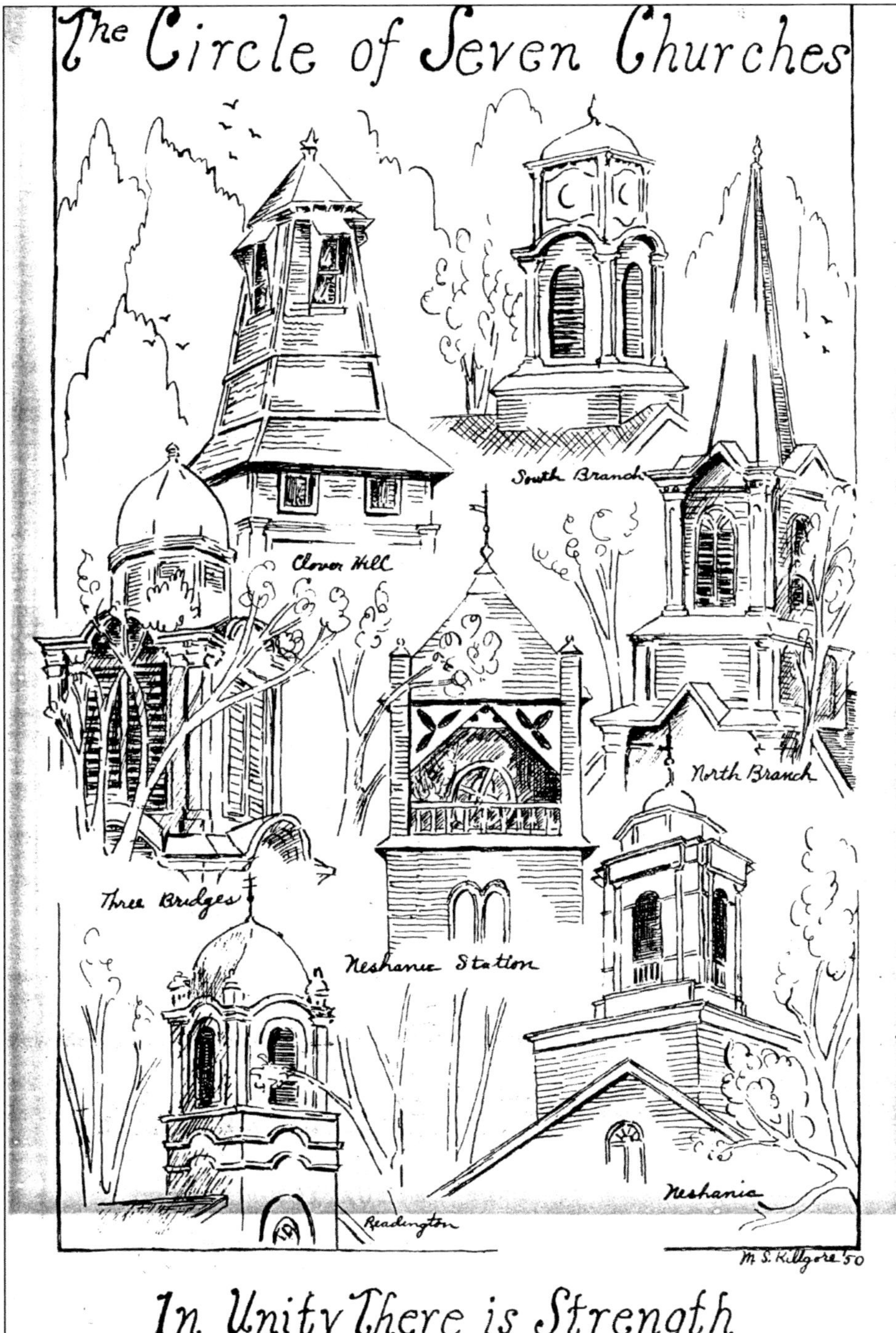

The Circle of Seven Churches, organized in 1939, was an active group of local Protestant churches that shared in many services and related church activities, such as concerts and Lenten services. (1950 Program, sketch by Mary Kilgore; courtesy of June Stryker Amerman.)

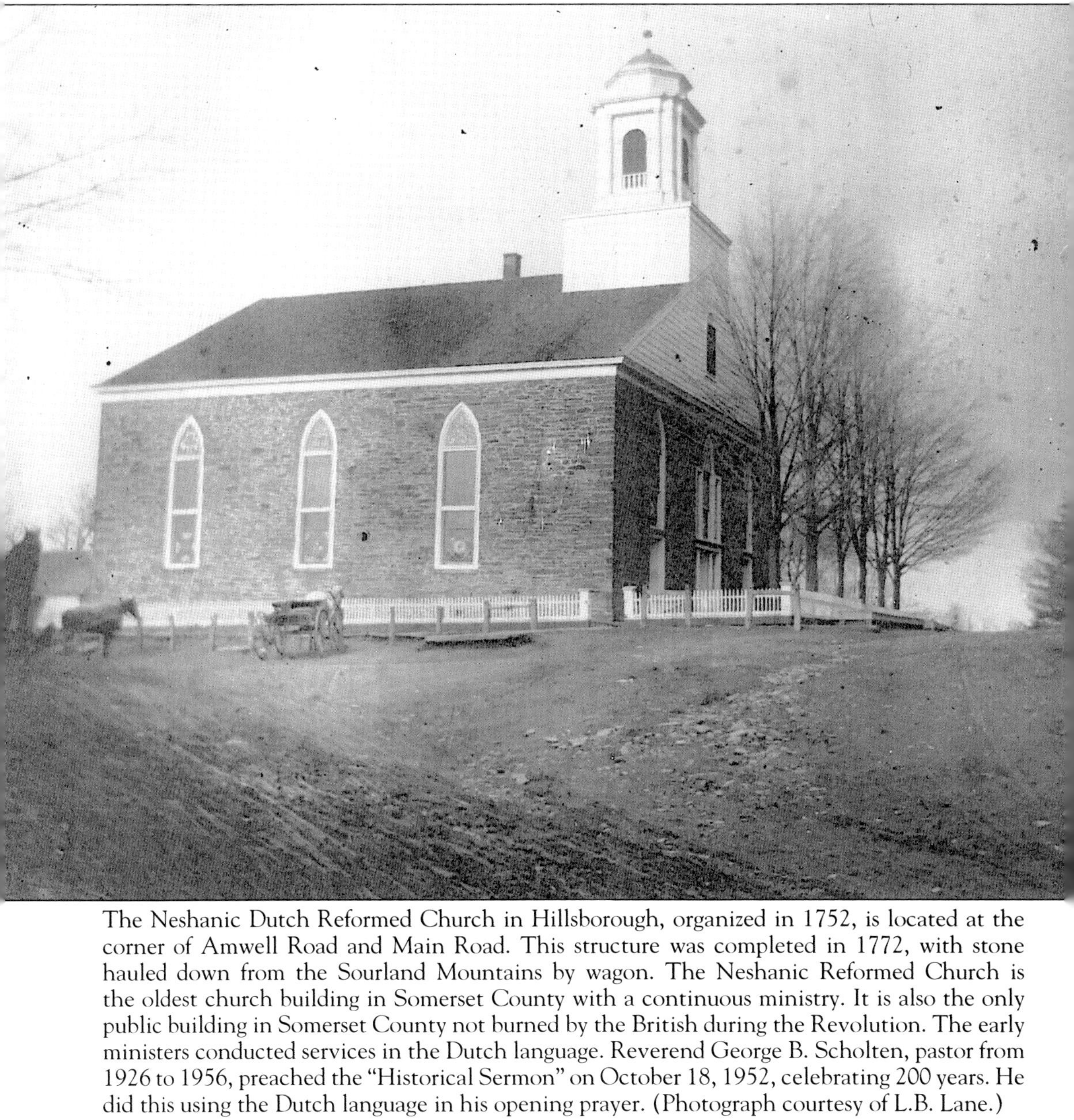

The Neshanic Dutch Reformed Church in Hillsborough, organized in 1752, is located at the corner of Amwell Road and Main Road. This structure was completed in 1772, with stone hauled down from the Sourland Mountains by wagon. The Neshanic Reformed Church is the oldest church building in Somerset County with a continuous ministry. It is also the only public building in Somerset County not burned by the British during the Revolution. The early ministers conducted services in the Dutch language. Reverend George B. Scholten, pastor from 1926 to 1956, preached the "Historical Sermon" on October 18, 1952, celebrating 200 years. He did this using the Dutch language in his opening prayer. (Photograph courtesy of L.B. Lane.)

Since its founding in 1628, on the island known today as Manhattan, the Reformed Dutch Church has adopted as its seal an adaptation of the coat of arms of Prince William of Orange. Prince William was defender of the faith and leader of the struggle for religious freedom and national independence of the Netherlands. A beautiful walnut, hand-carved replica of the seal, dedicated in the 1980s, hangs in this church today. (Photograph courtesy of the Neshanic Reformed Church.)

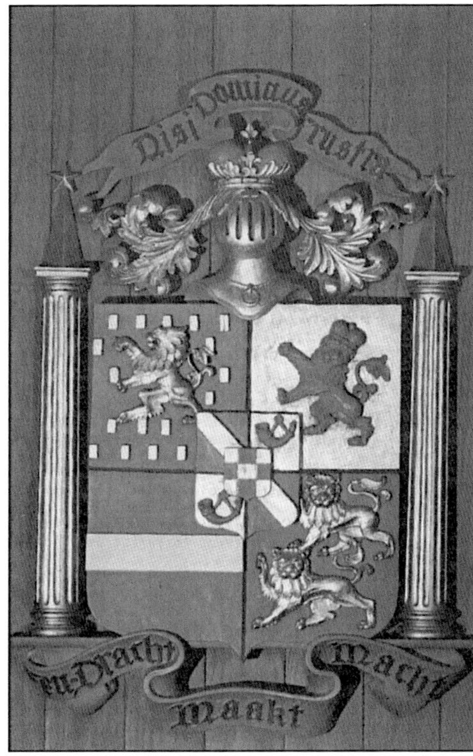

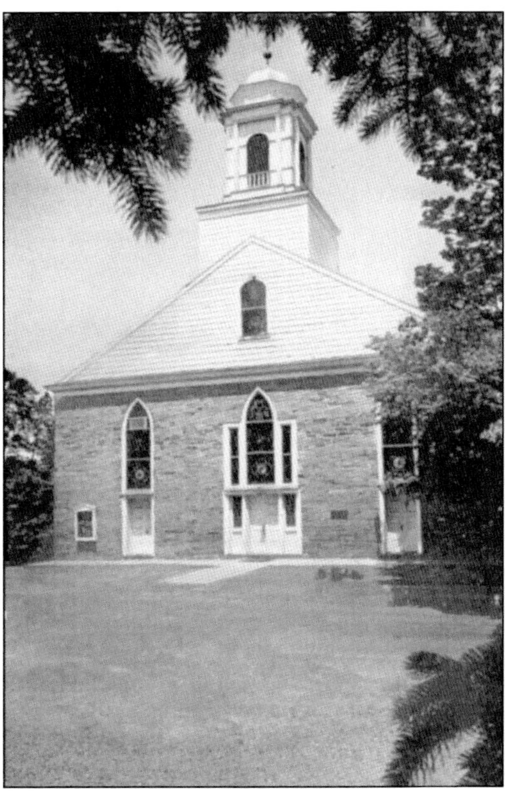

This postcard picture, taken in 1952, represents the Neshanic Reformed Dutch Church. (Courtesy of the Neshanic Reformed Church.)

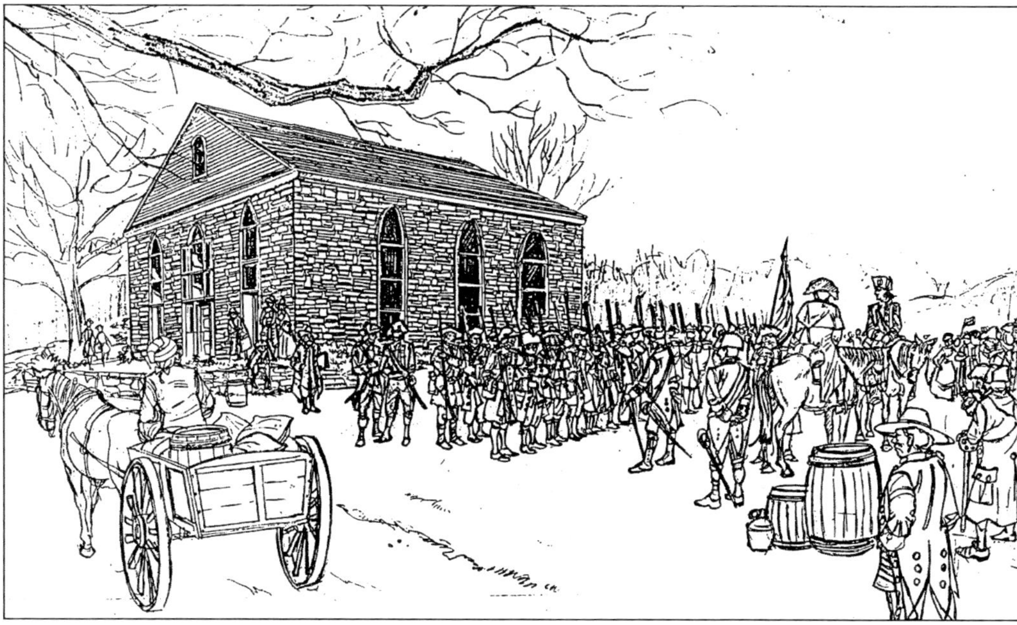

The First Somerset Minutemen, illustrated in this *c.* 1775 sketch, are forming at Neshanic Reformed Church to march off in response to General Washington's call to arms. (Sketch by John Albright, courtesy of Charles Stone.)

NESHANIC REFORMED CHURCH
Reverend Dr. Richard J. Tiggelaar, Pastor
P. O. Box 657, Neshanic Station NJ 08853-0657
(908) 369-4542

SOMERSET MINUTEMEN ROSTER

MAY 1775

Captains: John Ten Eyck, Ryner Veghte

Lieutenants: Peter D. Vroom, John Brokaw

Second Lieutenant: Jacobus Quick

Ensign: Joakim Quick

Sergeants: Minne DuBois, Andrew Van Middlesworth, Hendrick Post, Peter Quick, Benjamin Taylor, Abraham Van Arsdale

Corporals: Peter Brokaw, Jacobus Bergen, Thomas Coevert

Fifer: Bergen Coevert

Privates:
Jacobus Amerman
Albert Amerman
John Amerman
Thomas Auten
John Brokaw (Lieutenant when killed at Germantown)
Abraham Brokaw
George Brokaw
Jacob Cook
Jacob W. Cook
Jacobus Corshow
Peter Ditmars
Nicholas DuBois
William Griggs
Augustus Hartshough
Harmon A. Hoagland
Lucas Hoagland
Peter Hoagland
Dirck Huff
Abram Low
Peter Leyster
Hugh McAllum
Peter Perlee
Thomas Skillman
Abram Stryker
Jonathan Spader
Albert Stothoff
Willet Taylor
Abram Tayler
Garret Van Arsdale
John Van Dyke
William Van Dyke
Tunis Van Middflesworth
Jacobus Van Nuys
Coert Van Waggoner
Jacobus Voorhees
Rynier Veghte
Peter Voorhees
Peter Vroom
Jacob Winter
Coert Van Voorhees

The May 1775 Somerset Minutemen Roster is shown here. Note that many of the same families' descendants remain residents of the area today. (From *History of Troop 1776, Boy Scouts of America* by Harold DeHart.)

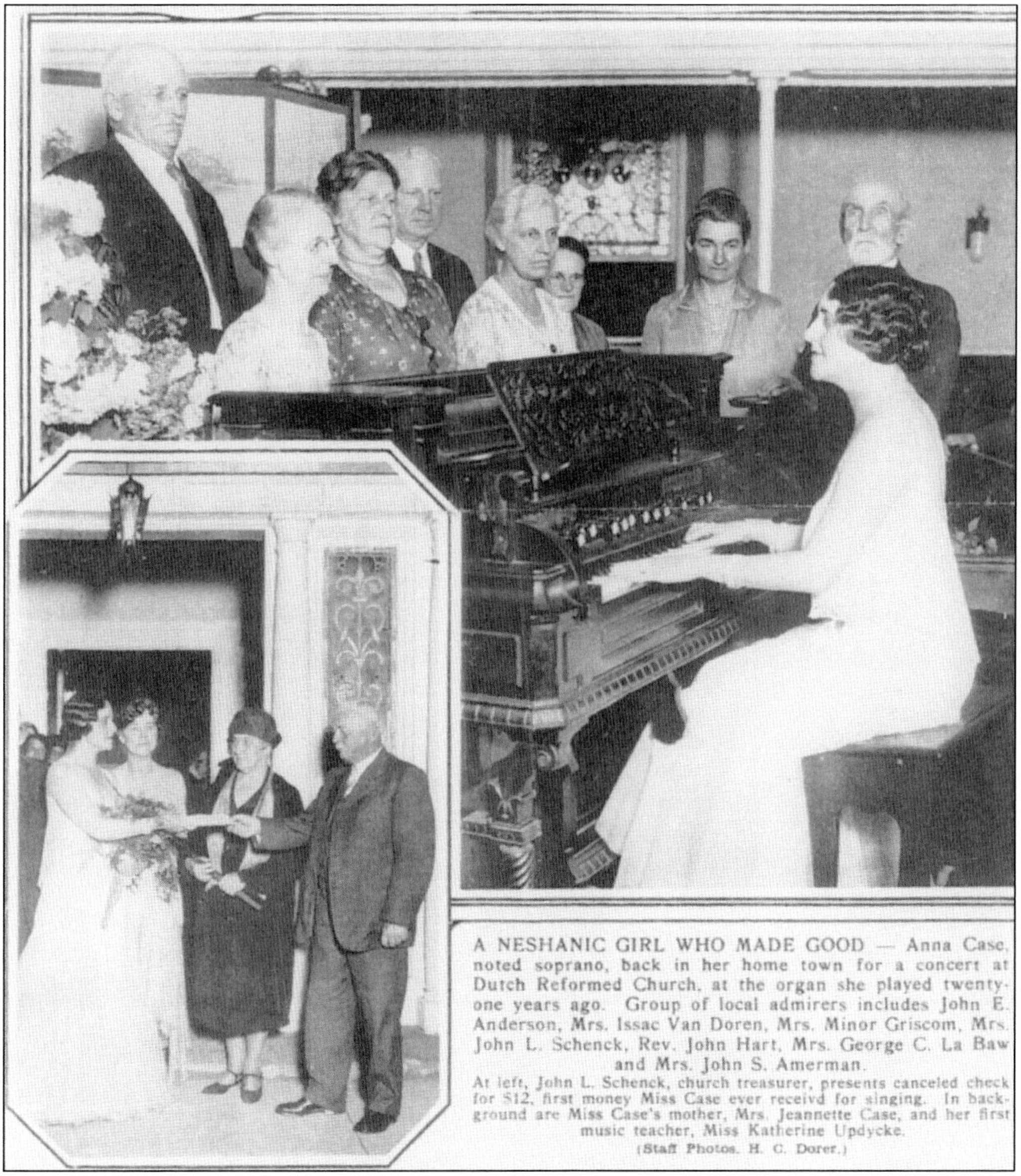
A NESHANIC GIRL WHO MADE GOOD — Anna Case, noted soprano, back in her home town for a concert at Dutch Reformed Church, at the organ she played twenty-one years ago. Group of local admirers includes John E. Anderson, Mrs. Issac Van Doren, Mrs. Minor Griscom, Mrs. John L. Schenck, Rev. John Hart, Mrs. George C. La Baw and Mrs. John S. Amerman.

At left, John L. Schenck, church treasurer, presents canceled check for $12, first money Miss Case ever receivd for singing. In background are Miss Case's mother, Mrs. Jeannette Case, and her first music teacher, Miss Katherine Updycke.

(Staff Photos. H. C. Dorer.)

Anna Case, noted soprano from South Branch, is shown here playing the Reformed Church organ at a recital in 1930. The organ was one of many placed in area churches by the Andrew Carnegie Foundation. (Photograph from the Newark Sunday Call, courtesy of June Stryker Amerman.)

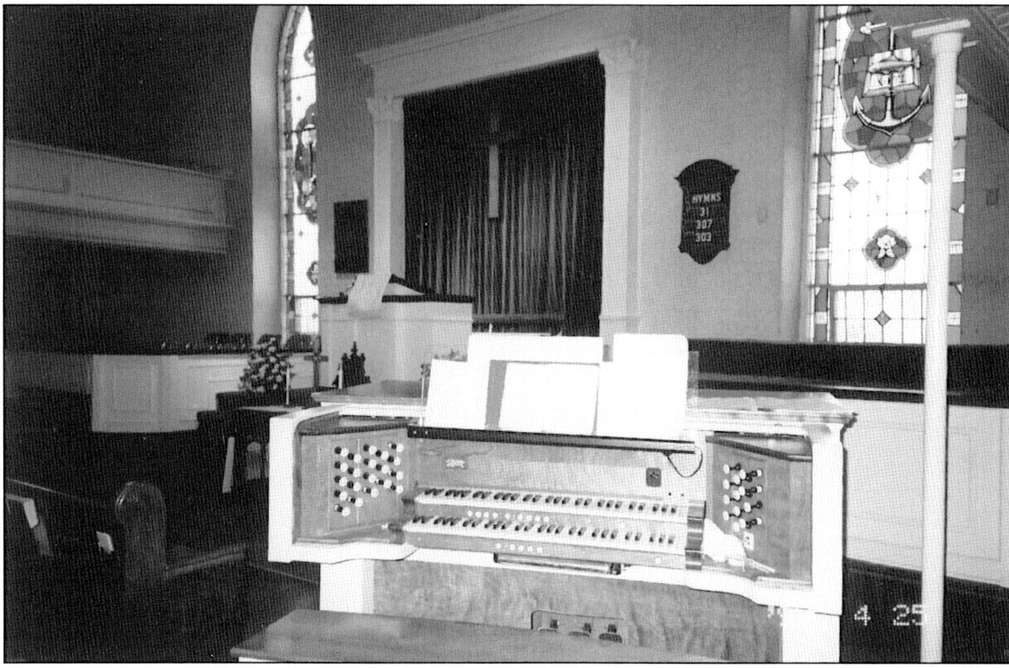

A new organ, placed in the Neshanic Reformed Church, was dedicated to Alida Kip Totten on May 23, 1982, and renamed as the "Harry S. and Alida K. Totten Memorial Organ" in 1984. (Photograph courtesy of the Neshanic Reformed Church.)

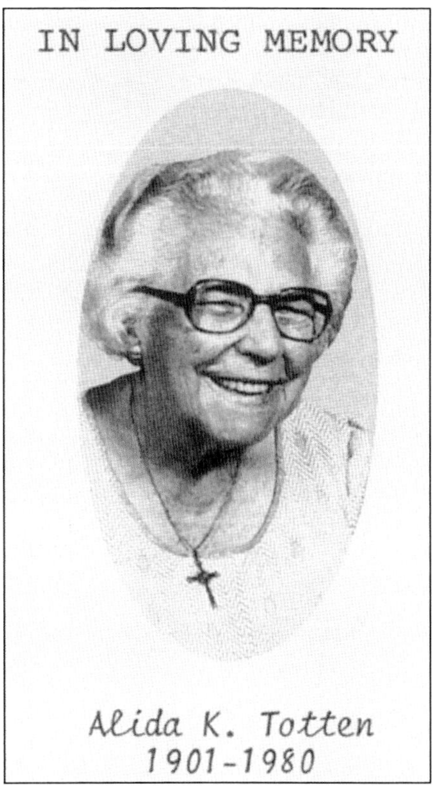

This small portrait is of Alida Kip Totten, 1901–1980. (Photograph courtesy of the Neshanic Reformed Church.)

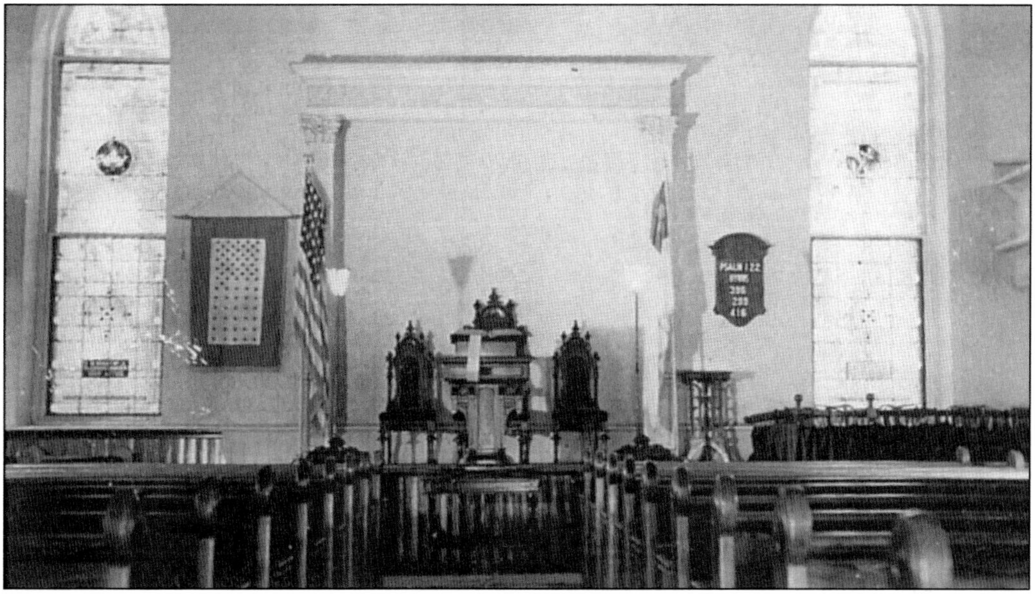

This interior view of Neshanic Reformed Church shows the pulpit area, including the WW II servicemen's star flag. Each star represented a member in the armed forces. The stained-glass windows were replaced with new windows in 1963. (Photograph courtesy of the Neshanic Reformed Church.)

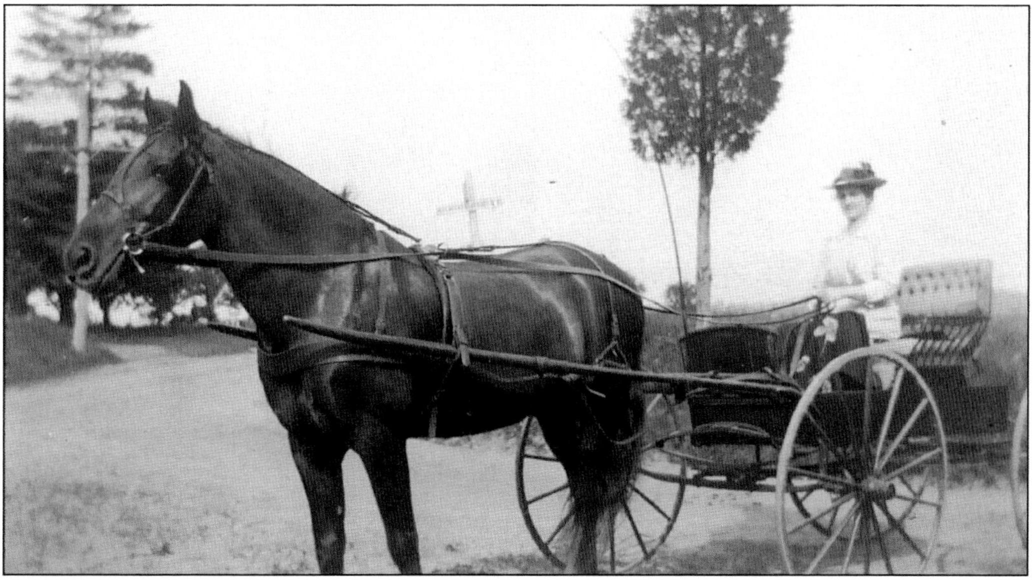

Mabel Stryker Neary is shown here on her way to church on Amwell Road, at the corner of Wertsville Road, around 1910. (Photograph courtesy of G.W. Amerman.)

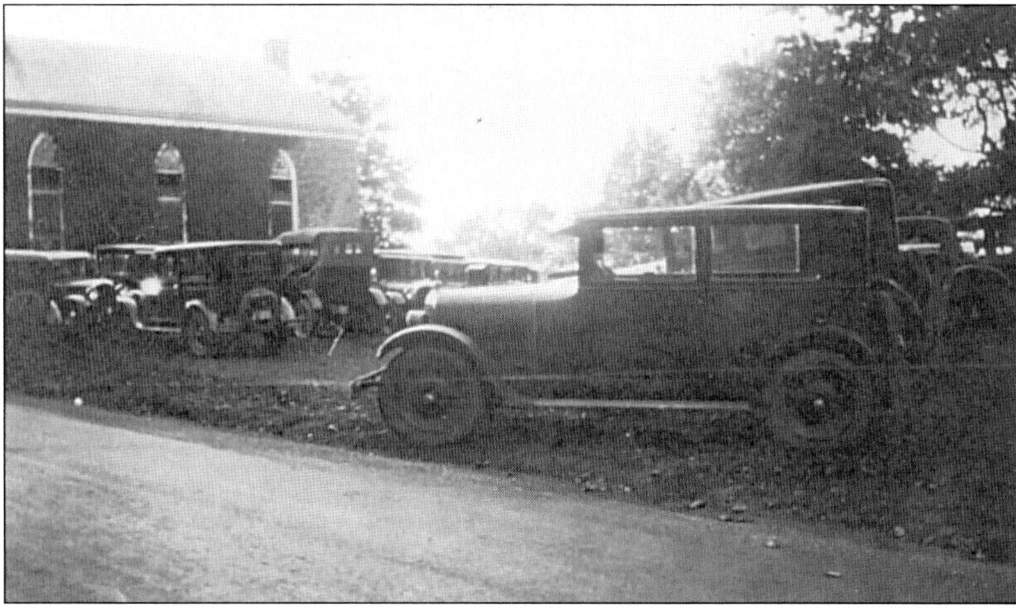

Neshanic Reformed Church parking lot is shown here at the time of the 175th Anniversary on October 26, 1927. (Photograph courtesy of the Neshanic Reformed Church.)

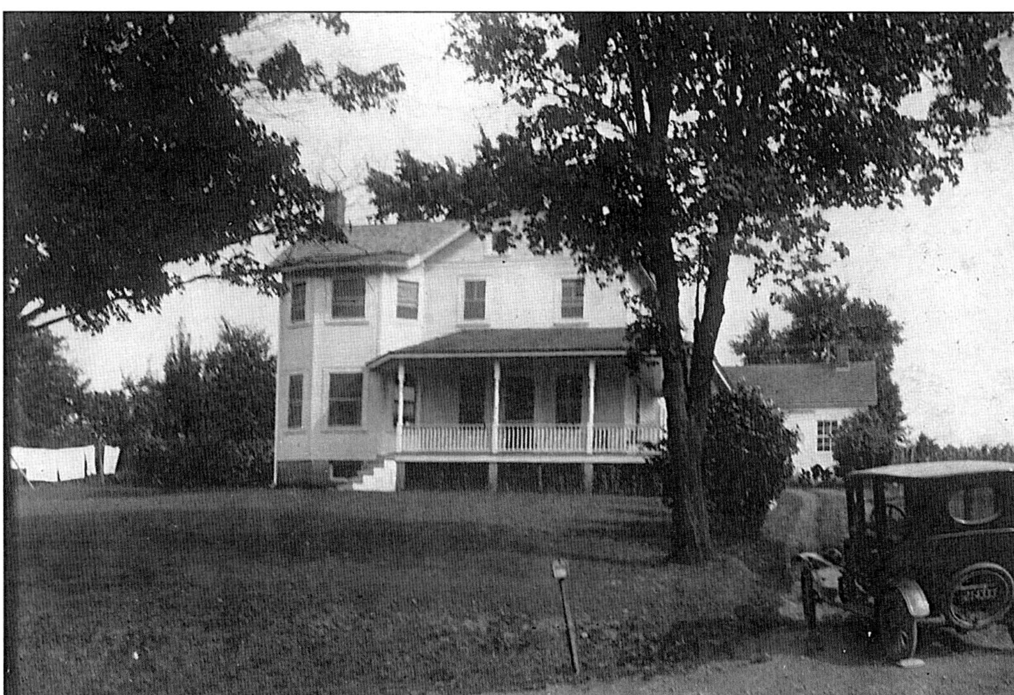

Pictured here is Neshanic Reformed Church's fourth parsonage at 722 Amwell Road, opposite the church parking area. It was the residence of five pastors. The car shown is that of Reverend Dr. John Hart in 1924. (Photograph courtesy of L.B. Lane.)

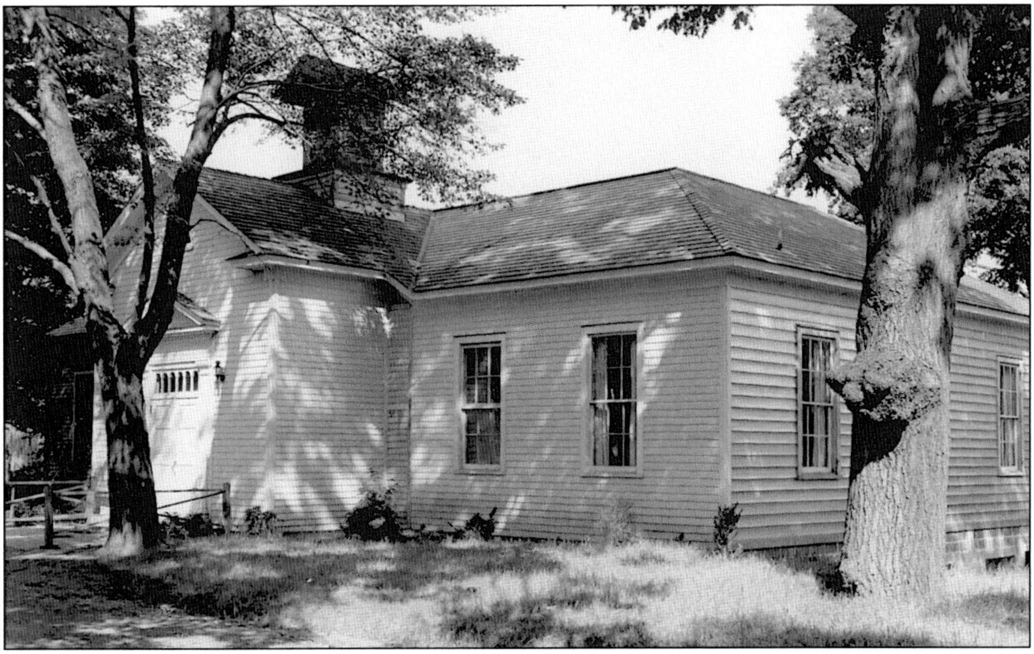

This is Brookside Hall, Neshanic Reformed Church Sunday school, shown in the mid-1950s. This view shows how the church enlarged the original one-room school, whose belfry is still showing and contains the bell. (Photograph courtesy of Stanley Wood.)

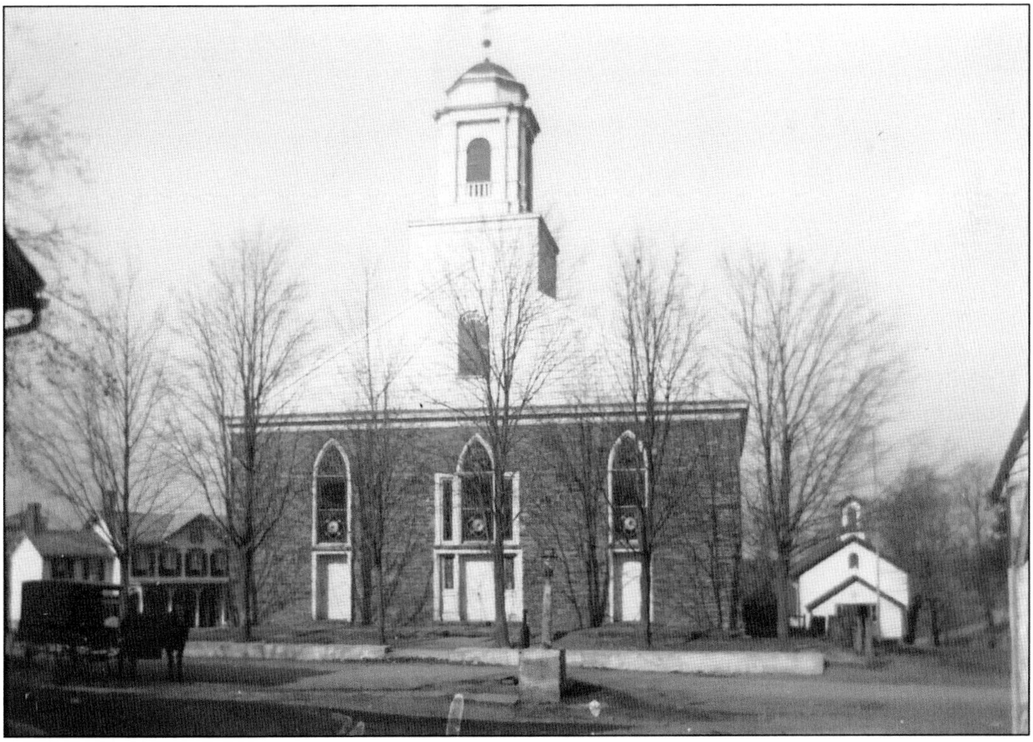

This c. 1900 postcard view of the Neshanic Reformed Church shows Dr. Andersen's home to the left and the original one-room school on the right. (Photograph courtesy of L.B. Lane.)

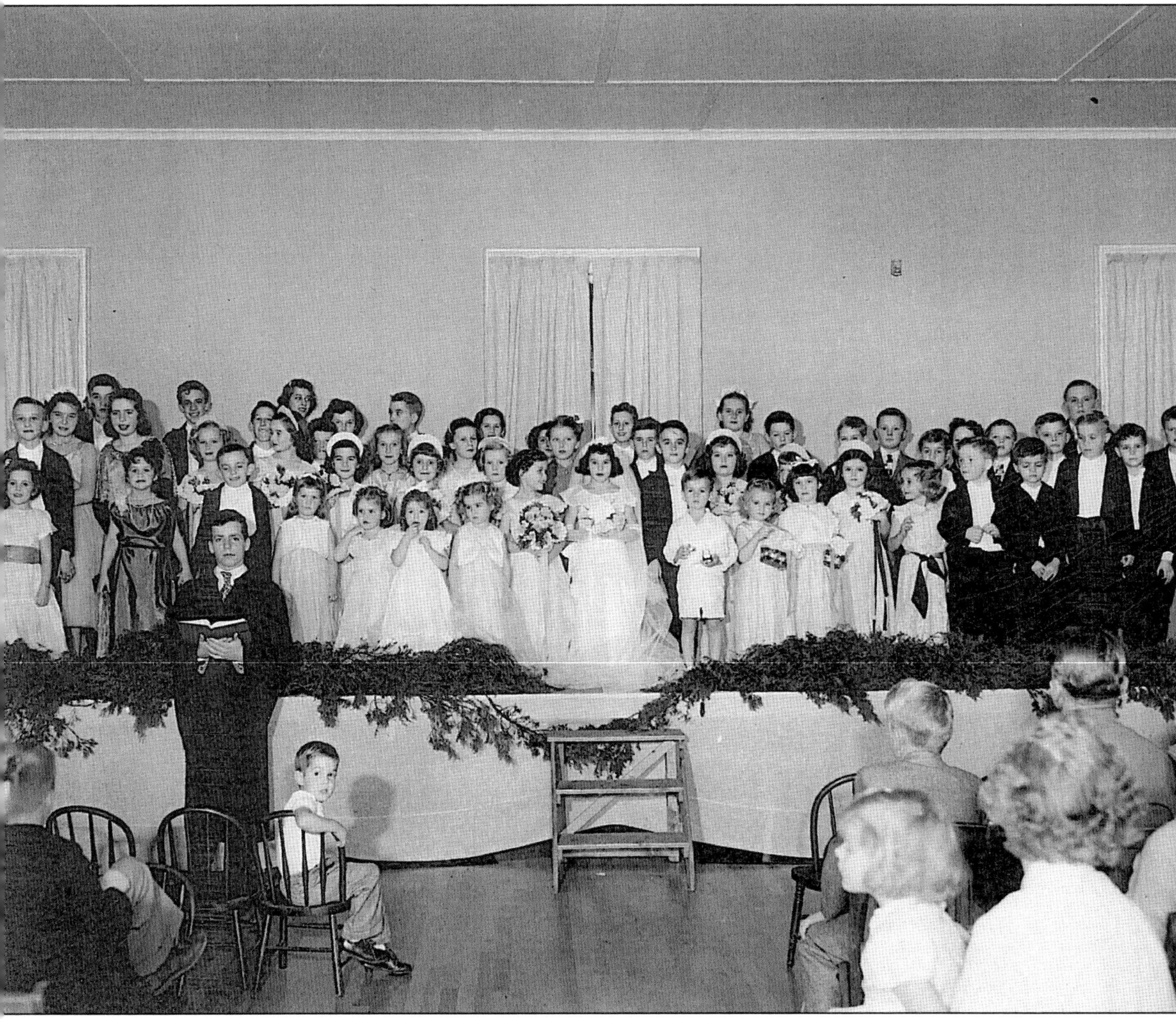

A Tom Thumb wedding, performed by Sunday school students in October 1950, is shown here shortly after Brookside Hall auditorium was enlarged. The participants were as follows: Marjorie Shepherd, bride; George Wallace, groom; David Totten, minister. (Towne Studio Photograph, courtesy of Rev. George Scholten.)

Four

RAILROADS

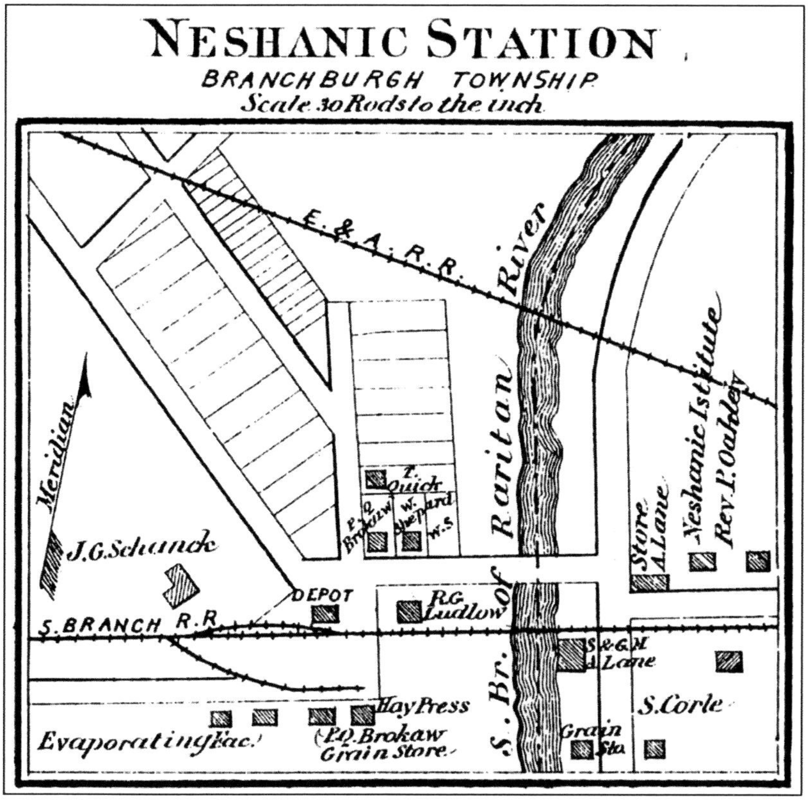

This 1875 map shows the Villa Sites subdivision by John G. Schenck, which was Somerset County's first registered subdivision. By the mid-19th century, the railroads were already a major presence in Neshanic Station, with the Easton and Amboy Railroad (later the Lehigh Valley Railroad) on the east side of the village and the South Branch Railroad (later the Central Railroad of New Jersey) on the west.

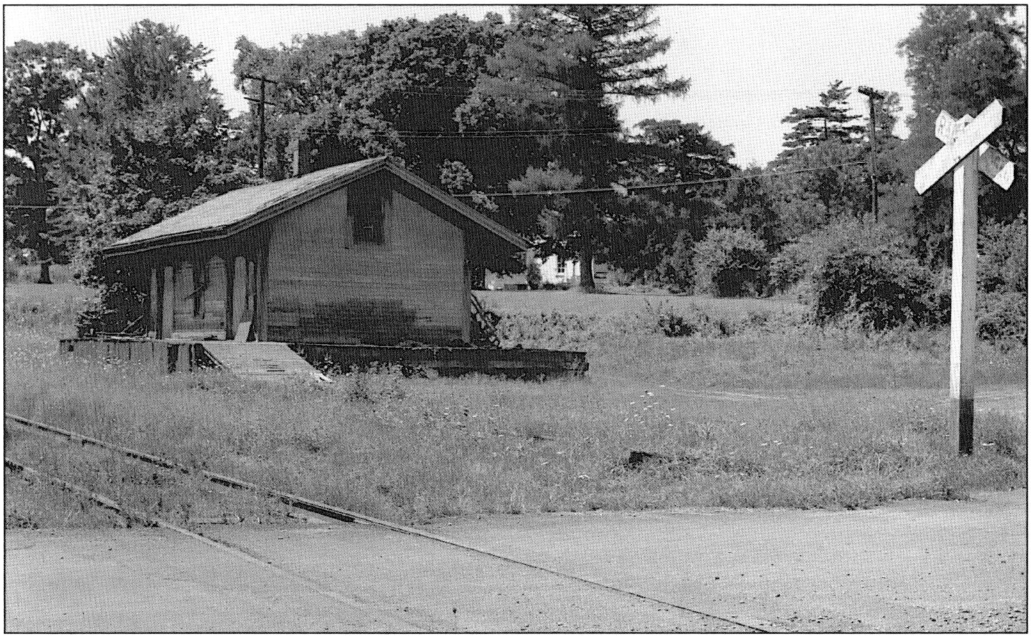

This freight station, now long gone, served the Central Railroad of New Jersey near the passenger station. It was one of several stations that served the immediate area of Neshanic Station. It was here, around the turn of the century, that wagons of peaches were unloaded for shipment to New York City. (Photograph courtesy of Walt Kostro.)

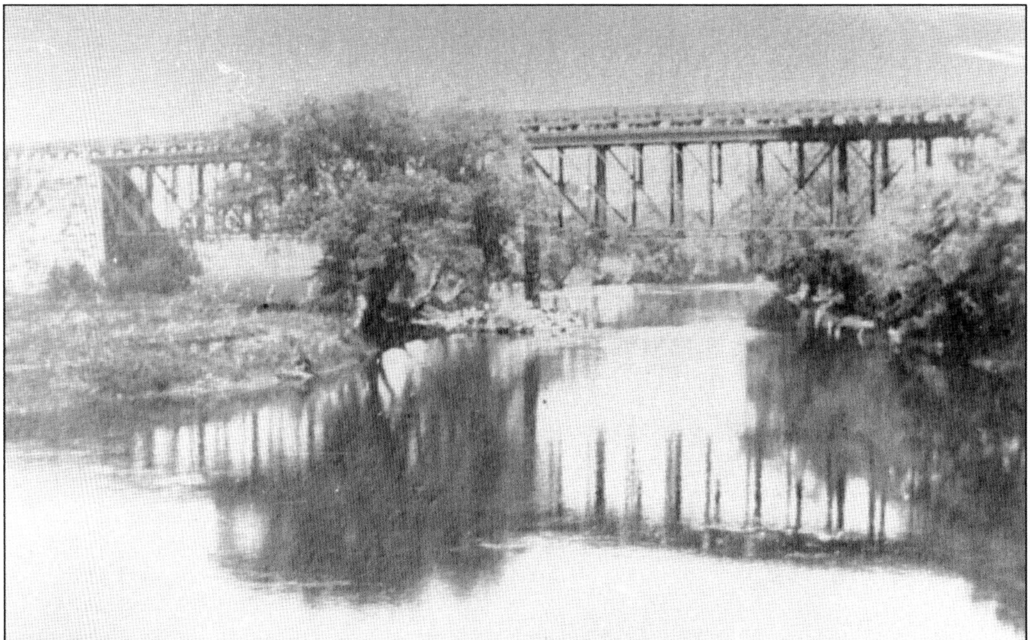

This is the only picture known to exist of the original bridge over the south branch of the Raritan River, which was built for the Easton and Amboy Railroad and later replaced. Trainloads of peaches, such as the one pictured here, were shipped regularly to New York from Neshanic Station. (Photograph courtesy of the Neshanic Station Historical Society.)

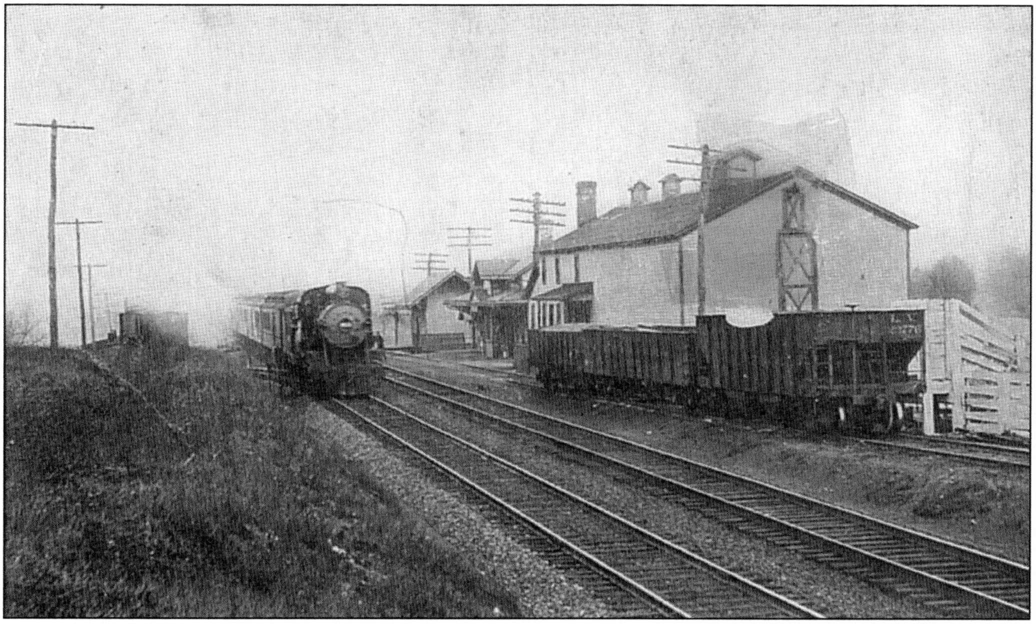

This passenger station on the Lehigh Railroad tracks stood next to a local creamery, both of which are now gone. They stood across the tracks from the Shurts feed store, now the Neshanic Farm, Home, and Garden Store (on Fairview Drive). Another Lehigh Station was located less than a mile away, across the river, on the Hillsborough side. (Photo postcard courtesy of Robert Yuell.)

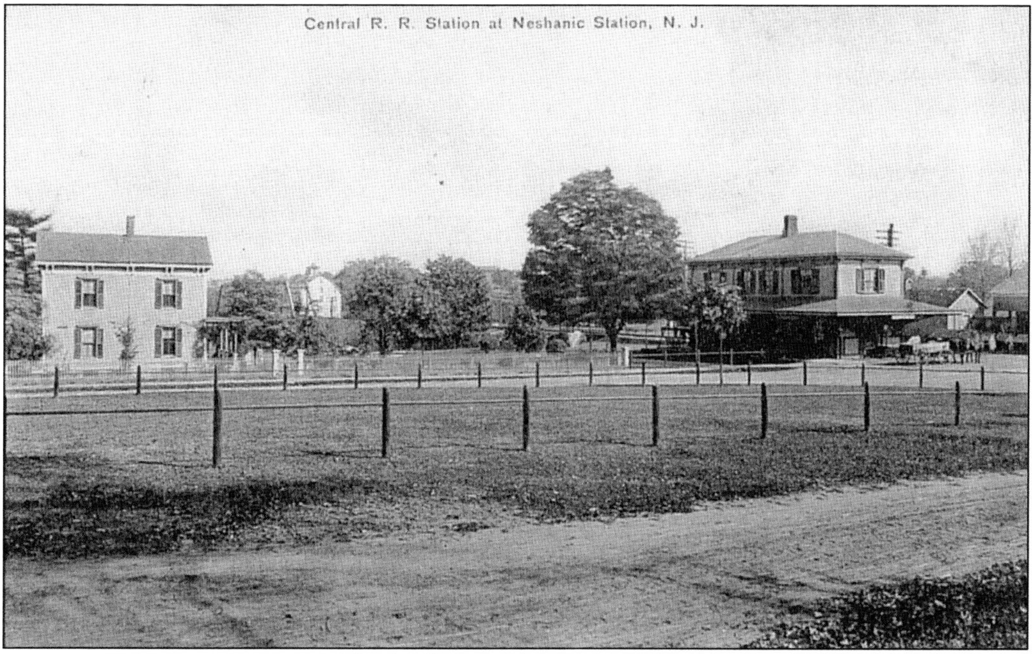

This postcard shows the center of the village in 1906, before the fire that destroyed a number of the buildings shown here. The grassy parcel of property in the foreground is now the site of the post office. (Photo postcard courtesy of Robert Yuell.)

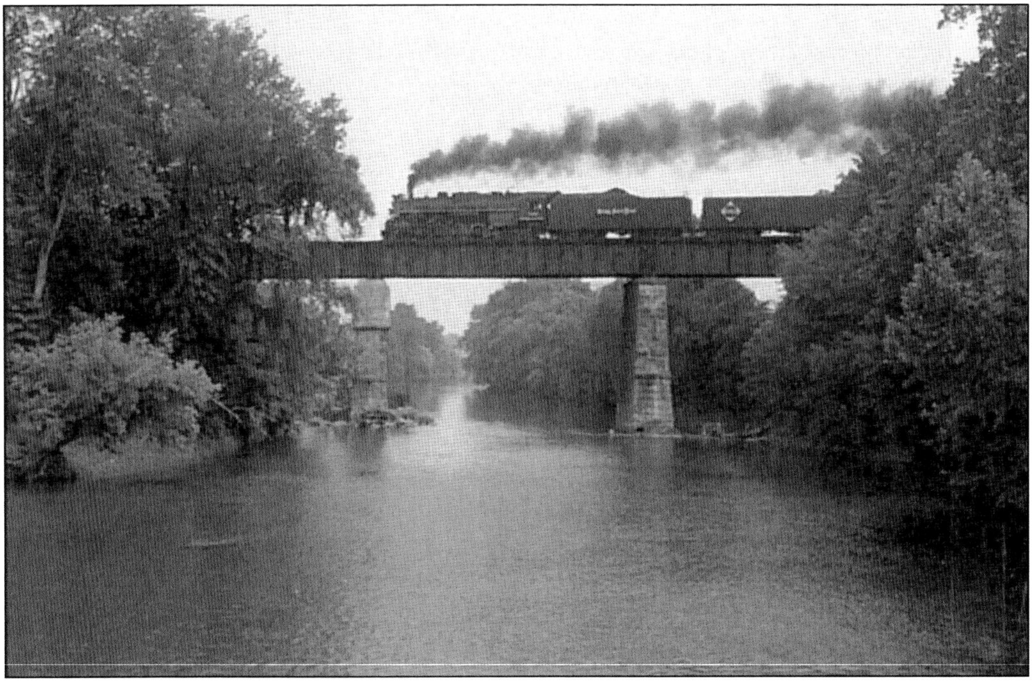

By the time of this picture, trees had grown along the riverbank. The railroad cars shown here were noticeably larger than those shown in an earlier picture, but coal was still king. (Photograph courtesy of Joan Levering.)

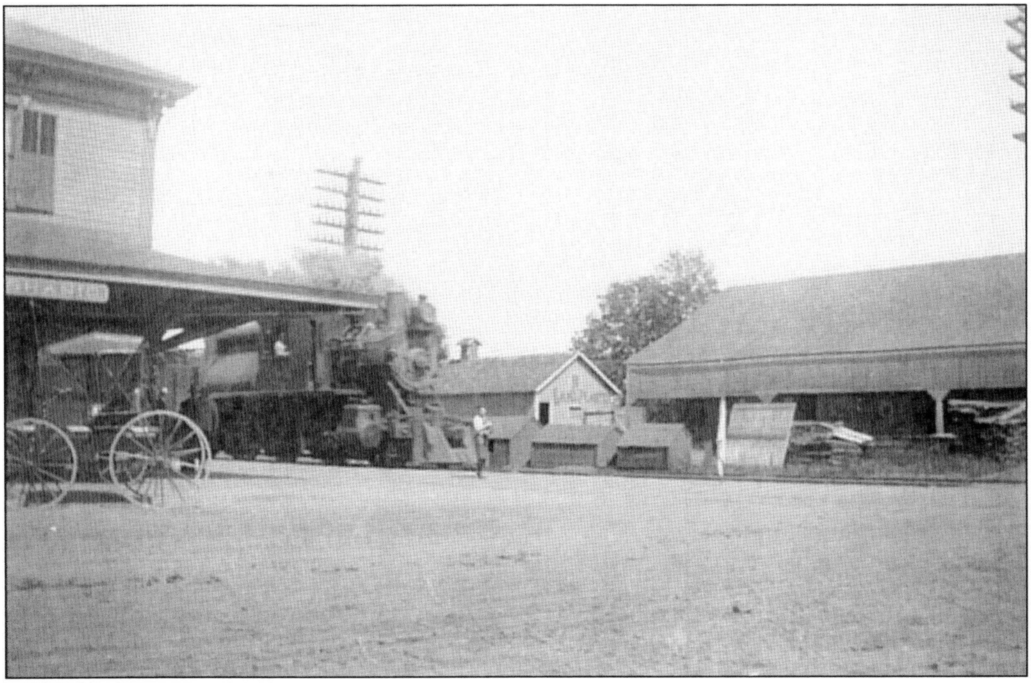

This *c.* 1908 postcard of the Central Railroad of New Jersey at Neshanic Station shows the creamery (with cupola), where the 1910 fire started; the J.S. Amerman Co. hay press; and rail cars under the overhang. (Photo postcard courtesy of Robert Yuell.)

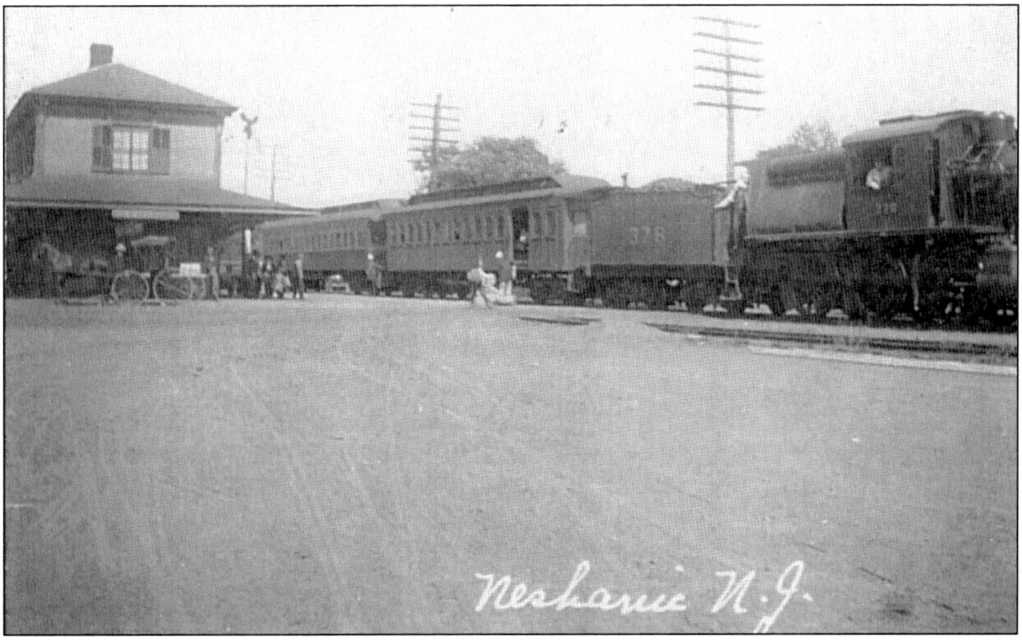

Camelback engines like the ones shown above, with the engineer's cab straddling the engine, were a common sight in Neshanic Station from the turn of the century into the 1940s. (Photo postcard courtesy of Robert Yuell.)

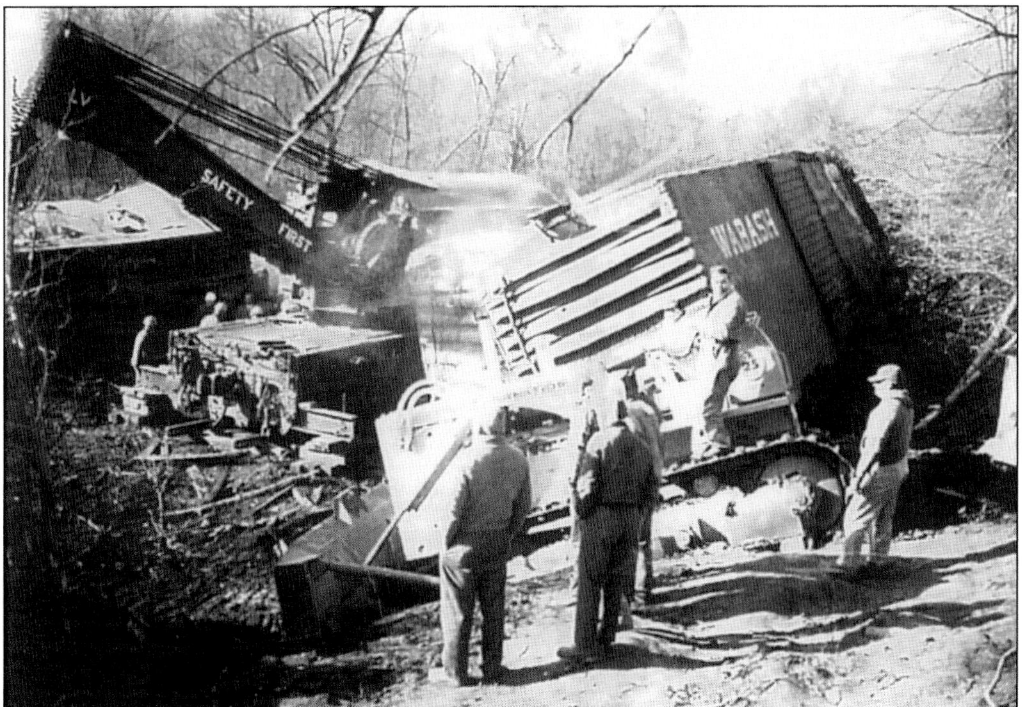

Train wrecks, like this one in the 1950s, were not common in the area of Neshanic Station. The tracks of both railroads were very straight approaching the village, but equipment failures and operator error took a toll. (Photograph courtesy of the Toles family.)

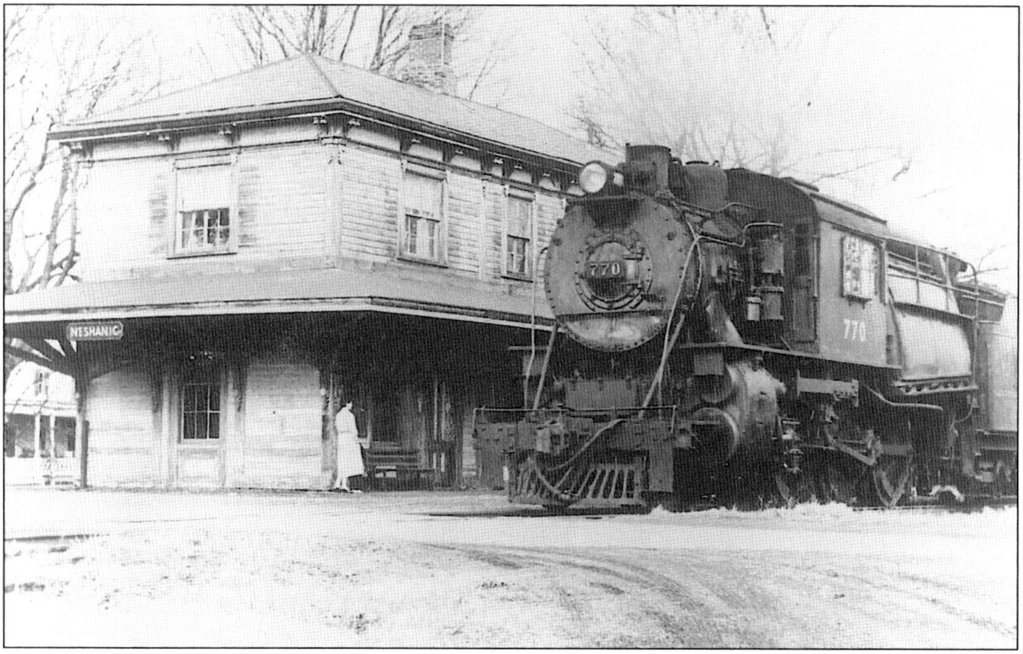

The approaching demise of the Central Railroad of New Jersey is evident from this 1952 photograph. The station is in obvious disrepair and the camelback engine is probably over 40 years old, but until 1953, you could still commute from Neshanic Station to New York (or to Somerville or Flemington!). (Photograph courtesy of Walt Kostro.)

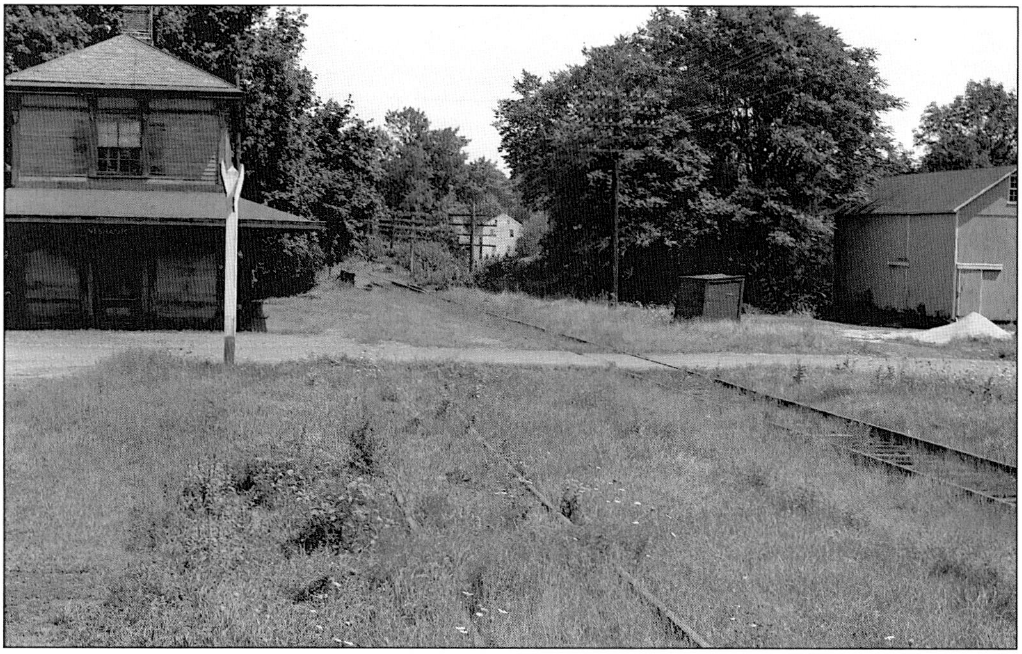

Within a year of the end of passenger service (and a few years before the end of freight service), grass had started to take over the right of way. The mill and the telegraph wires can be seen in the background. Today, the telegraph wires are gone, and the mill has now become a residence after restoration. (Photograph courtesy of Walt Kostro.)

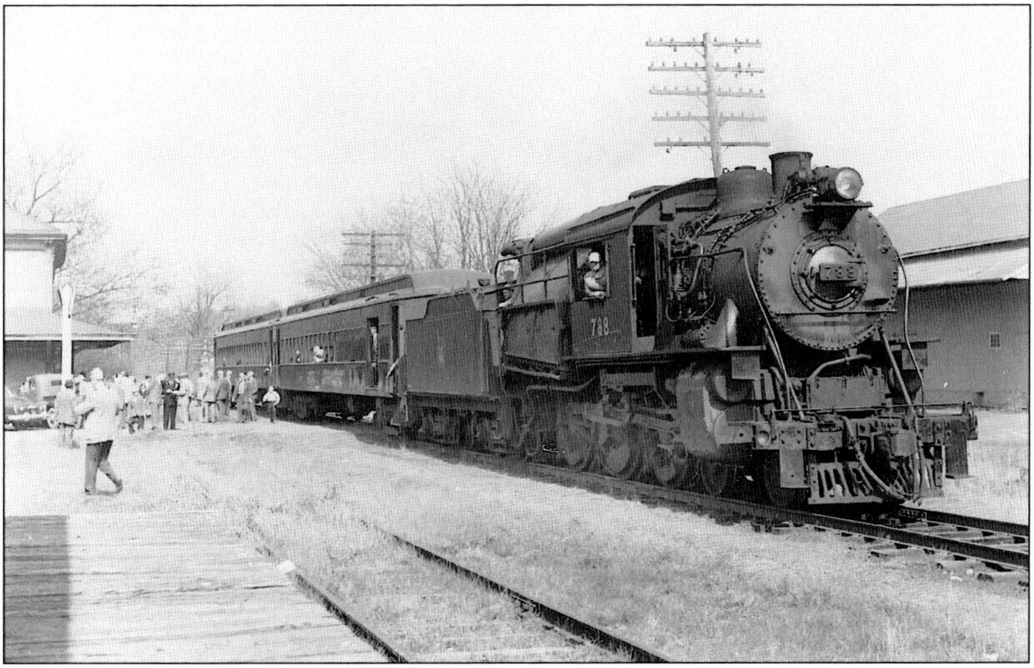

This scene shows passengers boarding at Neshanic Station for the last run to Flemington on April 24, 1953. (Photograph by Homer R. Hill.)

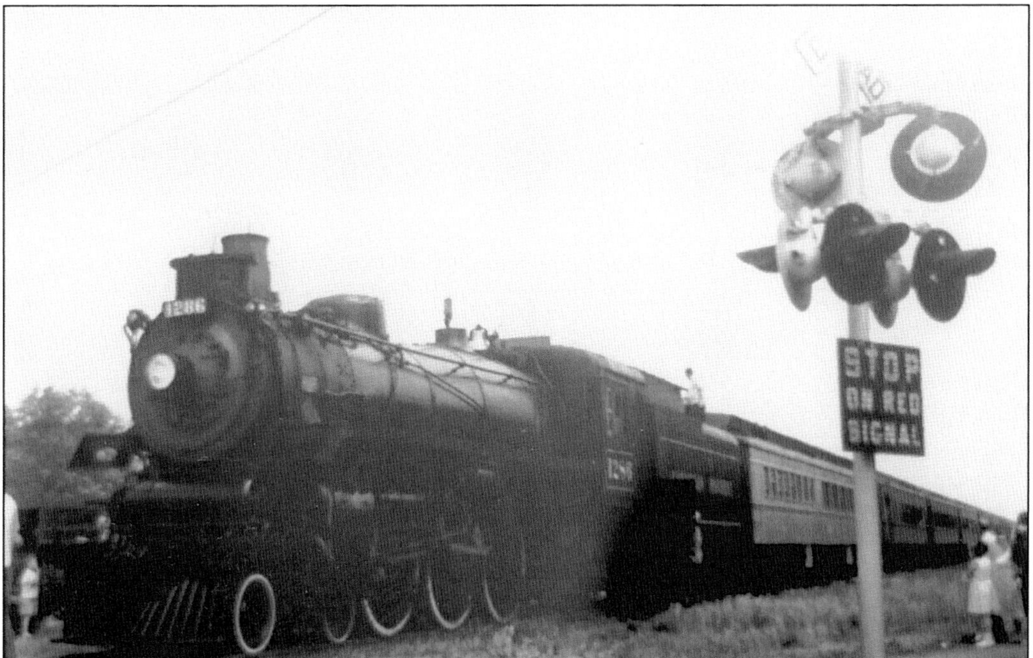

The Hunterdon County Agriculture Commission annual excursion to West Point and Bear Mountain, via Circle Line Ferry boats, is shown here pulled by engine number 1286 at Neshanic Station. These were the longest passenger trains seen on the South Branch Line with two runs of 10 to 12 cars each. (Photograph courtesy of Somerset County Historical Society.)

NEW YORK TERMINAL—Foot of Cortlandt or Desbrosses Streets (Pennsylvania R. R. Ferries).
BROOKLYN TERMINAL—Foot of Fulton Street (Brooklyn Annex Boats).

LEHIGH VALLEY RAILROAD SYSTEM.

EASTON & AMBOY R. R.

AND CONNECTIONS.

Anthracite Coal used.] [Insuring Cleanliness and Comfort.

TAKING EFFECT JANUARY 31, 1897—SUBJECT TO CHANGE.

WESTWARD.

STATIONS.	51	17	o 1	78	21	9	o 25	o 28	75	o 29		77	45	65	83	79	8	7	5	71	SUNDAY TRAINS. 617	1	659	45	o 8	5
NEW YORK.........Lv.	a. m.	a. m.	a. m.	a. m.	a. m.	noon	p. m.	p. m.	p. m.	p. m.		p. m.	p. m.	p. m	p. m.	p. m.	p. m.	p. m.	p. m.	p. m.	a. m.	a. m.	p. m.	p. m.	p. m.	p. m
Cortlandt or Desbrosses Sts...		6.40	8.20	9.00	10.50	12.00	12.40	1.40	2.30	4.10		4.20	5.20		6.10	6.30	7.00	8.30	9.00	11.50	7.00	8.15		5.20	7.00	9.00
Brooklyn ..P.R.R Anx Lv.		6.05	8.00	8.48	10.30	11.45	12.05	1.27	2.15	3.46		3.46	5.03		5.47	6.14	6.40	7.48	8.45	11.08		8.00		5.03	6.40	8.45
Jersey City ....Lv.		6.52	8.33	9.16	11.03	12.14	12.55	1.53	2.44	4.22		4.33	5.34		6.22	6.42	7.14	8.43	9.14	12.03	7.12	8.33		5.34	7.14	9.12
Newark—Market St........		s 7.06	s 8.47	s 9.33	s11.16	s12.23	s 1.08	s 2.07	s 3.58	s 4.34		s 4.46	s 5.47		s 6.36	s 6.55	s 7.28	s 8.58	s 9.26	s12.15	s 7.25	s 8.48		s 5.50	s 7.28	s 9.24
Newark-Frelinghuysen Ave		f7.11		f9.38	f11.22		f1.13		f3.03			f4.51	f5.52							f12.24	f7.29			f5.52		
Jersey City, Washington St																										
Edgewater Junction.....																										
Avenue D..............																										
Waverly Avenue.........		7.14		9.39	11.23		1.14		3.04			f4.52	f5.53			f7.03		9.10		12.26	7.30			f5.53		
Elizabeth Junction.....		7.16	p8.54	9.41	11.25		1.16	2.16	3.06			4.54	5.56		6.47	7.05			9.35	12.28	7.32	f8.54		5.56		9.35
Saybrook..............		f7.17		f9.42	f11.26		f1.17		f3.07			f4.55	f5.57			f7.06			e9.38	12.29	f7.33			f5.57		e9.38
Morris Avenue..........		7.19		9.44	11.29		1.20		3.09			4.57	6.00			7.08				f12.32	7.35			6.00		
Roselle................		7.23		9.47	11.32		1.24	e2.20	3.13			5.01	6.04		6.53	7.11			9.40	12.36	7.39	v 8.56		6.04		9.40
Faitoute...............		7.25		9.49	11.35		1.25		3.15			5.03	6.06			7.13				12.3-	7.41			6.06		
South Cranford.........		7.27		9.51	11.37		1.28		3.17			5.05	6.08		6.56	7.15			v9.43	12.40	7.43			6.08		v9.43
Picton.................		7.29		9.54	11.39		1.30	w	3.19			5.08	6.11		v 6.59	7.18			v9.45	12.43	7.46			6.11		v9.45
Ash Brook..............		7.33		9.58	11.43		1.34		3.23			5.12	6.15			7.22			v9.48	12.47	7.50			6.15		v9.48
Potters Crossing		f7.34		f10.00	f11.45		f1.35		f3.25			f5.14	f6.17			f7.24				f12.49	f7.52			f6.18		
Oak Tree		7.38		10.02	11.47		1.38		3.28			5.17	6.19		v 7.04	7.27			v9.52	12.51	7.55			6.19		v9.52
Perth Amboy, State St. Lv	6.25	7.23	8.45		11.30	11.30		2.05		4.20			6.00								7.35	8.35	1.55	5.45		
Perth Amboy, Dublin Cross	6.27	7.25	8.47		11.32	11.32		2.07		4.22			6.02								7.37	8.37	1.57	5.47		
Eagleswood............	f6.29	f7.27	f8.49		f11.34	f11.34		[illegible]		[illegible]			f6.04								[illegible]	[illegible]	[illegible]	[illegible]		
Ford's.................	6.32	7.30	8.52		11.37	11.37		2.12		4.27			6.07								7.42	8.42	2.02	5.52		
Valentine's............	f6.34	f7.32	f8.54		f11.39	f11.39		f2.14		f4.29			f6.09								f7.44	f8.44	f2.04	f5.54		
Metuchen...............	6.38	7.36	8.58		11.43	11.43		2.18		4.32			6.13								7.48	8.48	2.08	5.58		
Perth Junction.........	6.40	7.38	9.00		11.45	11.45		2.20		4.34			6.15	6.40							7.50	8.50	2.10	6.00		
So. Plainfield.........	6.45	7.44	9.10	10.07	11.54	12.52	1.44	2.34	3.34	4.58		5.22	6.25	6.45	7.10	7.32	7.52	9.32	9.58	12.55	8.01	9.10	2.15	6.25	7.52	9.58
New Market.............		7.49		10.11	11.59		1.48	2.38	3.38			5.26	6.30		7.15	7.36			v10.01	1.02	8.06	v 9.13		6.30		v10.01
West Dunellen..........		7.51		10.13	12.01		1.50		3.40			5.28	6.32			7.38				1.04	8.06			6.32		
Bound Brook............		7.56	9.18	10.18	12.06		1.56	2.43	3.45			5.32	6.37		7.21	7.42			10.07	1.09	8.13	9.18		6.37		10.07
Hillsboro..............		8.00			f12.10		f2.00						f6.41								8.18			f6.41		
South Somerville		f8.03			f12.13		f2.03						f6.44								f8.21			f6.44		
Flagtown...............		f8.10			f12.20		f2.10						f6.51								f8.29			f6.51		
Neshanic...............		8.14			12.24		2.14						6.55								8.33			6.55		
West Neshanic..........		f8.16			f12.26		f2.16						f6.57								f8.35			f6.57		
Woodfern...............		f8.18			f12.28		f2.18						7.00								f8.37			7.00		
Three Bridges..........		8.22			12.32		2.22						7.05								8.41			7.05		
Flemington Junction....		8.27	9.38		12.37		2.27	3.05		5.25			7.10		7.43				v10.30		8.46	9.38		7.10		v10.30
Flemington...........Ar.		8.32	9.44		12.42		2.32	3.10		5.30			7.15		7.48						8.50			7.15		
Flemington ....Lv.		8.20	9.25		12.32		2.20	3.00		5.20			7.05		7.35						8.40			7.05		
Stanton................		8.32			12.42		f2.32						f7.16								8.51			f7.15		
Bunnyside..............		f8.34			f12.44		f2.34						f7.17								f8.53			f7.17		
Landsdown		8.40			12.50		2.38	3.14		5.32			7.21		7.52						8.59			7.21		
Clinton..............Ar.		8.53			12.55		2.42	3.19		5.37			7.26		7.57						9.05			7.26		
Clinton..............Lv.		8.35			12.45		2.30	3.08		5.25			7.15		7.45						8.54			7.15		
Pittstown............Ar.		10.10			1.55		3.40	3.40		6.15											9.25					
Pittstown............Lv.		8.15			12.25		2.05	2.05		4.00			6.45		6.45						7.35			6.50		
Grandin................		8.43			12.53		f2.41						f7.24								9.02			f7.24		
Jutland................		8.47			12.57		2.45						7.28								9.06			7.28		
Pattenburg		8.53			1.03		2.51						7.34								9.12			7.34		
West Portal		8.57			1.07		2.55						7.39								9.16			7.39		
Bloomsbury		9.02			1.12		3.00	3.30					7.43								9.21			7.43		
Kennedy		f9.09			f1.19		f3.06						f7.49								f9.26			f7.49		
Whitaker...............		f9.12			f1.22		f3.09						f7.51								f9.31			f7.51		
Phillipsburg (Stockton St).		9.16			1.26		3.13						7.56								9.35			7.56		
Phillipsburg		9.18	10.13		1.28		3.15	3.43		5.57			7.58		8.18		f8.55		11.07		9.37	10.13		7.58	f8.55	11.07
EASTON ;.............Ar.		9.20	10.15		1.30	1.47	3.17	3.45		5.59			8.00		8.20		8.57	10.45	11.10		9.40	10.15		8.00	8.57	11.10
BETHLEHEM....... "		10.10	10.37		2.00	2.06	3.45	4.06		6.21					8.50		9.20	11.05	11.34		10.10	10.37		8.50	9.20	11.34
ALLENTOWN....... "		10.20	10.55		2.12	2.19	4.13	4.18		6.33					9.00		9.35		11.55		10.20	10.55		9.00	9.35	11.55
READING ....Ar.		1.43	1.43				5.50	5.50							10.50											
CATASAUQUA...... "		10.32	11.03		2.32		4.23	4.27		6.40					9.12				12.07		10.32	11.03		9.12		12.07
SLATINGTON...... "		10.58	11.22		2.58		4.46	4.45		7.00					9.40				12.28		10.58	11.22		9.40		12.28
POTTSVILLE, via Liz.Cr.Junct. "					4.23					8.17																
LEHIGHTON....... "		11.16			3.16		4.59	4.59		7.16									f12.44		11.16					f12.44
MAUCH CHUNK..... "		11.25	11.45		3.25	3.00	5.06	5.06		7.24							10.20	12.02	12.53		11.25	11.45			10.20	12.58
E. MAUCH CHUNK "		11.27	o		3.30		5.12	5.12		o											11.27	o			o	
GLEN ONOKO...... "			o				[illegible]	[illegible]		o												o				
PENN HAVEN JCT. "			o							[illegible]							[illegible]					o			o	
													p. m.								a. m.	a. m.		p. m.		

(Column 9: BLACK DIAMOND EXPRESS. Column 7: This train leaves stations New York to Bethlehem, inclusive, daily except Sundays; stations west of and including Mauch Chunk, daily except Mondays. Column 71: New York and Brooklyn stations west of and including ... Sundays only.)

; Dining station. v Stops to let off passengers from New York, Jersey City, Newark or Elizabeth Junction. f Stops only on signal. p Stops to take on passengers for Easton and points west. o Passengers taking train 1, 3, 23 or 29 for points marked thus (o) and points on Coal Branches to which branch trains run must change cars at Mauch Chunk. w Stops on Saturdays to let off passengers from New York or Newark. e Stops to let off passengers from New York and Newark. A.M. Time in light type, P.M. in heavy type. s Stops to take on passengers.

PULLMAN AND CHAIR CAR SERVICE.

Train No. 1—Parlor Car Philada. to Buffalo. Chair Car New York to Wilkes-Barre. Dining Car Easton to Buffalo. Sundays—Sleeping Car New York to Buffalo.
Train No. 29.—Pullman Buffet Parlor Car New York to Wilkes-Barre and Chair Car Philadelphia to Hazleton.
Train No. 23.—Chair Car New York to Wilkes-Barre.
Train No 33—Chair Car New York to Slatington.
Train No. 3—Sleeping Cars New York to Chicago, via Grand Trunk Railway System, Philadelphia to Buffalo; New York to Toronto.
Train No. 5—Sleeping Cars New York to Buffalo and Wilkes-Barre; Philadelphia to Chicago via Grand Trunk Railway System.
Train No. 9—Black Diamond Express, Combined Cafe and Dining Car, Day Coaches and Parlor Car, New York to Buffalo, and Day Coach Philadelphia to Buffalo.
Train No. 7.—Weekdays—Sleeping Car New York to Buffalo.

ROLLIN H. WILBUR, GENERAL SUPT, SOUTH BETHLEHEM, PA.
W. B. SMITH, GEN'L EAST. PASS'R AGENT, 235 Broadway, NEW YORK.
CHAS. S. LEE, GENERAL PASSENGER AGENT, PHILADELPHIA, PA.
A. W. NONNEMACHER, ASST. GEN'L PASS'R AGT., SOUTH BETHLEHEM, PA.

Pictured here is the 1897 Easton and Amboy Railroad schedule of the Lehigh Valley Railroad System, showing the two Neshanic stations. (Courtesy of Robert Yuell.)

Five

Neshanic Volunteer Fire Company

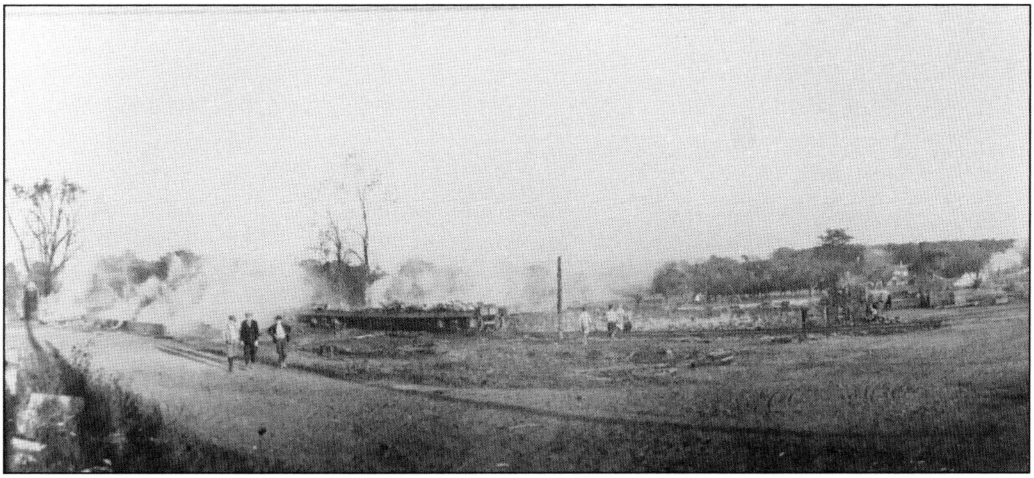

The need for a local fire company became evident in 1910, when a major blaze destroyed the eastern edge of the village. The fire started in a creamery by the Central Jersey Railroad. The boiler that exploded is by the large tree on the left of the picture. Two rail cars were consumed by the blaze at the J.S. Amerman hay press building. The lumberyard, Holcombe's Hotel, and the Schenck farm (to the far rear) were all destroyed. (Photograph courtesy of G.W. Amerman.)

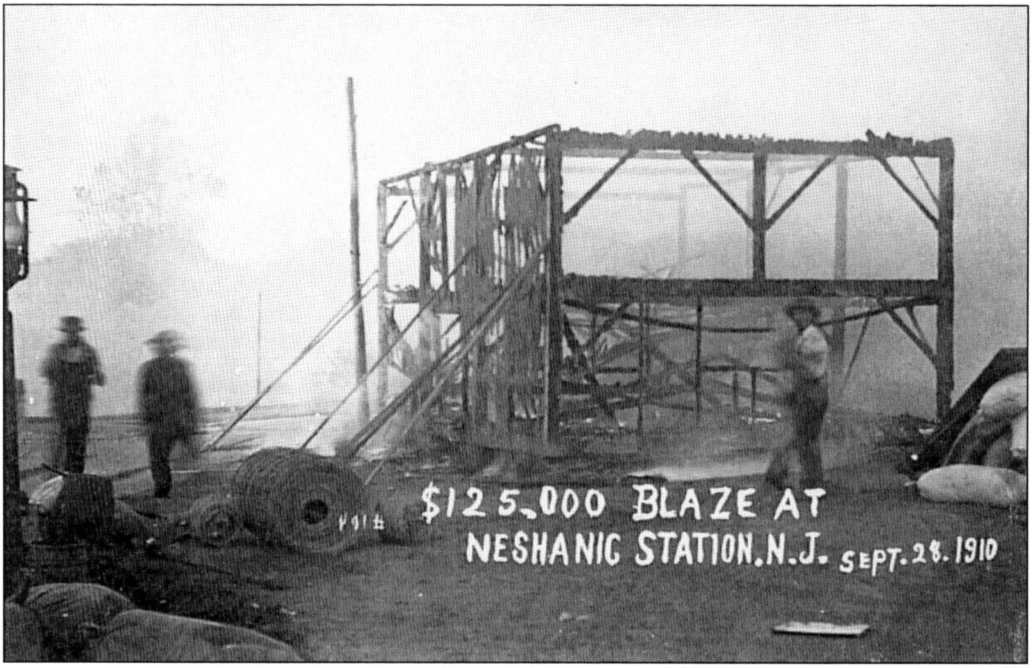

Over the two days following the fire, the creamery building, shown here ablaze on September 28, 1910, attracted hundreds of people who flocked to see the devastation. (Photo postcard courtesy of Robert Yuell.)

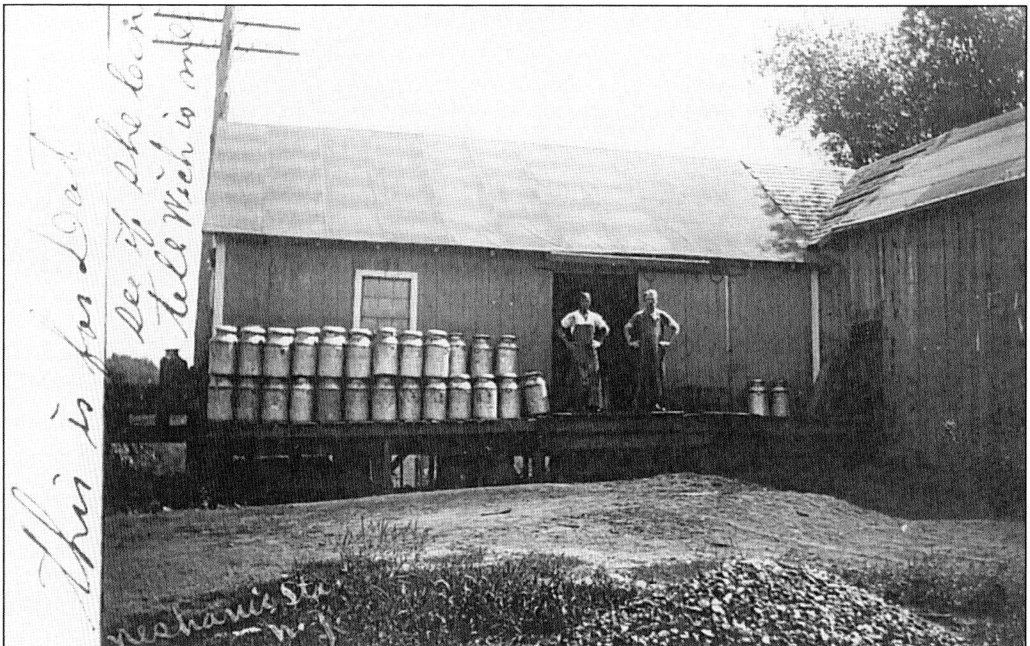

This postcard is dated 1907 and depicts the creamery by the Central Jersey Railroad Station during its active days. (Photo postcard courtesy of Robert Yuell.)

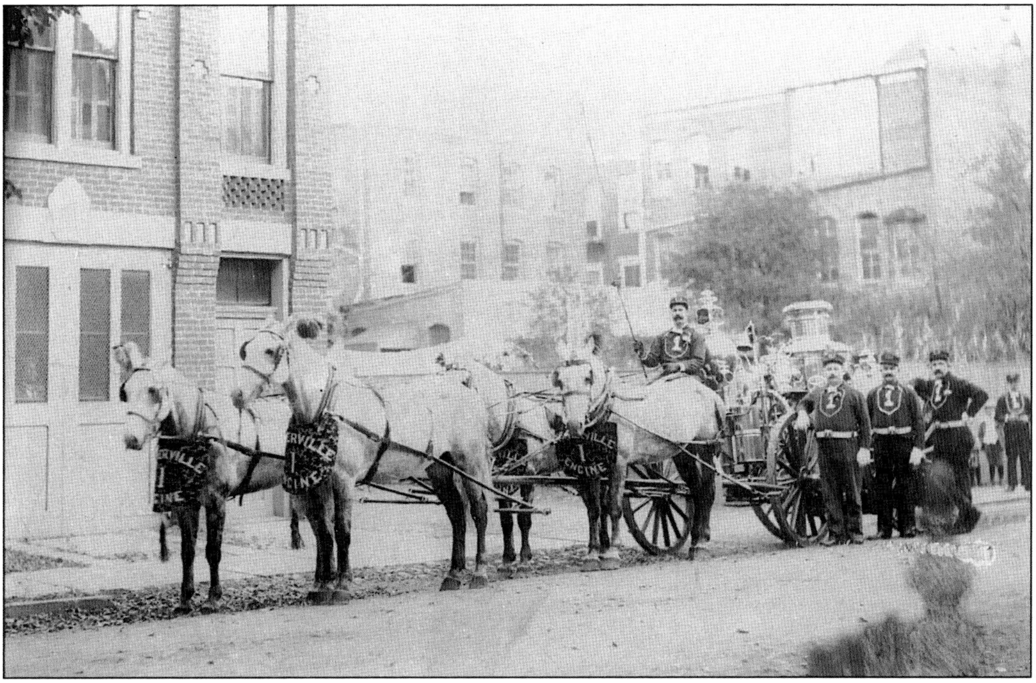

Somerville Engine Co. No. 1 was brought by special flatcar train to Neshanic to help quell the embers of the coal yard fire over the two days after the fire began. This engine returned to Neshanic in the early 1990s during an antique fire equipment muster sponsored in Neshanic. (Photograph by Charles F. Karbowski, courtesy of Somerville Firemen's Museum.)

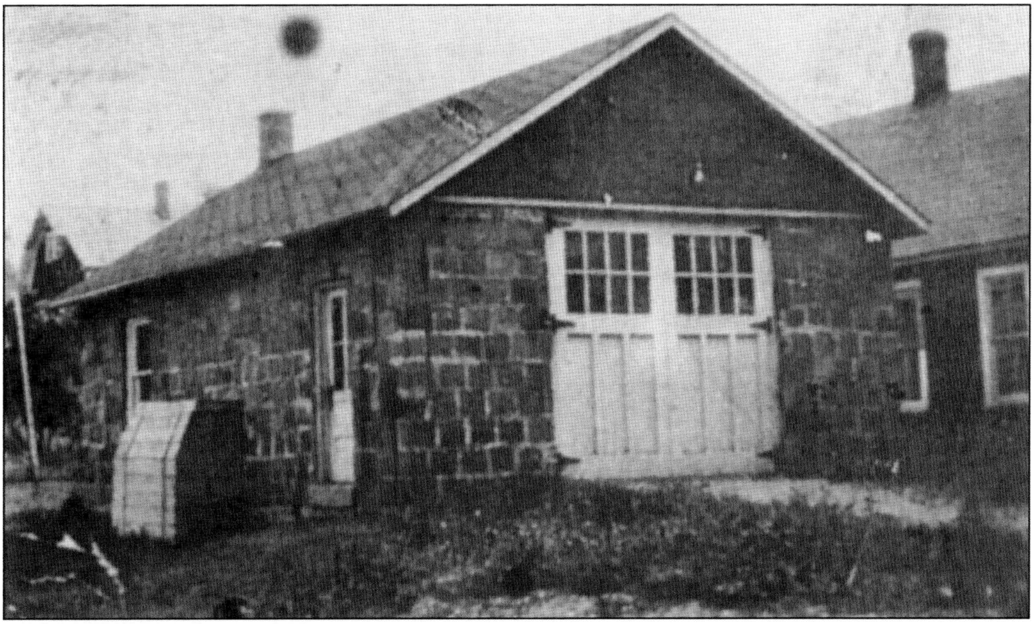

The first firehouse, a 20-by-30-foot garage, was built in 1928. Most of the funds were raised by the Ladies Auxiliary, chaired by Mrs. J.S. Covert. Many events were held, including suppers and auctions, and much labor was volunteered during the construction of the firehouse. (Photograph courtesy of Neshanic Volunteer Fire Co.)

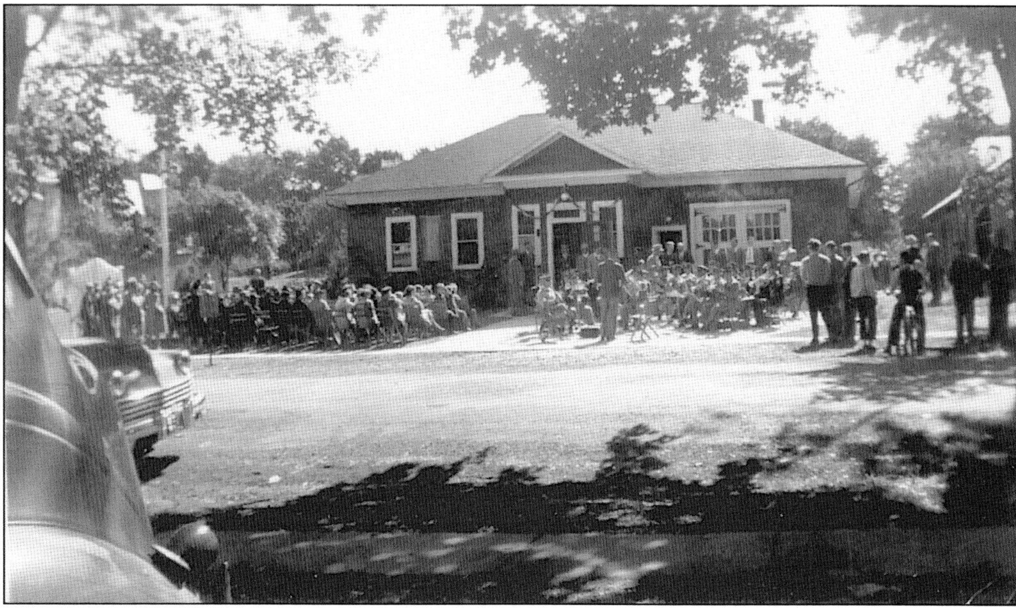

In 1933, an auditorium and kitchen were added to the firehouse. These provided the company space to hold other fund-raising events, as well as suppers and card parties. During the 1930s, the fire company also held a week-long carnival near the Fairview School by Marshall Street. This photograph shows the Blawenburg Band playing during the dedication ceremonies. (Photograph courtesy of Neshanic Volunteer Fire Co.)

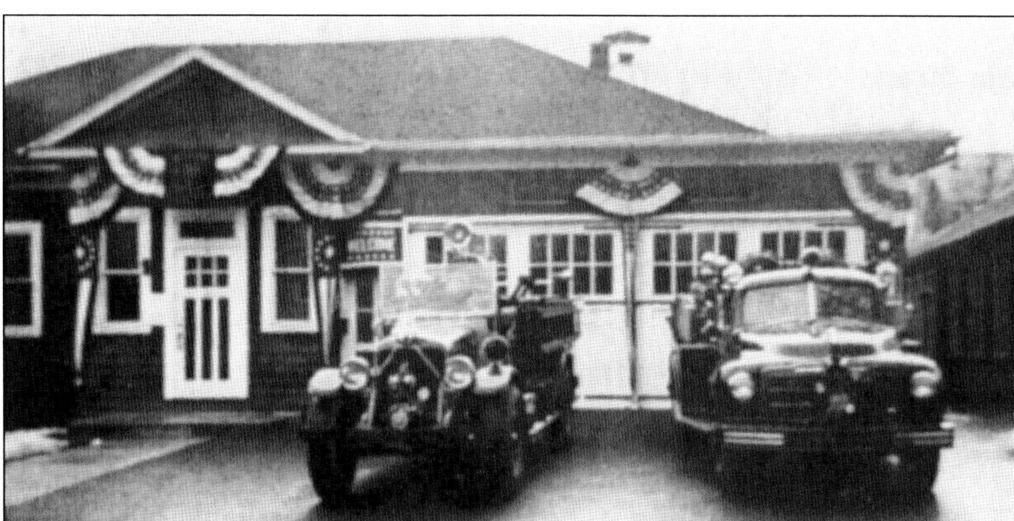

A third addition, started in 1949 and completed in 1951, housed the original Pirsch pumper and the 1950 Studebaker utility pumper. (Photograph courtesy of Neshanic Volunteer Fire Co.)

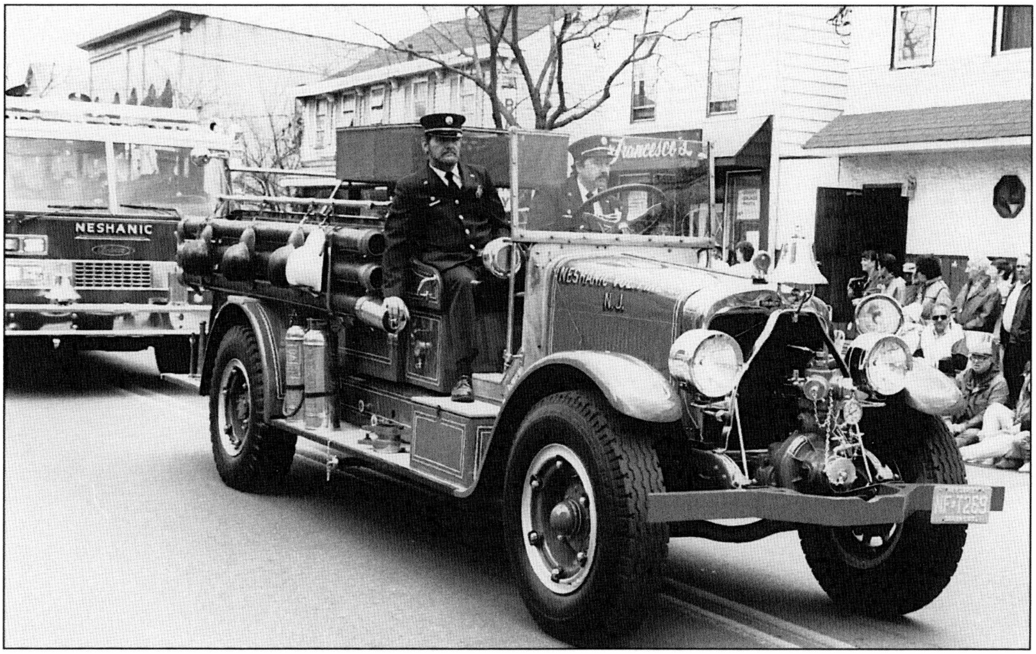

The Neshanic Volunteer Fire Co. and its 1929 Pirsch pumper are shown here in the Raritan Basilone Day Parade in 1988. The pumper, with the first Hahn International pumper, was retired in 1963. Shown here are Len Brown and Tom Van Glahn (driving). (Photograph by Doug Merrill.)

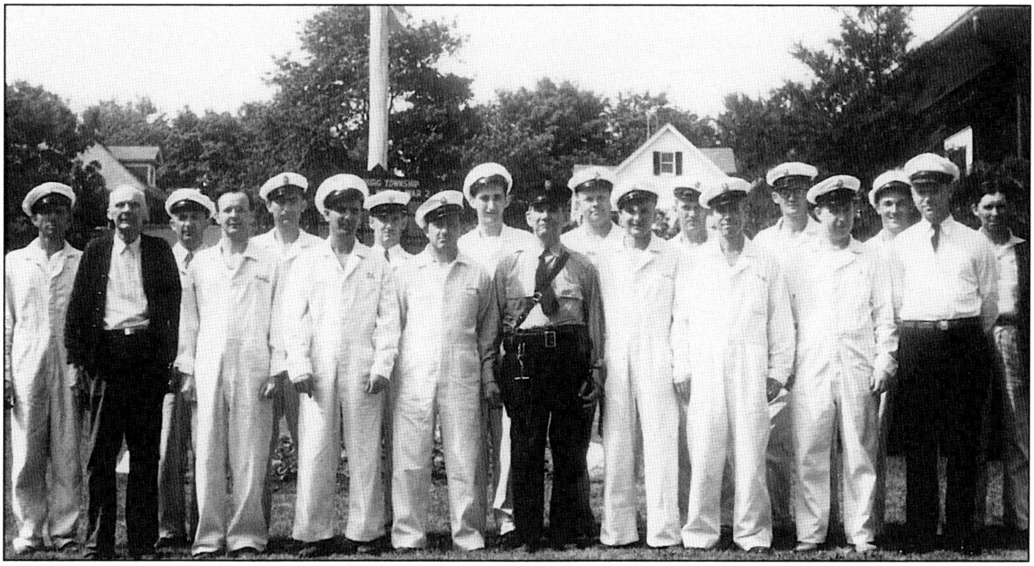

The 1951 Neshanic Volunteer Fire Co. members, showing their first uniforms, are ready for the Lions Club Memorial Day Parade and service. Fire company members shown here, from left to right, are as follows: Simon Nevius, John R. Gaddis, Varian Quick Jr., Ralph Ricker, Irving Covert, Peter Emery, Larry Lee, Harold Van Glahn, Joseph Berger, Irving Connett, George Covert, Bill Amerman, John O'Brien Jr., Max Gwin, Andrew Deak, Robert Strong, Clark Scully, Harold O'Brien, and Henry Schuler. (Photograph courtesy of Neshanic Volunteer Fire Co.)

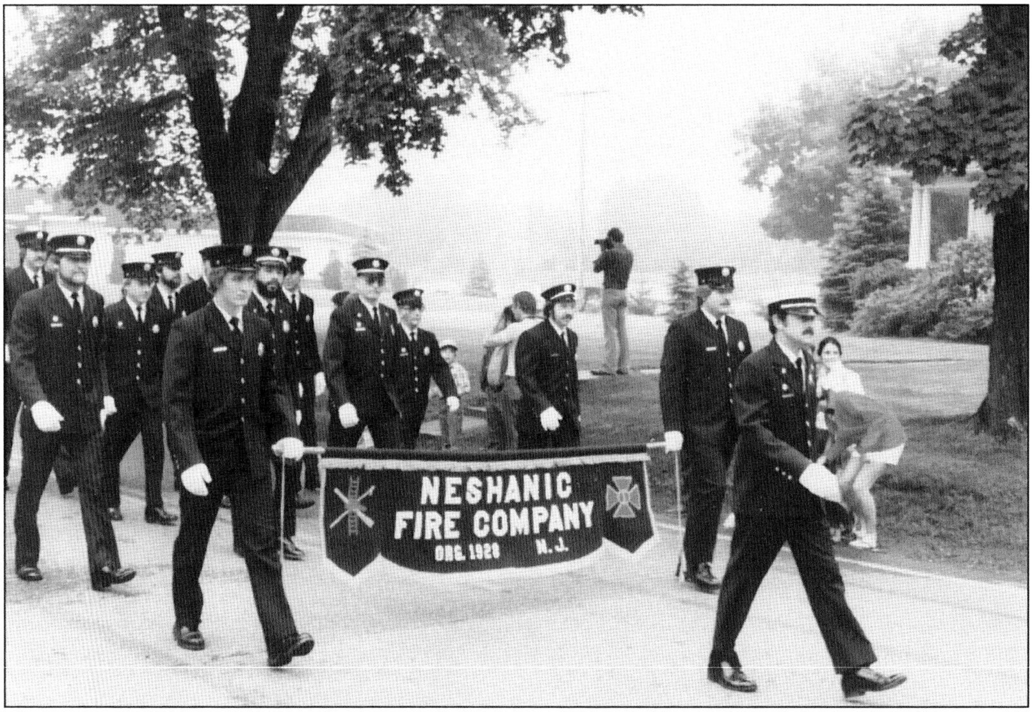

The 1982 Firemen's Parade is shown here starting down Maple Avenue, from the firehouse, with Chief Jack Knower leading the crew. (Photograph courtesy of Alma Quick Deak.)

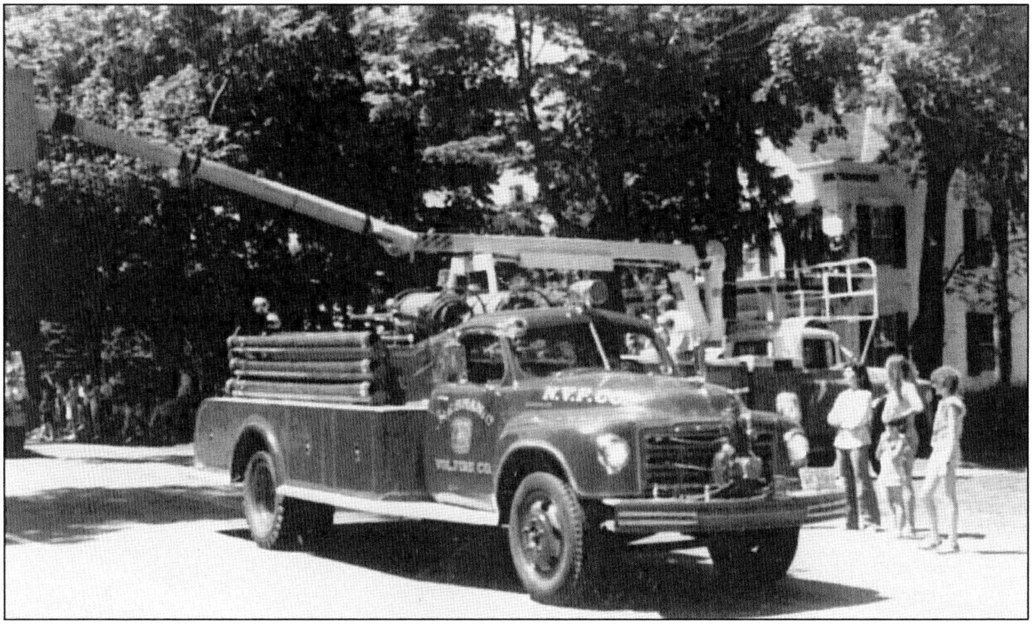
The 1950 Studebaker pumper is shown here passing in review under a cable television camera boom truck on Maple Avenue in 1978. Retired in 1968, this pumper came out of storage and was loaned to Hillsborough Fire Co. No. 2 in 1972, while one of the company's pumpers was being repaired. It was the last time the truck was in service. (Photograph courtesy of G.W. Amerman.)

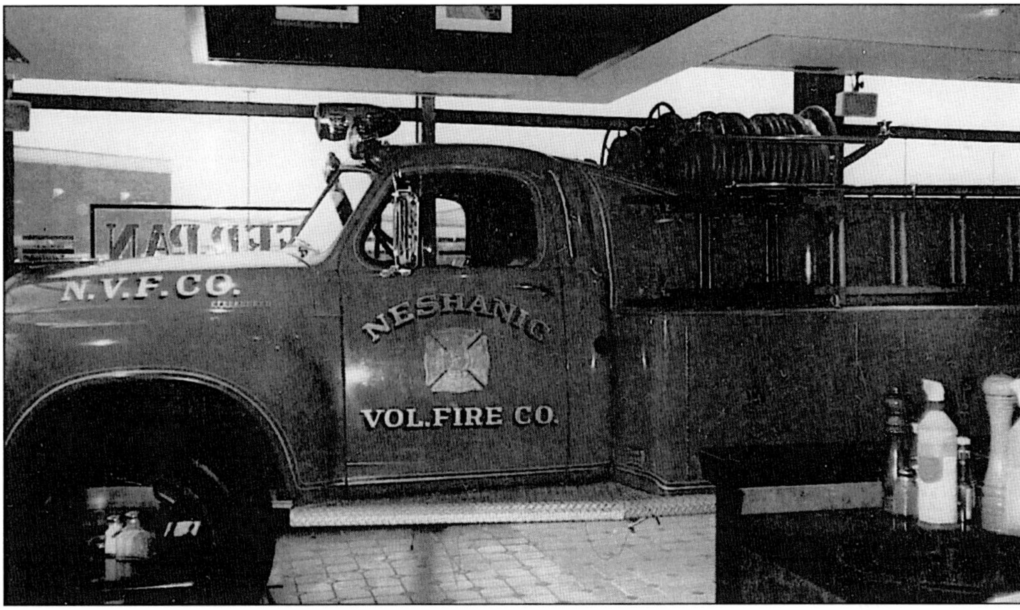

Neshanic's Studebaker, with its 500-gallon-per-minute, front-mounted pump, became much traveled. Since it was unique as a Studebaker firetruck, it was included in many antique firetruck musters. Here the firetruck is shown in 1998, in England, where it serves in complete array (as part of the décor) in a deep pan pizza restaurant near Manchester, in the Bury-Lancaster Mall. (Photograph courtesy of Tom Van Glahn.)

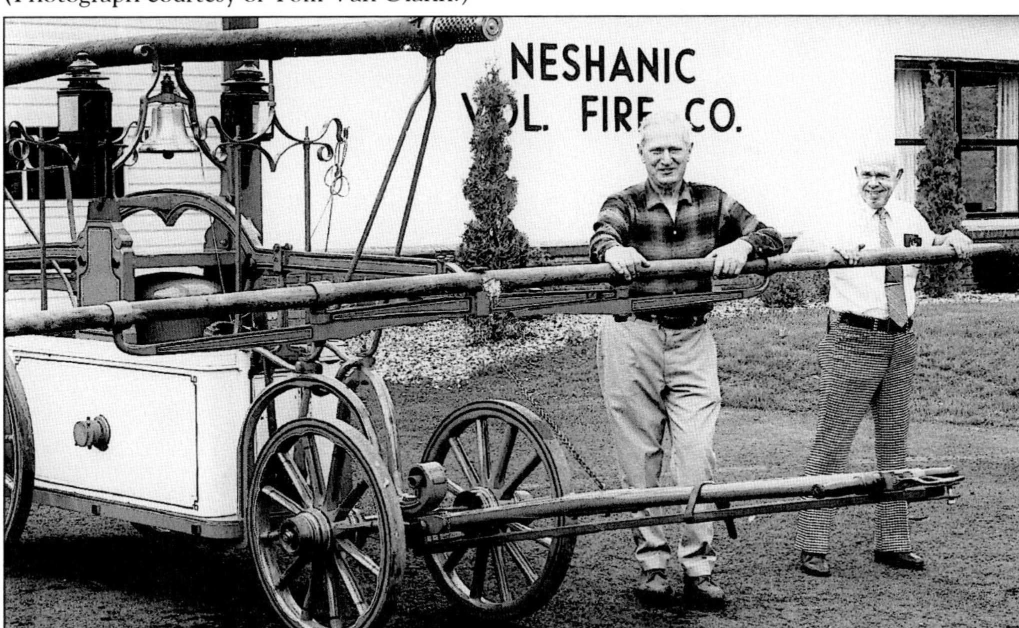

John O'Brien Jr. and Max Gwin pose by the Hunnewell pumper, restored by Mr. O'Brien for the Neshanic Volunteer Fire Company. This hand-drawn pumper has won many awards in parades and was still demonstrated in use during the 1990 antique equipment muster at the Firemen's Field. It still pumps with eight healthy men pulling the bars. (Photograph by Bob Young, courtesy of the Hillsborough Beacon.)

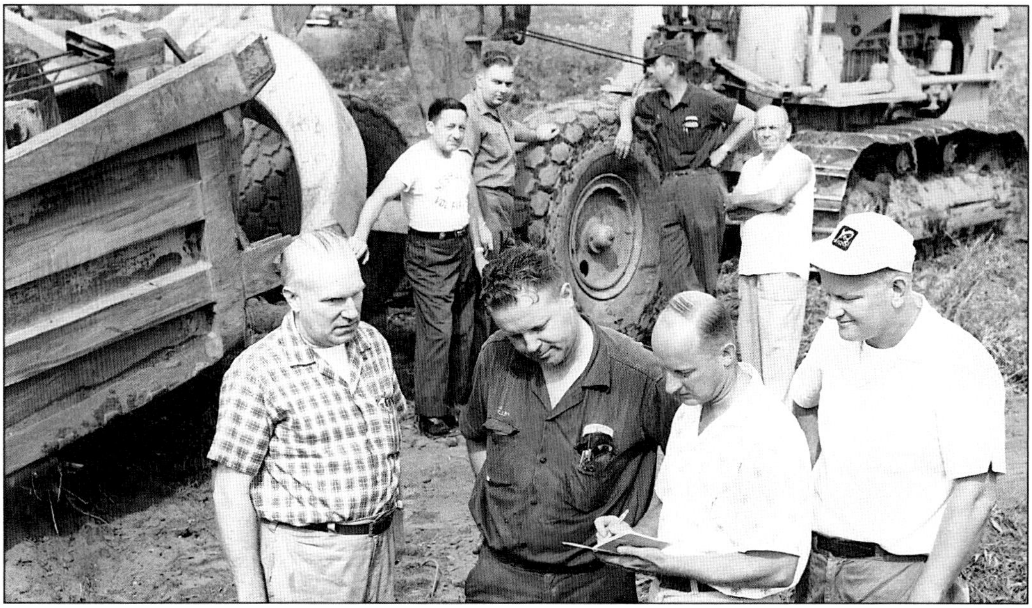

In 1958, Orville Shurts donated a large parcel of land on Maple Avenue to the Neshanic Volunteer Fire Company, and the new fire headquarters is located here. From 1958 to 1960, the fire company constructed a fire pond with a gravity hydrant system in the village. This picture shows the start of the excavation by Vollers Construction Co., from left to right, as follows: (front row) Branchburg Mayor Walter O'Brien, George Covert, Bill Amerman, and George Fenwick; (back row) Harold Van Glahn, Dave Bullock, Irving Covert, and Chris McTameny. (Photograph by Harvey Patterson, courtesy of Neshanic Volunteer Fire Company.)

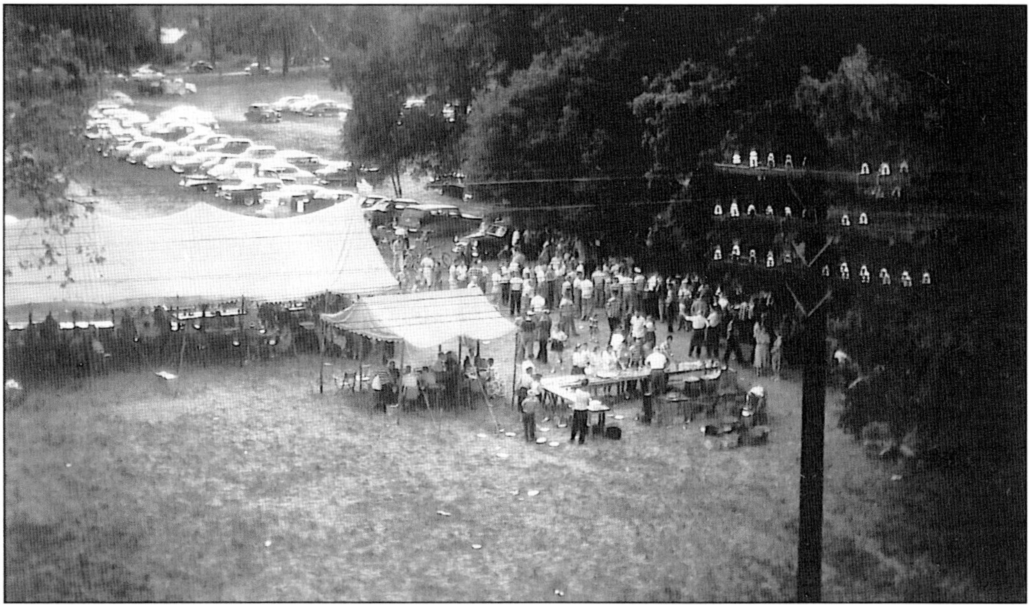

Neshanic Firemen's popular clambakes were held at various locations through the 1960s. This view, in the late 1950s, shows a clambake in the Firemen's Field across from the Neshanic Flea Market on Elm Street. The large tent was owned by the Neshanic Reformed Church and used for Harvest Home Suppers. (Photograph courtesy of the Toles family.)

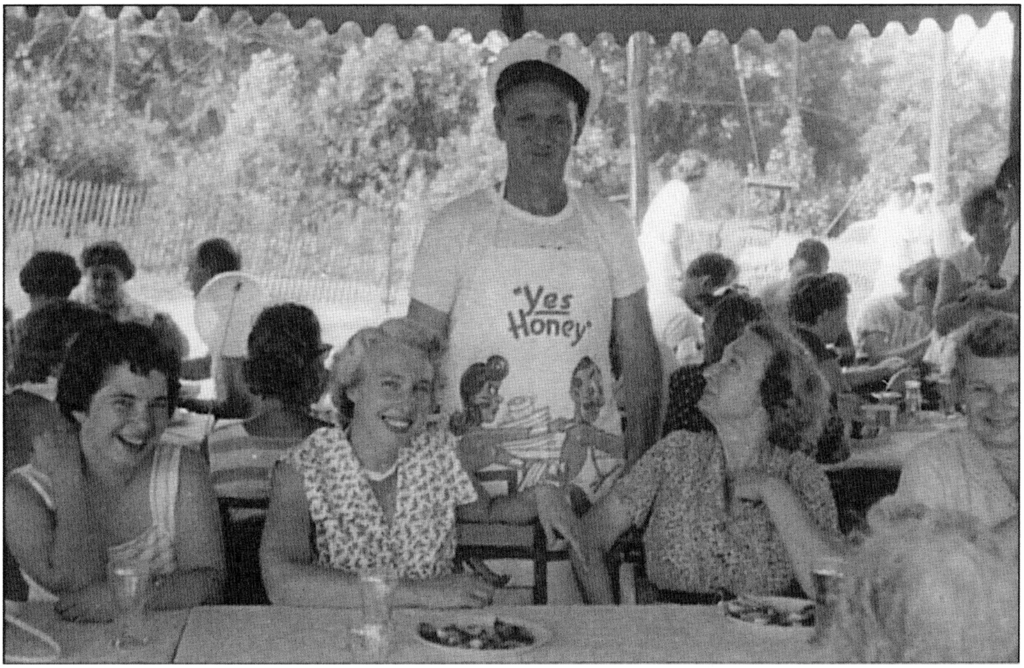

Fire Chief John O'Brien is shown here keeping some of the ladies supplied with clams and birch beer. The ladies shown here, from left to right, are as follows: June Amerman, Ruth Quick, Ruth Messig, and Edith Wargo. (Photograph by G.W. Amerman.)

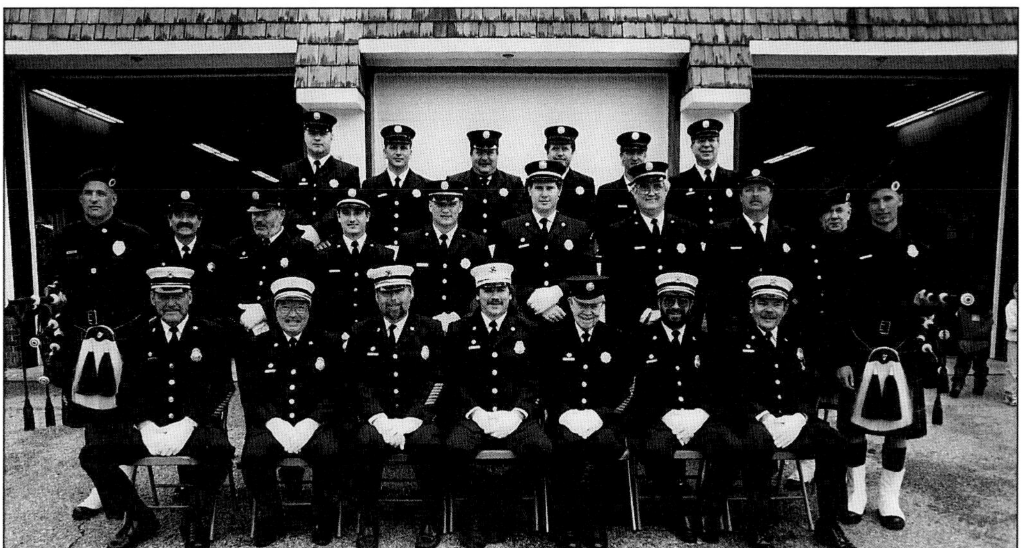

The 1998 Memorial Day celebration, at current headquarters, is shown here. Some of the participants are, from left to right, as follows: (first row) Len Brown, Thomas Van Glahn, Jim Covert, Darcy Marshall, Max Gwin, Joseph Cangelosi, and Thomas Bittle; (second row) Larry Booker, Emilio Suarez, John Hance, Chris Suarez, Dan Clerico, John Lazorchak, Bill Iden, Charles Davis, George Murphy, and Eric Jensen; (third row) Keith Covert, John Andreychak, Richard Bullock, David Gwin, Andy Preston, and Richard Malko. (Photograph courtesy of Neshanic Volunteer Fire Co.)

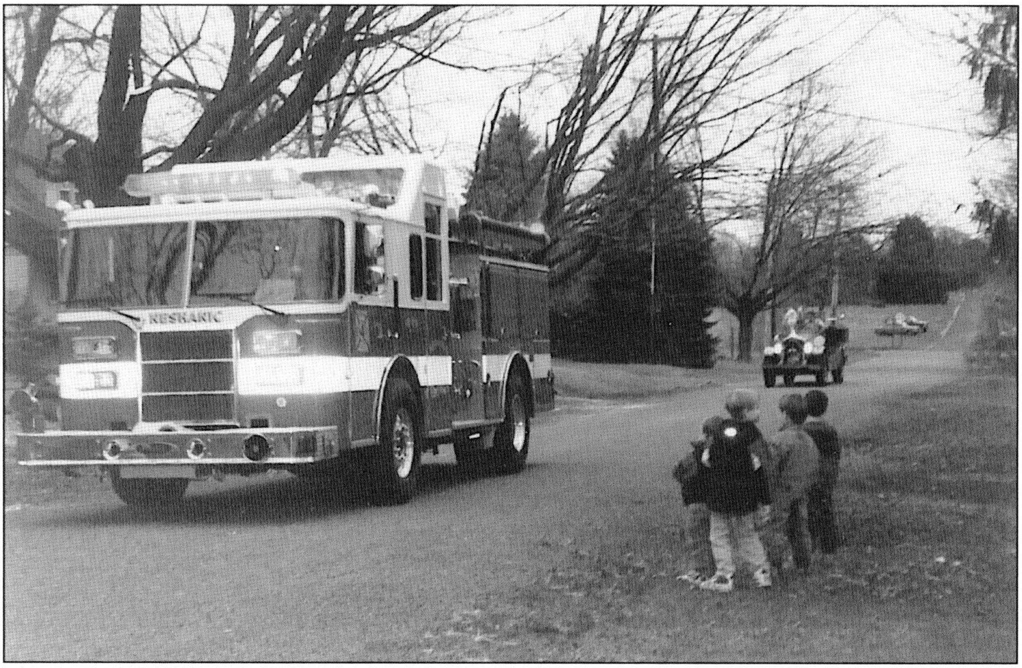

The weekend before Christmas, Santa appears in all of the Branchburg Township streets included in the area served by the Neshanic Volunteer Fire Company. Here, youngsters anxiously await his coming with candy canes, as he is preceded by the newest truck in the fleet. (Photograph by G.W. Amerman.)

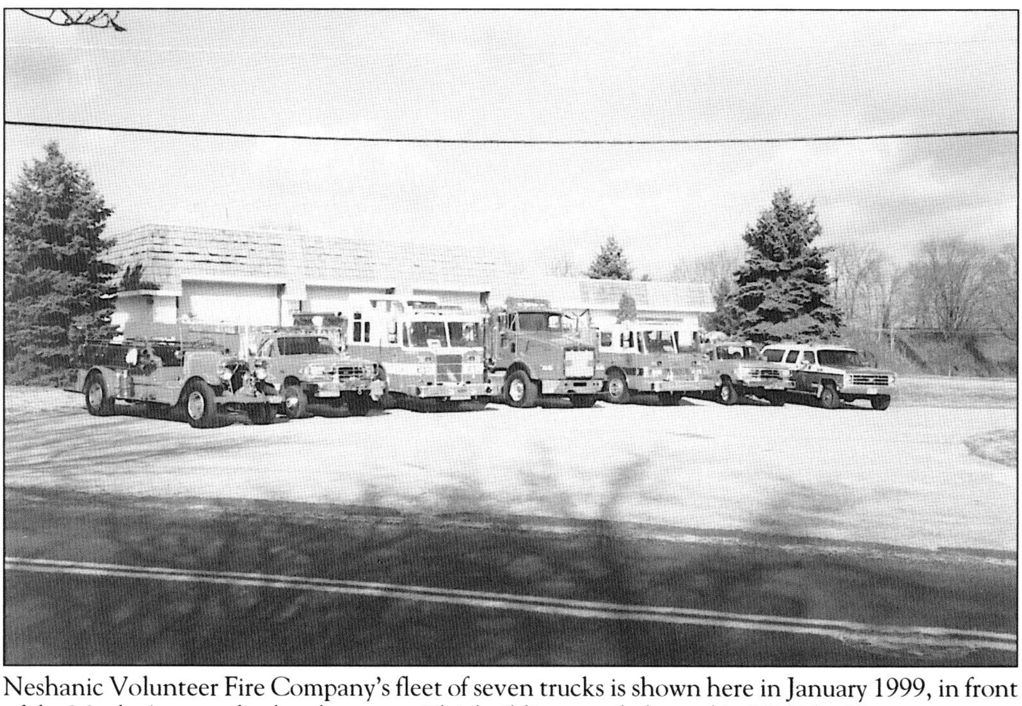

Neshanic Volunteer Fire Company's fleet of seven trucks is shown here in January 1999, in front of the Maple Avenue fire headquarters. This building was dedicated in 1977, by Congresswoman Millicent Fenwick. (Photograph by G.W. Amerman.)

Six

AGRICULTURE

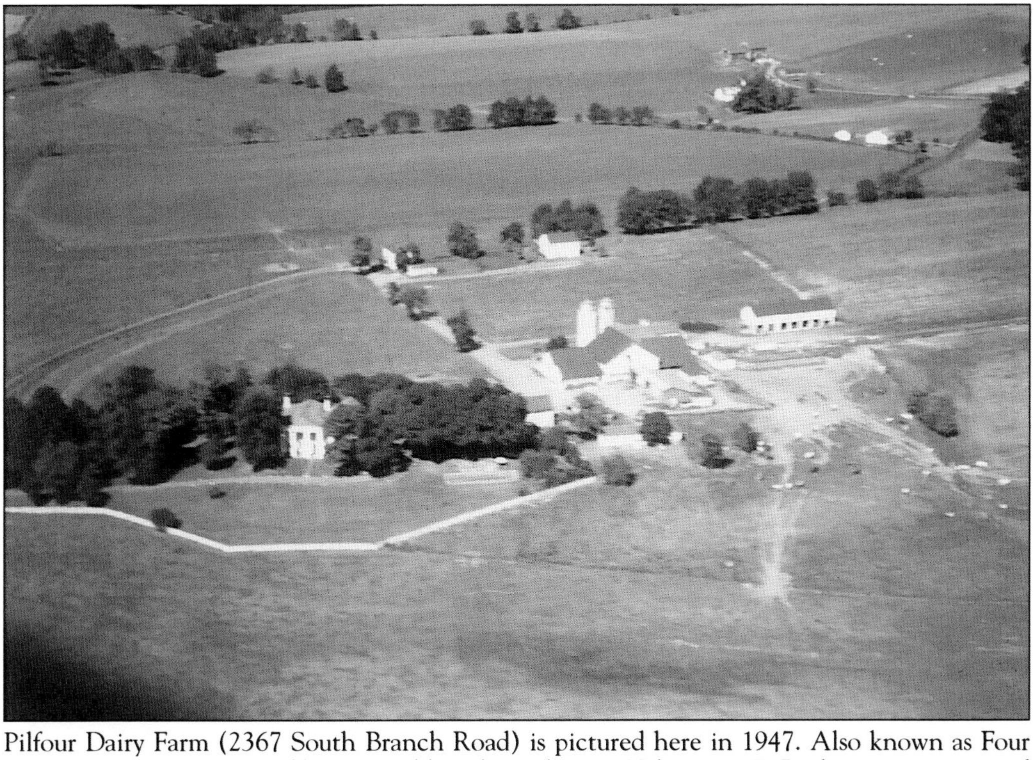

Pilfour Dairy Farm (2367 South Branch Road) is pictured here in 1947. Also known as Four Pillar Farm, it was operated by B.J. Goldsmith. Built in 1837 by Peter T. Beekman, it was owned in 1855 by Calvin Corle, who served as a New Jersey state senator in the 1870s. (Photograph courtesy of G.W. Amerman.)

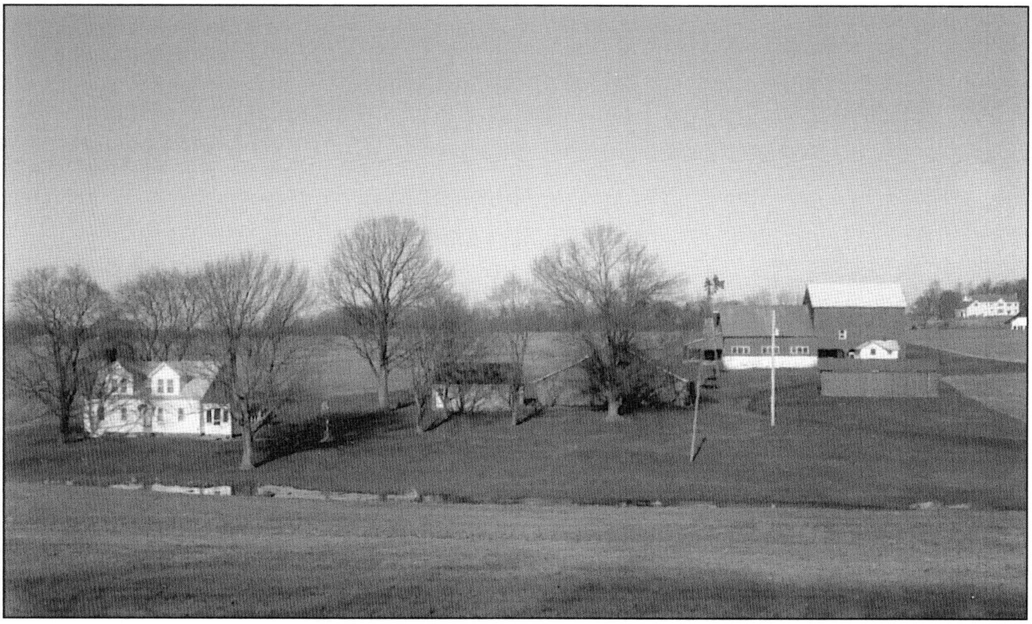

The Housel Farm, at 2352 South Branch Road, is a typical small dairy farm with a hay storage barn, poultry house, windmill, and machine shed. This farm is one of two very similar early farms in this area. Each had the same house plan, and the barns were built similarly on a hillside facing the southeast. (See photograph of Arch S. Amerman Farm.) (Photograph courtesy of G.W. Amerman.)

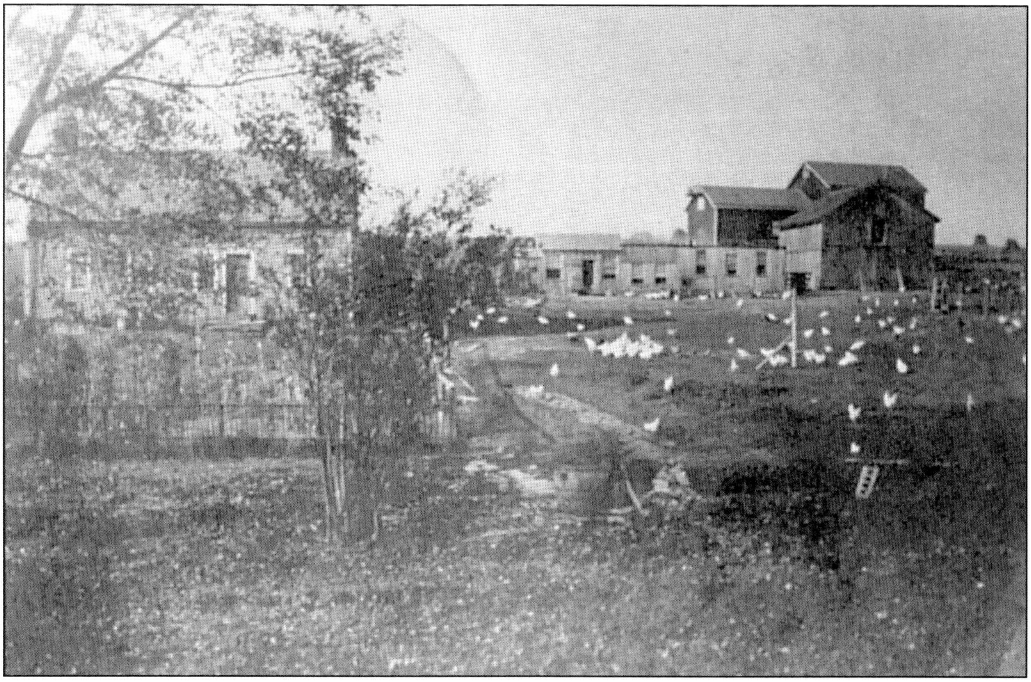

The Arch S. Amerman Farm is situated in Hillsborough, at 1140 River Road. (See description of the Housel Farm.) Mr. Amerman also owned the A.S.A. Feed Mill. (Photograph courtesy of Paul Kurzenberger.)

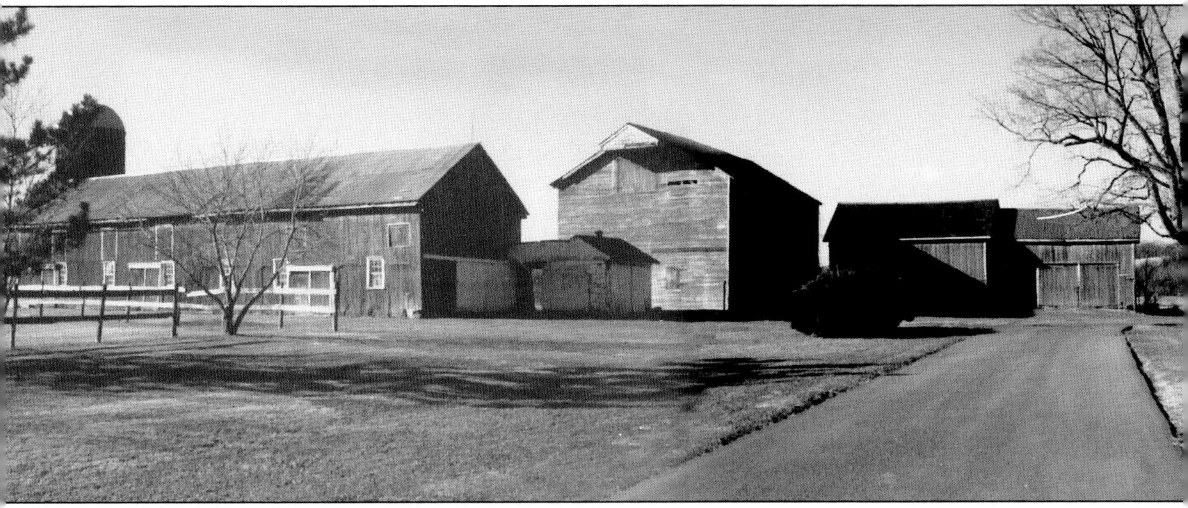

River Edge Stock Farm, seen here, is located on South Branch River Road in Neshanic and was in the Huff family for many generations. The farm was originally the property of Tunis Huff, who owned about 500 acres of land in Neshanic. His daughter Sarah married John G. Schenck, who laid out the town of Neshanic Station. Tunis's son Abram T. Huff became the owner of River Edge Farm. In 1903, the farm was purchased by John V. Huff. After his death in 1914, his widow and sons continued to operate the farm. In 1938, the farm had 40 Guernsey milk cows and a flock of 100 Cheviot sheep imported from England. (Photograph courtesy of G.W. Amerman.)

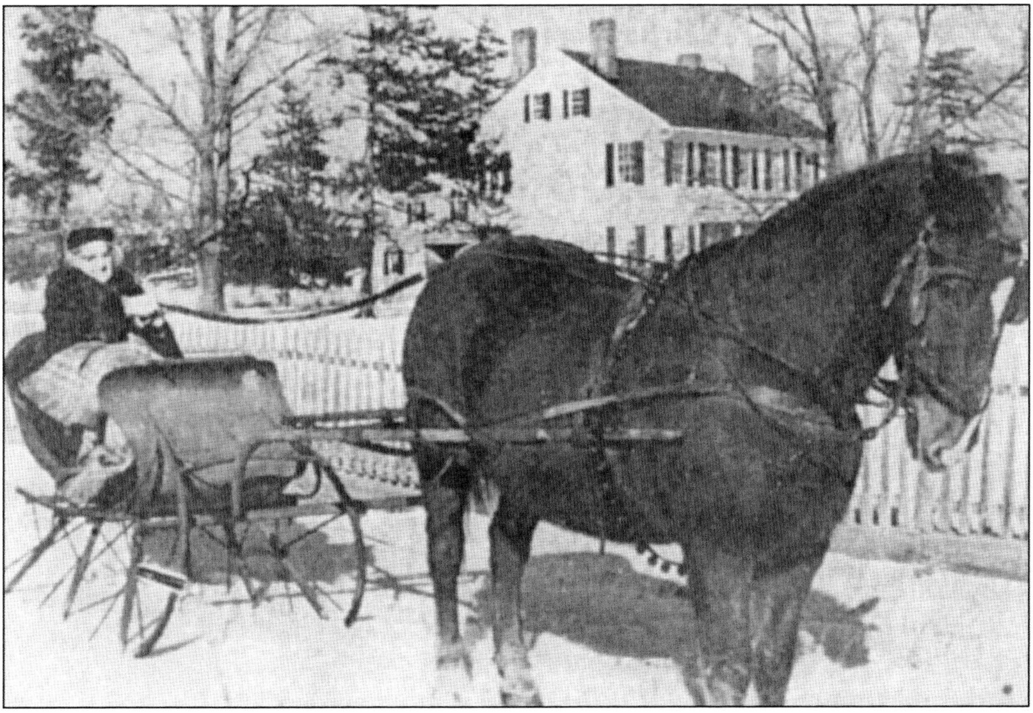

Anna Griscom, another descendant of the Huffs, is pictured here at the age of 91 in a December 1969 sleigh ride at the River Edge Farm. Mrs. Griscom was the mother of Mary Boughton of Neshanic Station. (Photograph courtesy of E. Saums.)

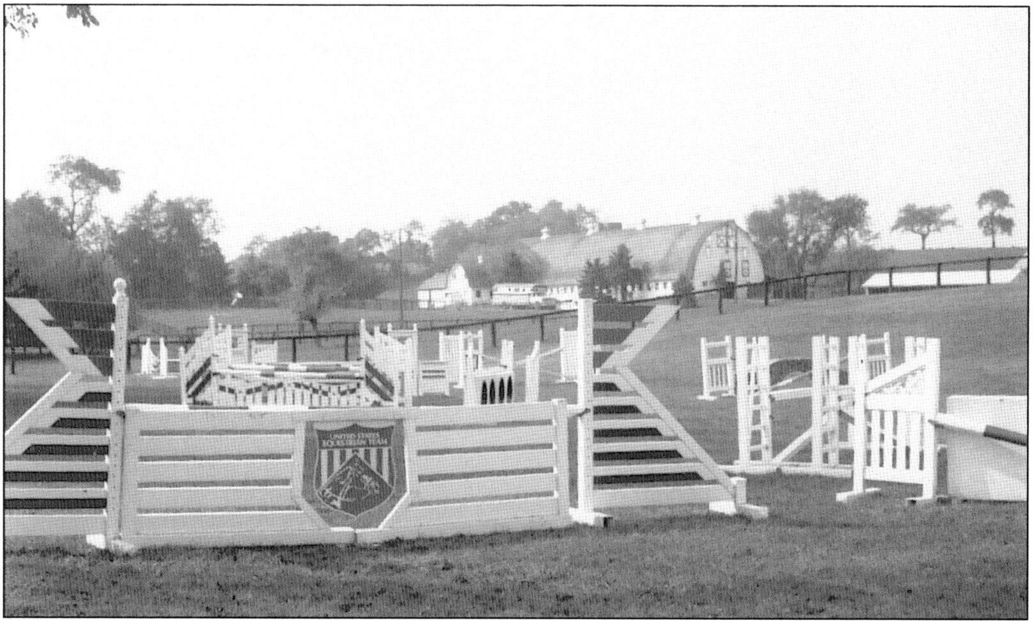

Halliday McCall's Opie Road farm is depicted here. Mr. McCall built the large dairy barn shown here after a fire destroyed earlier barns. The present owner is a trainer for the U.S. Olympic Equestrian team, and the barn and fields are used for horses. This is typical of the many changes taking place in agriculture in the area. (Photograph courtesy of G.W. Amerman.)

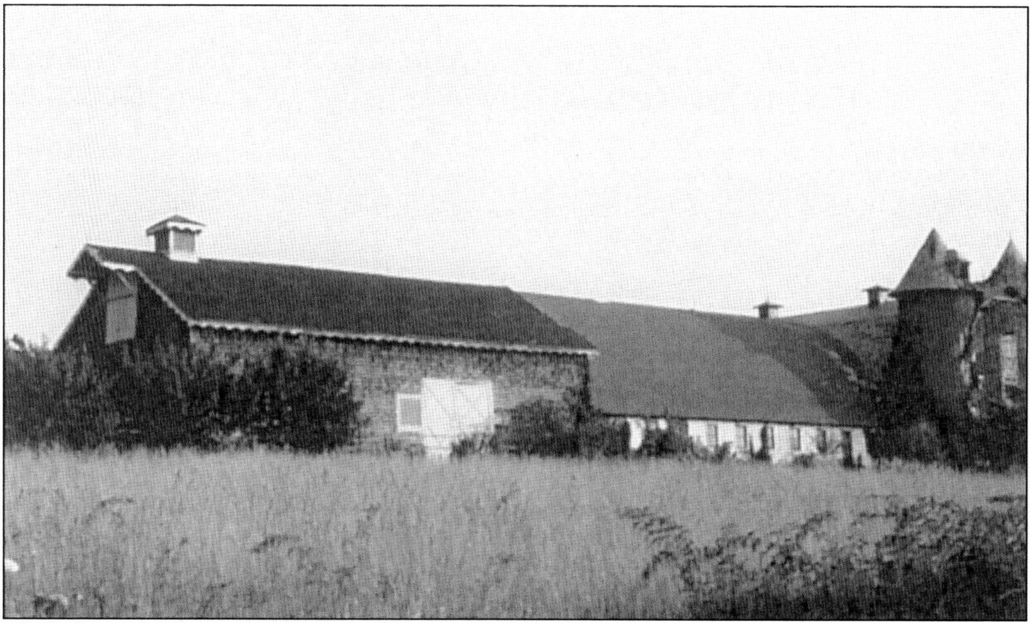

The Hastings Farm on Zion Road shows a typical Canadian double silo dairy barn built just prior to the start of the 20th century. Mr. Hastings had moved here from Richford, Vermont, a prominent French-Canadian dairy farm area. The middle barn was built in the 1950s by Berton J. Todd to house more dairy cows. The barn on the left was built by Mr. Hastings for hay storage, horse stalls, and machinery storage. (Photograph courtesy of G.W. Amerman.)

John Vermeulen, founder of John Vermeulen & Son Wholesale Nurserymen, emigrated from Holland and began his business in 1921, in Westbury, New York, before moving to Neshanic in 1947. (Photograph courtesy of J. Peter Vermeulen.)

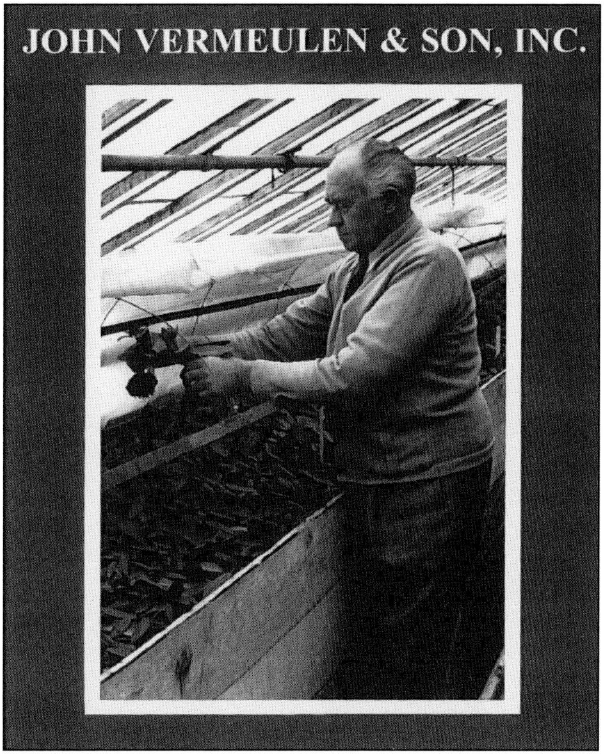

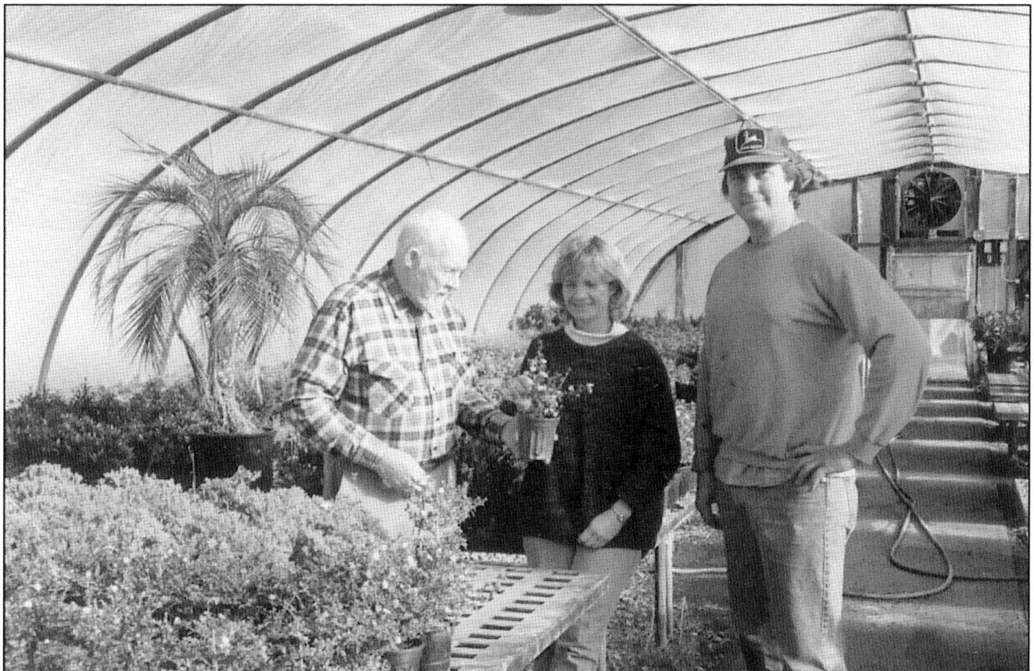

Three generations of the Vermeulen family have been involved in the nursery business in Neshanic. Pictured are John Vermeulen's son J. Peter and his grandchildren Nancy and Jeff. (Photograph courtesy of G.W. Amerman.)

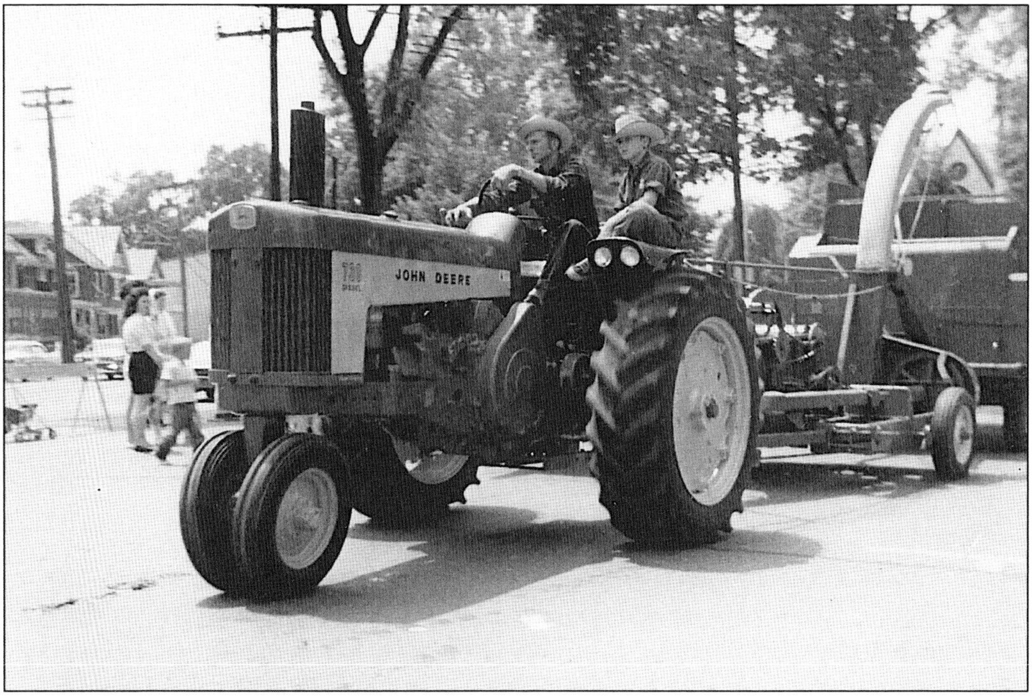

Simon Nevius and son David show off a John Deere 730 Diesel from J.S. Covert & Sons, in this *c.* 1958 photograph. (Photograph courtesy of M. Jane [Nevius] Brown.)

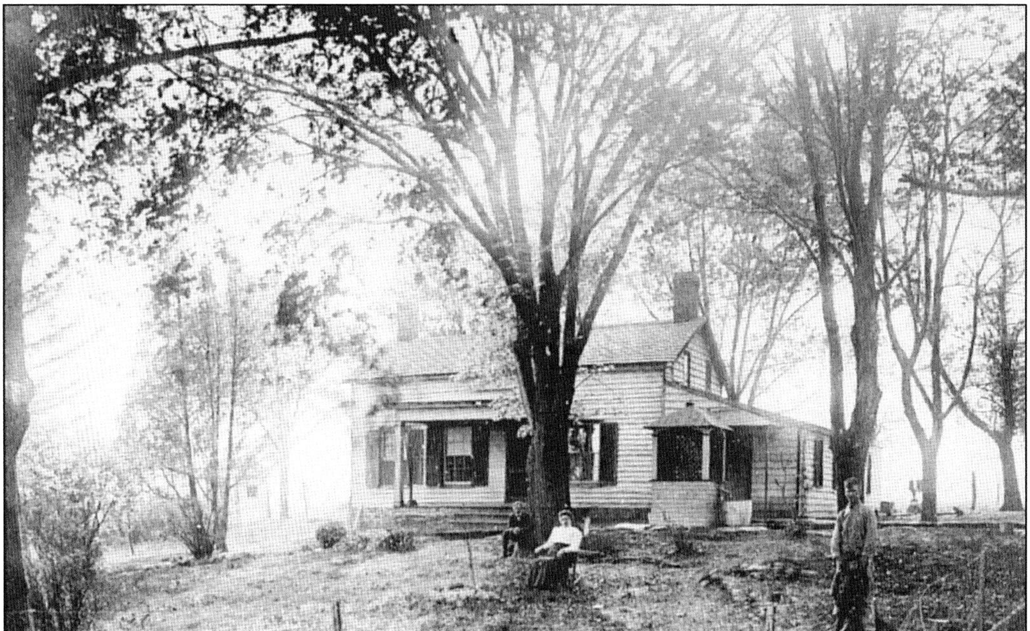

Hill Top Farm, off Pleasant Run Road, is shown in this *c.* 1903 photograph with its new owner Isaac Livingston Kip (seated on stump). (Photograph courtesy of Francis Totten.)

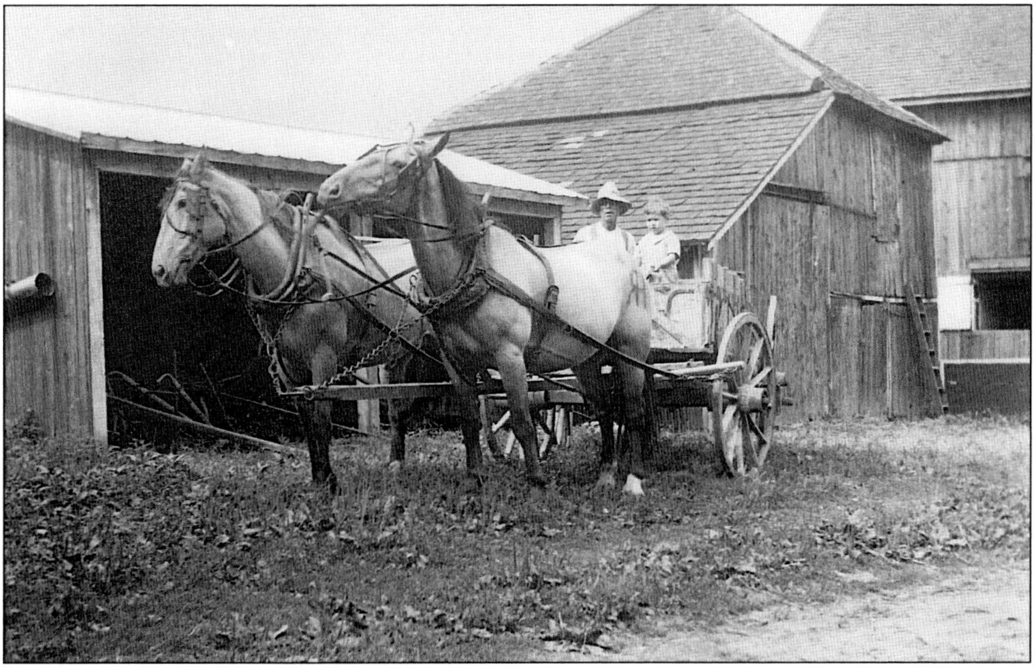

Isaac Livingston Kip (at 63 years of age) is pictured in May 1934, with grandson Francis Totten, aged two and a half years. The buckskin team of Bucky and Charlie were born and raised in the west, shipped east in 1932, and purchased by Mr. Kip. Note the brand on the left rump of Charlie. (Photograph courtesy of Francis Totten.)

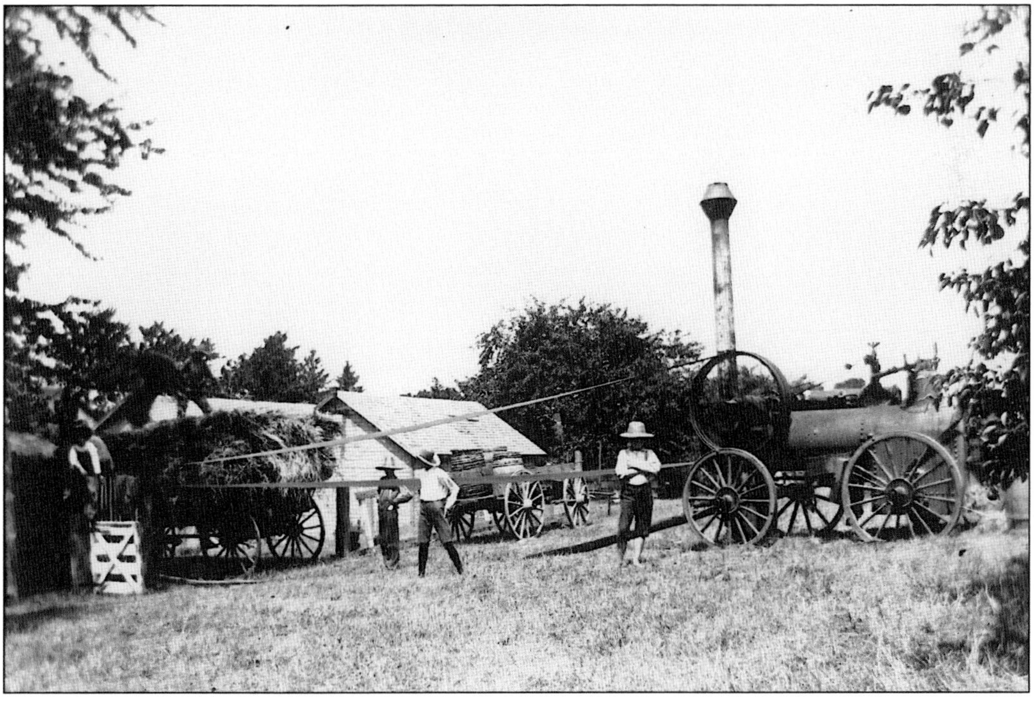

A wood-burning steam engine is shown here running a thresher at the Sebring Farm at 721 Amwell Road, *c.* 1890. (Photograph courtesy of L.B. Lane.)

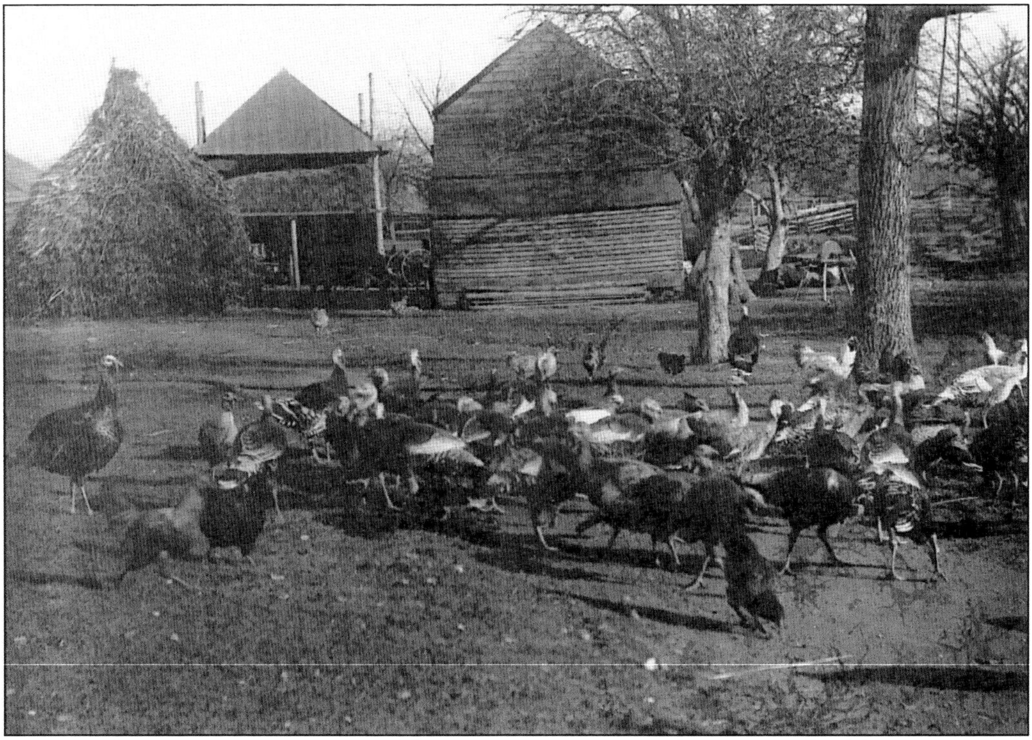

This *c.* 1890 image portrays poultry at large on the Sebring Farm (721 Amwell Road). Note the grinding wheel stone by the large tree. This photograph also affords a great view of an adjustable roof hay barrack, cornstalk thatch, and corncrib attached to the end of the barn. (Photograph courtesy of L.B. Lane.)

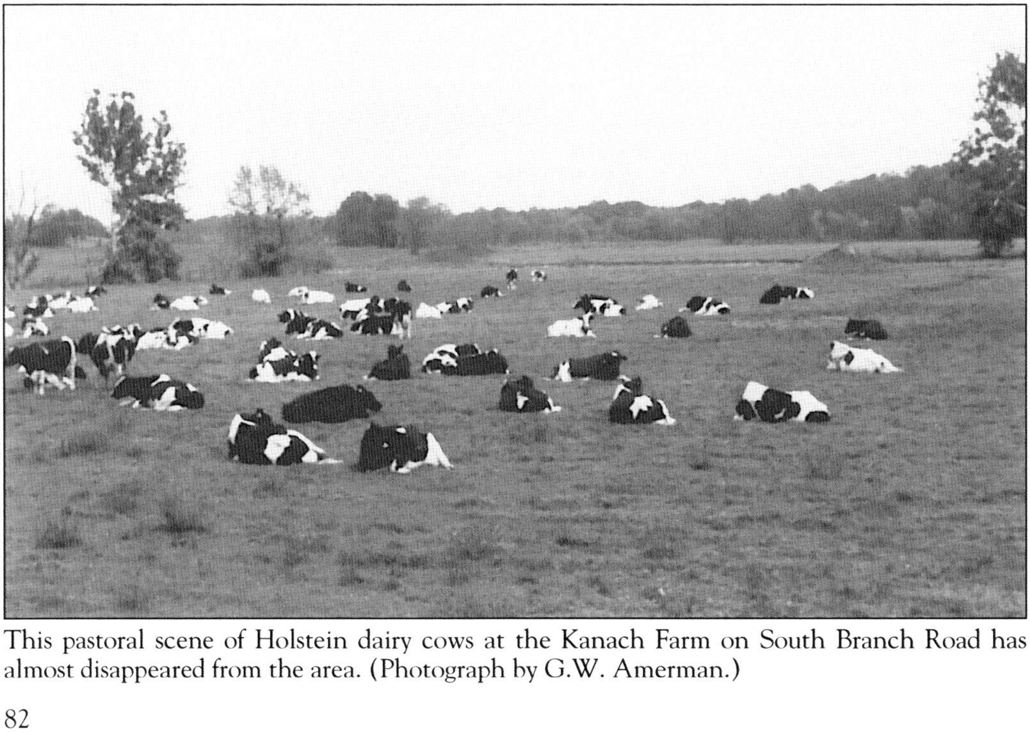

This pastoral scene of Holstein dairy cows at the Kanach Farm on South Branch Road has almost disappeared from the area. (Photograph by G.W. Amerman.)

Seven

Commerce and Industry

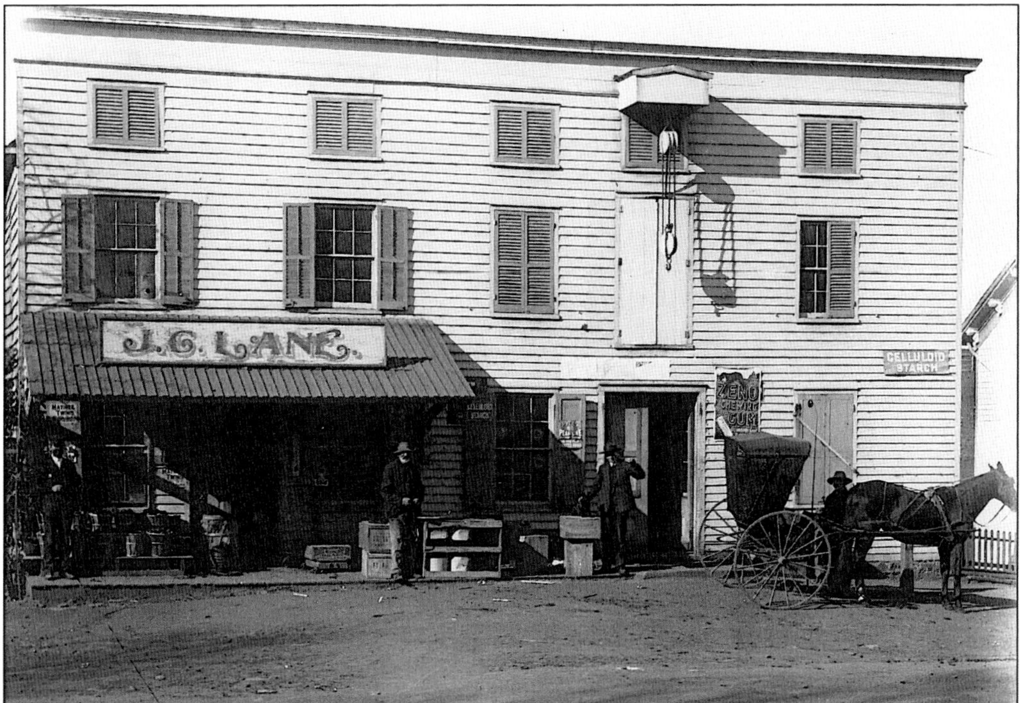

The John C. Lane Store stood at the corner of Amwell and River Roads, in Neshanic, next to Dr. Andersen's home. The store building burned on May 18, 1918. Today, the foundation is still visible between the Bassuk home and the Lane corner home. This photograph dates to 1900. (Photograph courtesy of L.B. Lane.)

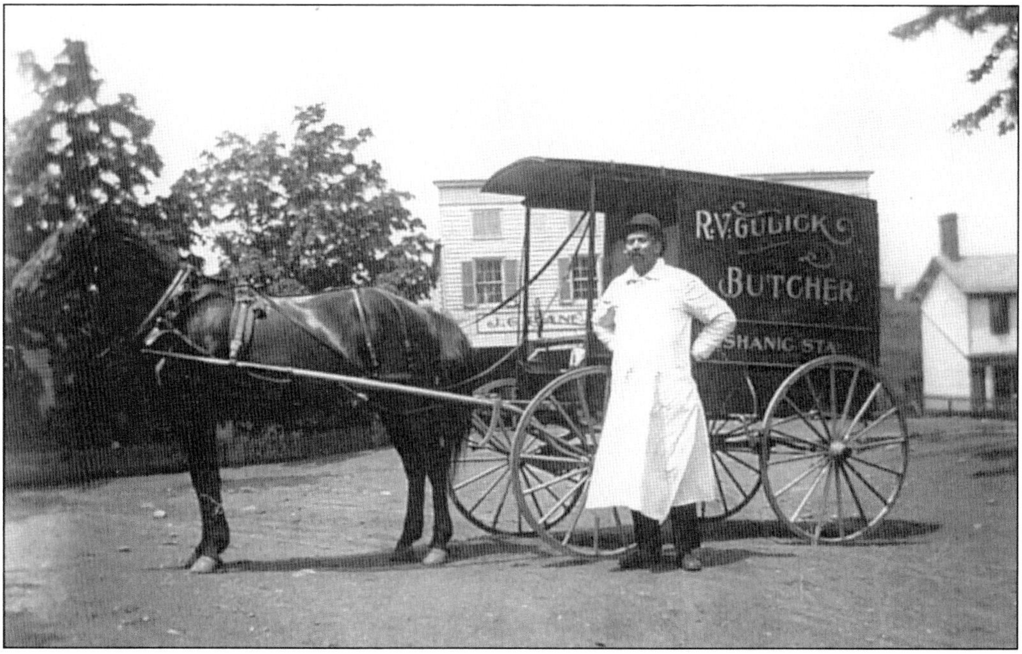

This c. 1904 photograph taken by Laura Lane shows Mr. R.V. Gulick, an early local butcher, with his retail delivery wagon at the corner near J.C. Lane's store and the Neshanic Reformed Church. (Photograph courtesy of L.B. Lane.)

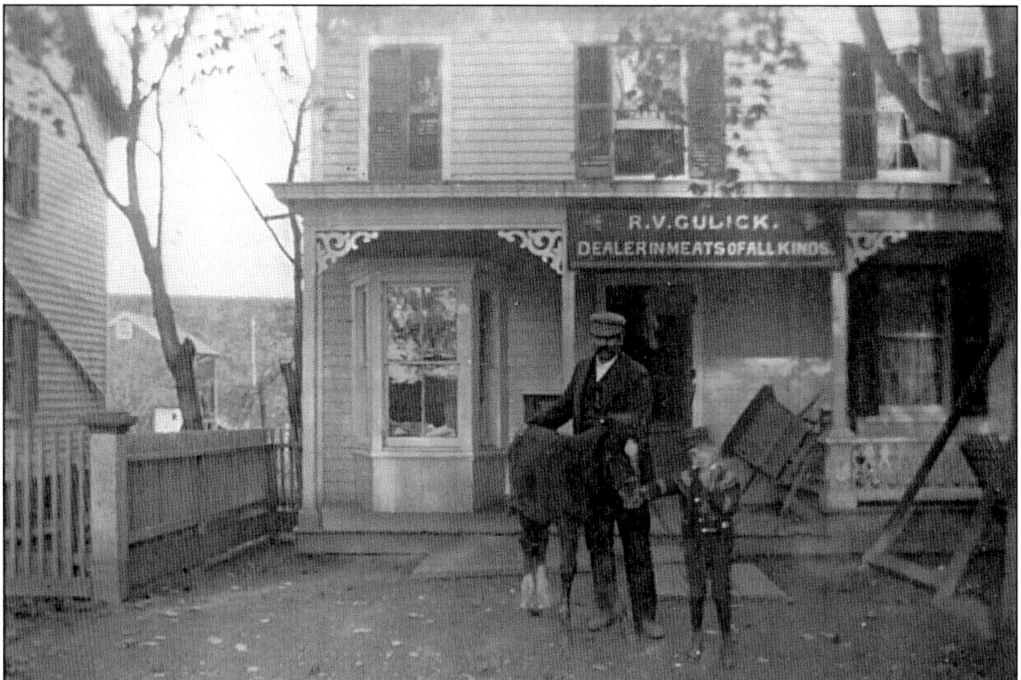

The R.V. Gulick local butcher shop was located at 405 Olive Street, in Neshanic Station, in the same building that housed the post office during the 1940s (when Mr. Willis Hoagland and Mrs. Edna McTameny were postmasters). (Photograph courtesy of L.B. Lane.)

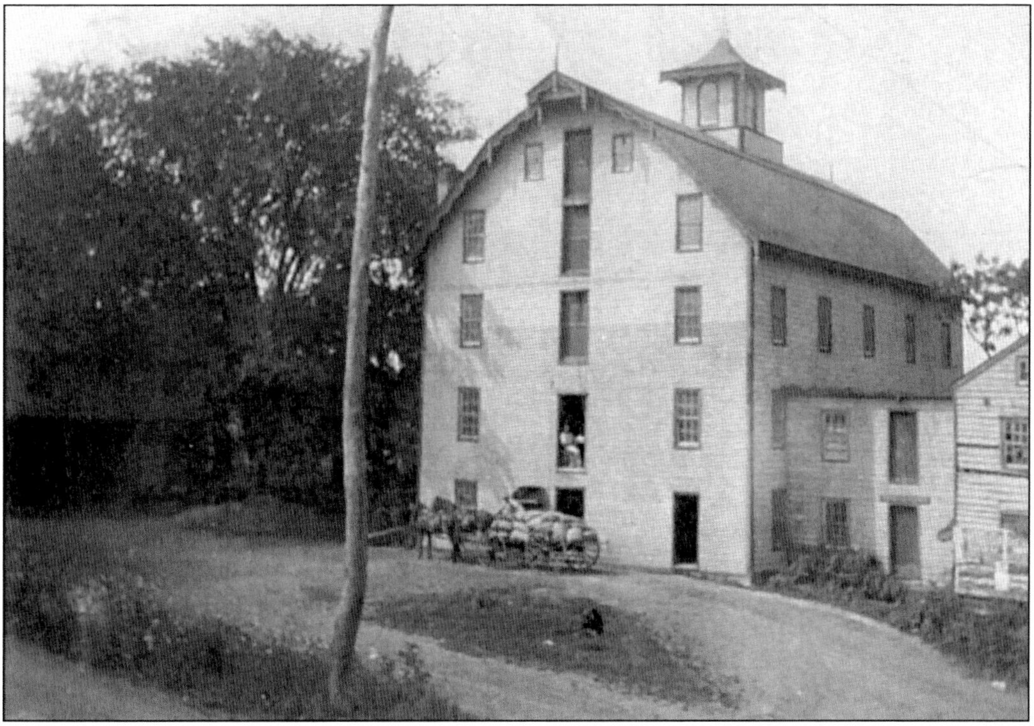

This *c.* 1904 photograph shows the A.S. Amerman Mill (at 1127 River Road) that burned in 1926, during a snowstorm. (Photograph courtesy of Neshanic Station Historical Society.)

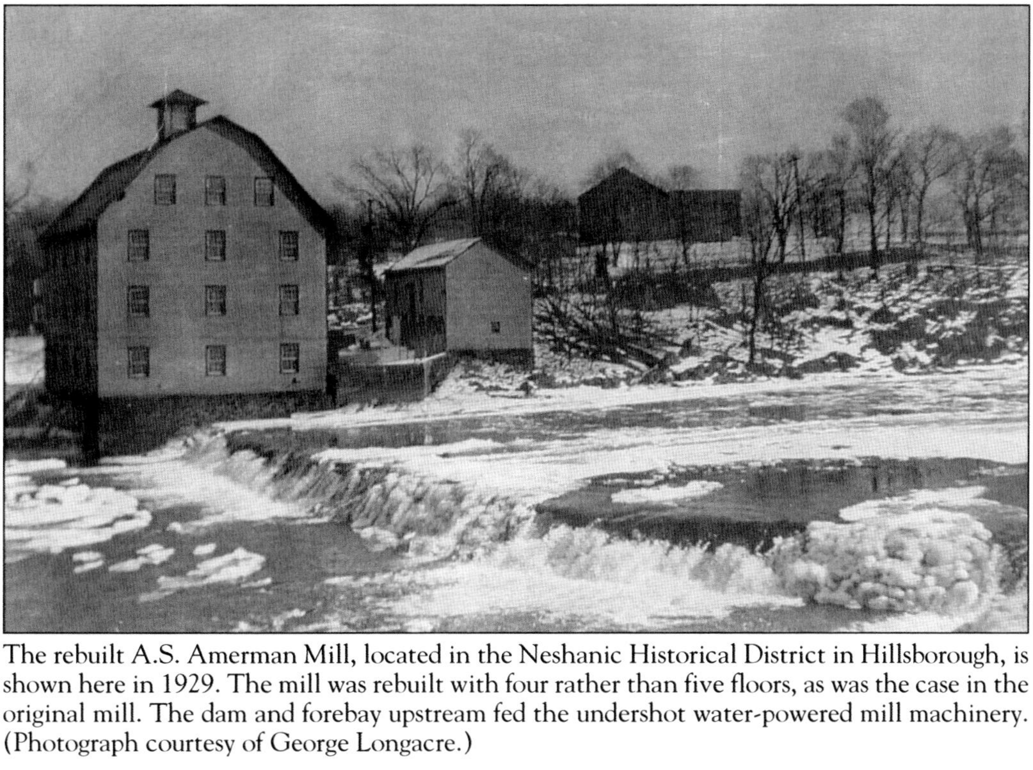

The rebuilt A.S. Amerman Mill, located in the Neshanic Historical District in Hillsborough, is shown here in 1929. The mill was rebuilt with four rather than five floors, as was the case in the original mill. The dam and forebay upstream fed the undershot water-powered mill machinery. (Photograph courtesy of George Longacre.)

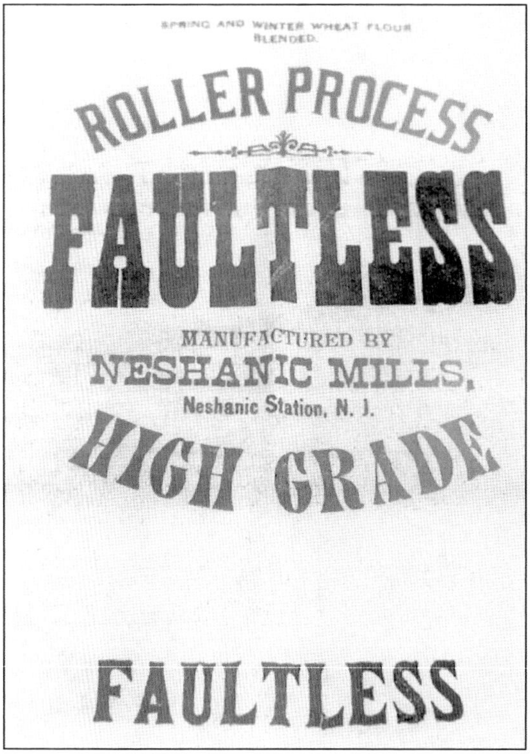

This flour bag shows the brand manufactured by the Neshanic Mill. (Photograph courtesy of G.W. Amerman.)

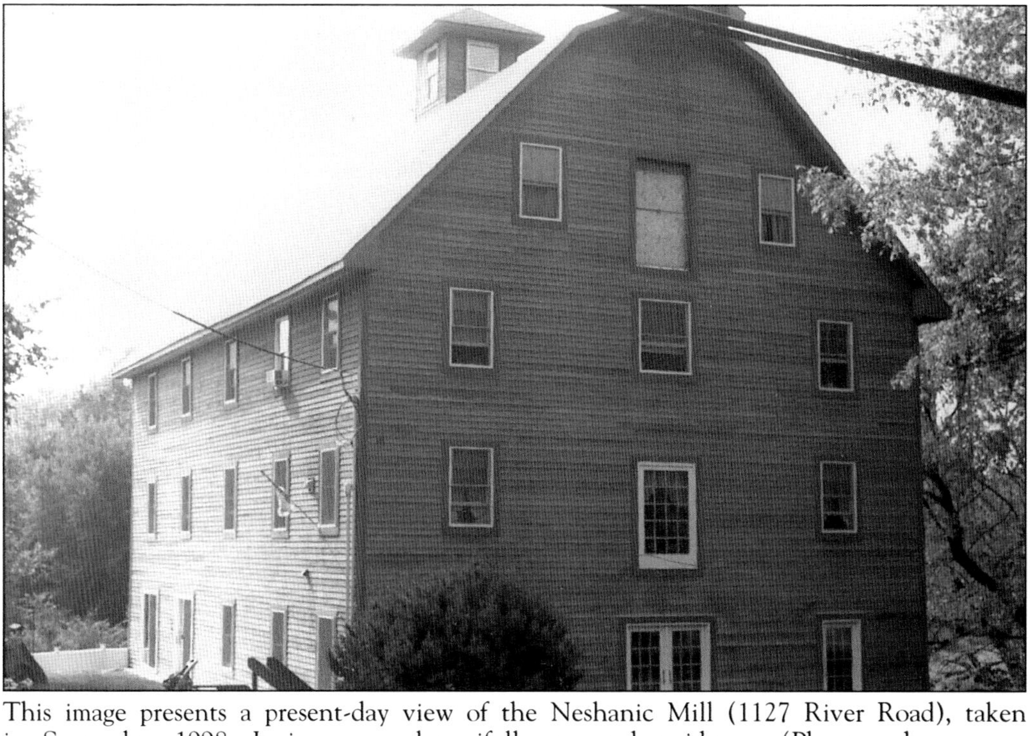

This image presents a present-day view of the Neshanic Mill (1127 River Road), taken in September 1998. It is now a beautifully restored residence. (Photograph courtesy of G.W. Amerman.)

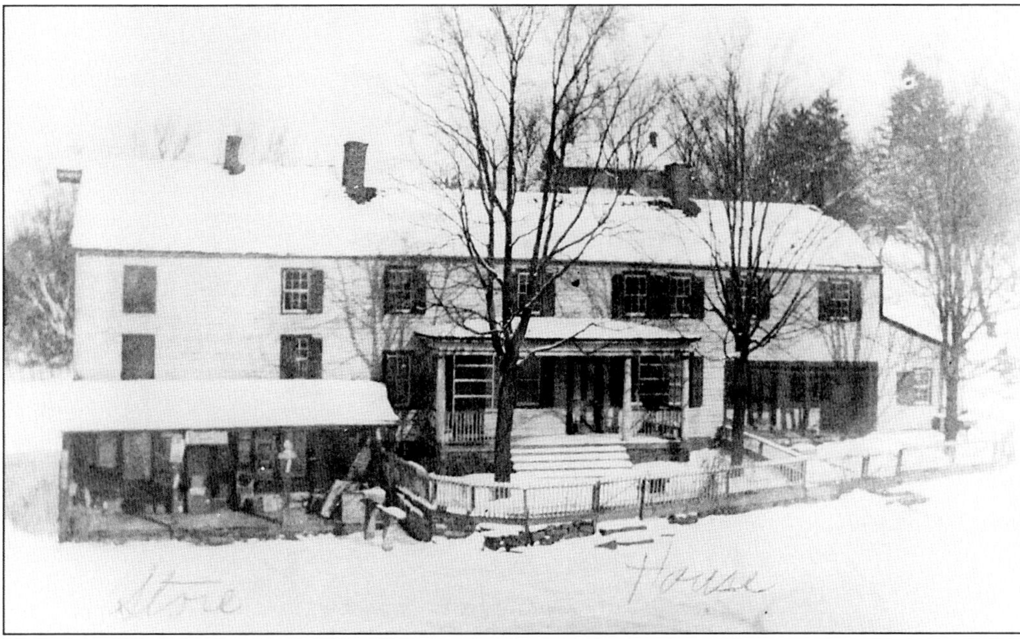

Andrew Lane's Mill and Store, with residence attached, was located at the River Road end of Mill Lane, just opposite the A.S. Amerman Mill. This photo postcard, taken in 1904, shows the Lehigh Valley Railroad Station at the top of the hill. At that time, there were two stations: this station and another called West Neshanic Station (located by the Shurts Feed mill on Fairview Drive). (Photograph courtesy of the Neshanic Station Historical Society.)

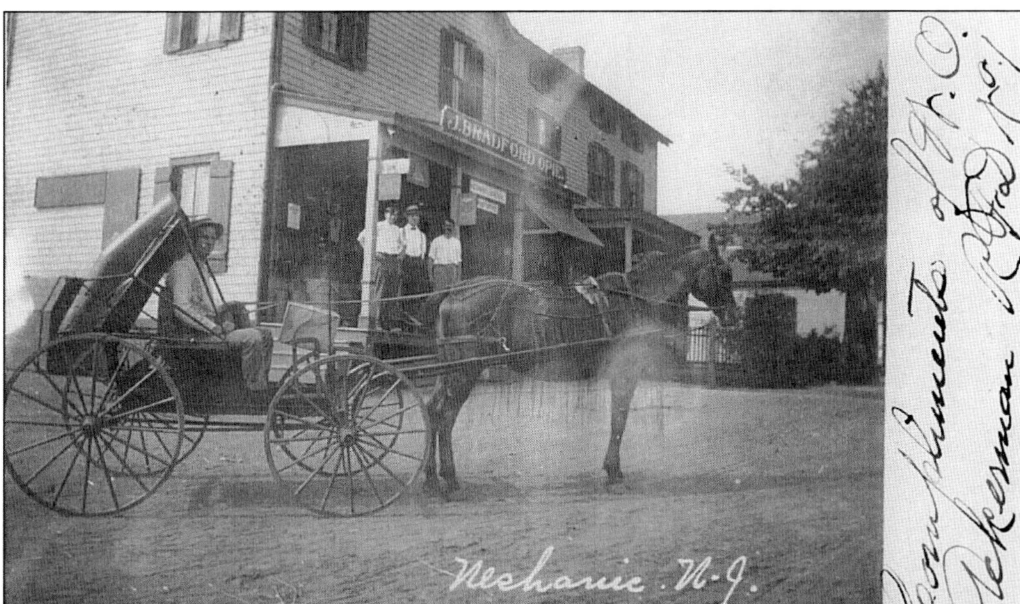

W.O. Ackerman, a Rural Free Delivery (RFD) mailman, is shown by the J. Bradford Opie General Store and Post Office with his horse and buggy in August 1909. (Photo postcard courtesy of Robert Yuell.)

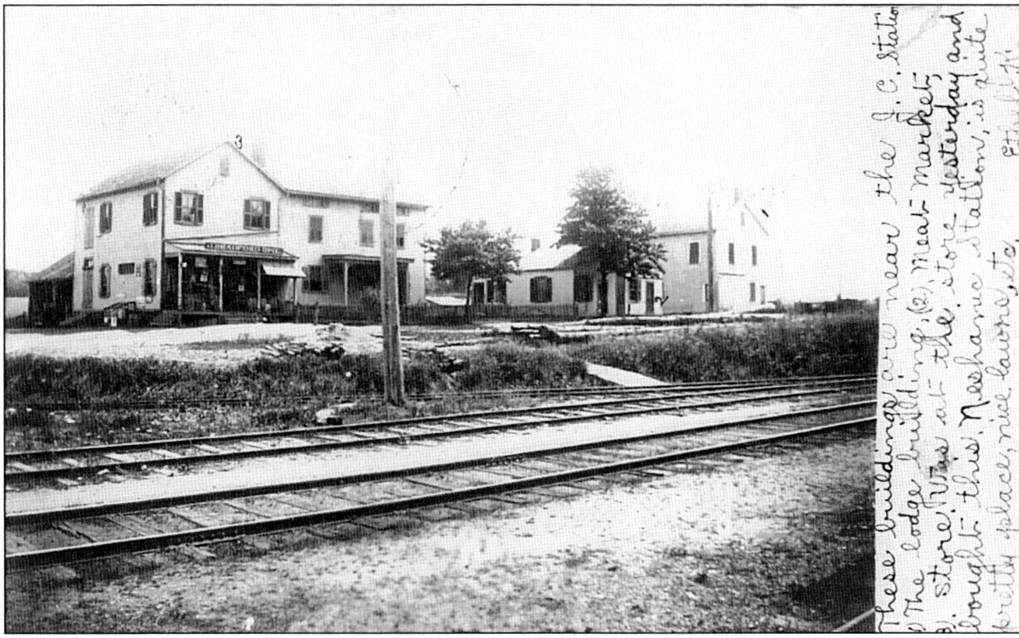

This view, from C.R.R. freight house, shows the Opie store with meat market (in middle) and Knights of Pythias Lodge (on right). Note the message card, postmarked April 13, 1908. (Photo postcard courtesy of Robert Yuell.)

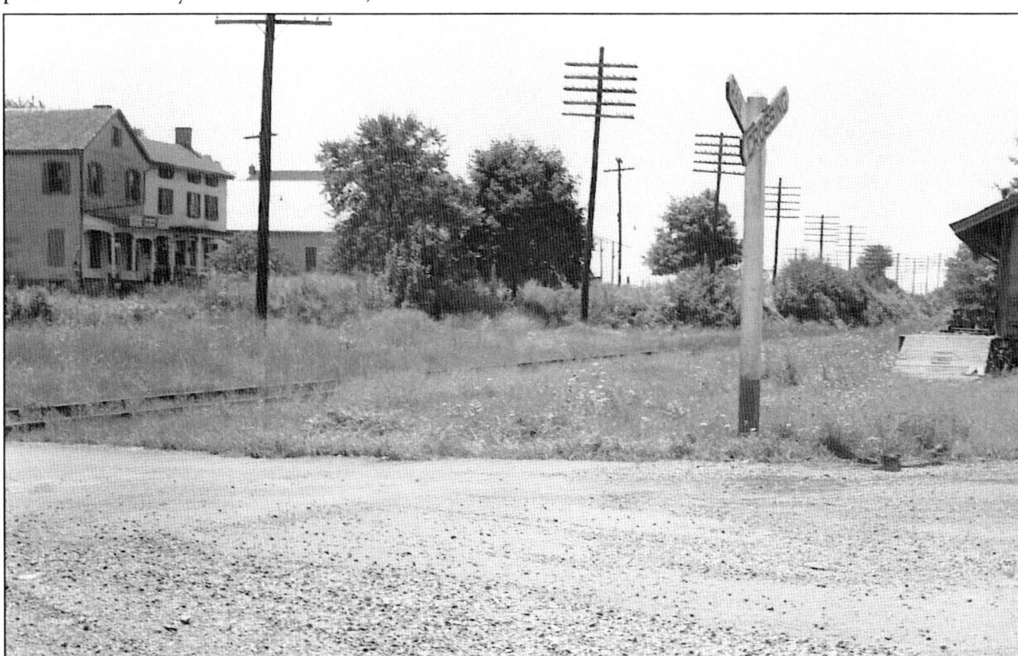

The J. Bradford Opie store, which he operated for 50 years, was continued by his cousin, V.W. Opie. Clark Scully operated a general store at this location for a few more years. Then Otho Saums and son Elmer Saums sold electrical appliances here while operating as Neshanic Electric Co. The building has now been restored as a residence. (Photograph courtesy of Walt Kostro.)

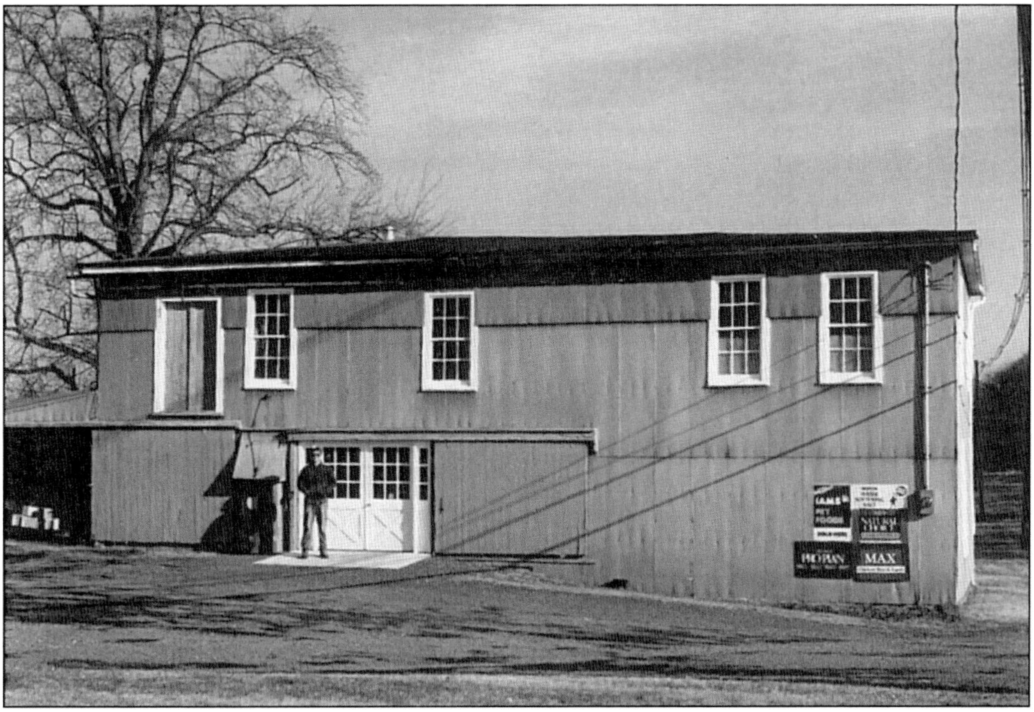

The Shurts Brothers' original building (101 Fairview Drive), which is still operating as Neshanic Station Farm and Garden, is owned by Walter Maze (pictured here by the door). This building was originally a cheese factory with a residence on the second floor. (Photograph by G.W. Amerman, 1998.)

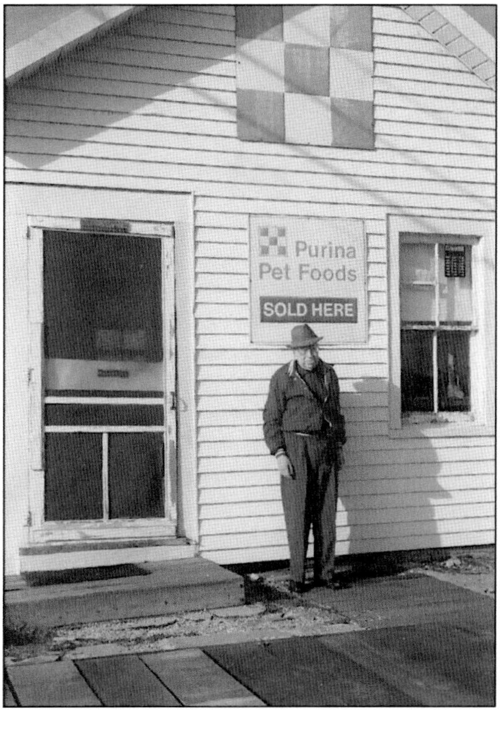

Orville Shurts (at the age of 95) is shown in this October 1998 photograph by the scalehouse and office, which he operated after the death of his father, Lester, and uncle, Andrew Shurts. Orville Shurts still stops in to check on business with Walter Maze. (Photograph by G.W. Amerman, 1998.)

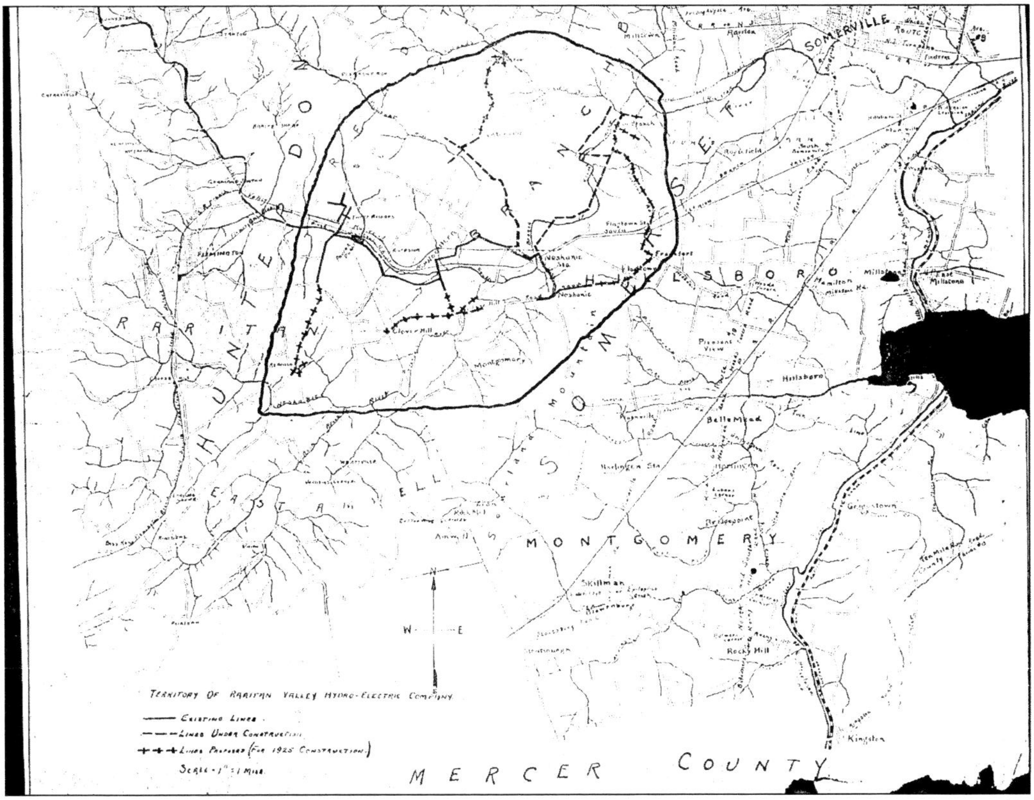

This is a map of the Raritan Valley Hydroelectric Co. started in 1922. Powered at the Higginsville Mill (below Three Bridges), the Raritan Valley Hydroelectric Co. supplied the first electricity to the villages of Neshanic and Neshanic Station with an undershot waterwheel. Founded by John S. Amerman, Harry V. Hoff, and Frank Van Syckle, the company was later incorporated into the NJ Power & Light Co. (Courtesy of Neshanic Station Historical Society.)

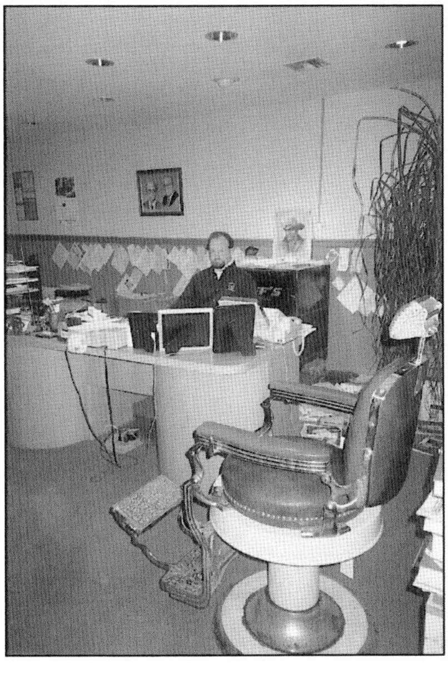

Hoff's Electrical Service at 421 Olive Street was started in 1948, by David F. Hoff, and is now celebrating 50 years in commercial and residential wiring service. The electric service began in one of D.C. R. Hoff's poultry houses. Starting with the firm in 1973, Douglas C. Hoff III is now the president. Here he proudly sits in his office with his great-grandfather Harry Barker's original barbershop chair as décor. (Photograph by G.W. Amerman, 1999.)

Michael Hausch, a blacksmith, is shown in this *c.* 1920 photograph at work by his forge. His shop was located on Mill Lane, just above Andrew Lane's Mill and Store. (Photograph courtesy of Mary Hausch Sixt.)

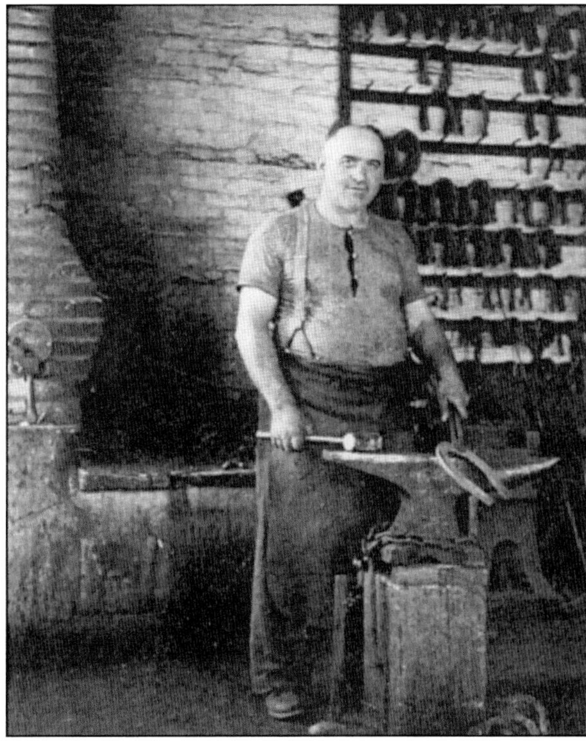

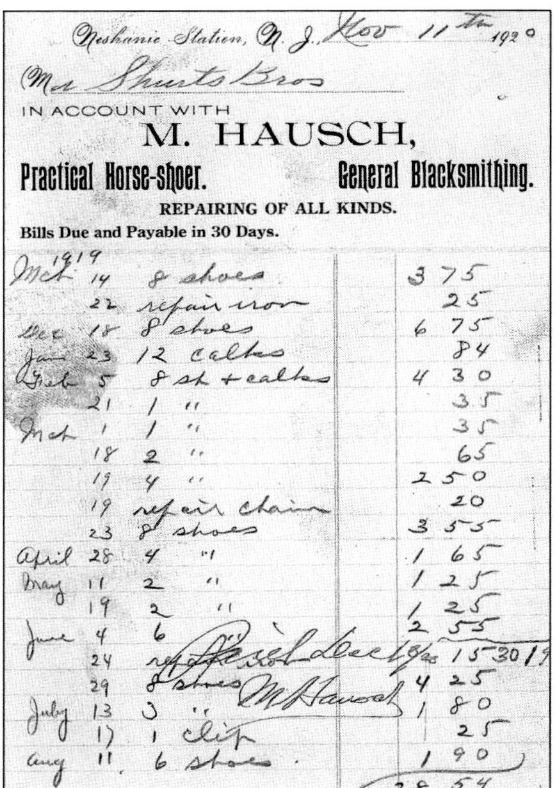

Neshanic Station, N. J. Nov 11th 1920

Mr Shurts Bros

IN ACCOUNT WITH

M. HAUSCH,

Practical Horse-shoer. **General Blacksmithing.**

REPAIRING OF ALL KINDS.

Bills Due and Payable in 30 Days.

1919 Mch	14	8 shoes	3 75
	22	repair iron	25
Dec	18	8 shoes	6 75
Jan	23	12 calks	84
Feb	5	8 sh + calks	4 30
	21	1 "	35
Mch	1	1 "	35
	18	2 "	65
	19	4 "	2 50
	19	repair chain	20
	23	8 shoes	3 55
April	28	4 "	1 65
May	11	2 "	1 25
	19	2 "	1 25
June	4	6 "	2 55
	24	repair	15 30
	29	8 shoes	4 25
July	13	3 "	1 80
	17	1 clip	25
Aug	11	6 shoes	1 90
			38 54

Rec'd Dec 1/20 M Hausch

This is one of Mr. Hausch's statements, for the Shurts Brothers' Mill, showing prices for horseshoes, chain repair, etc. over several months in 1920. (Courtesy of Orville Shurts.)

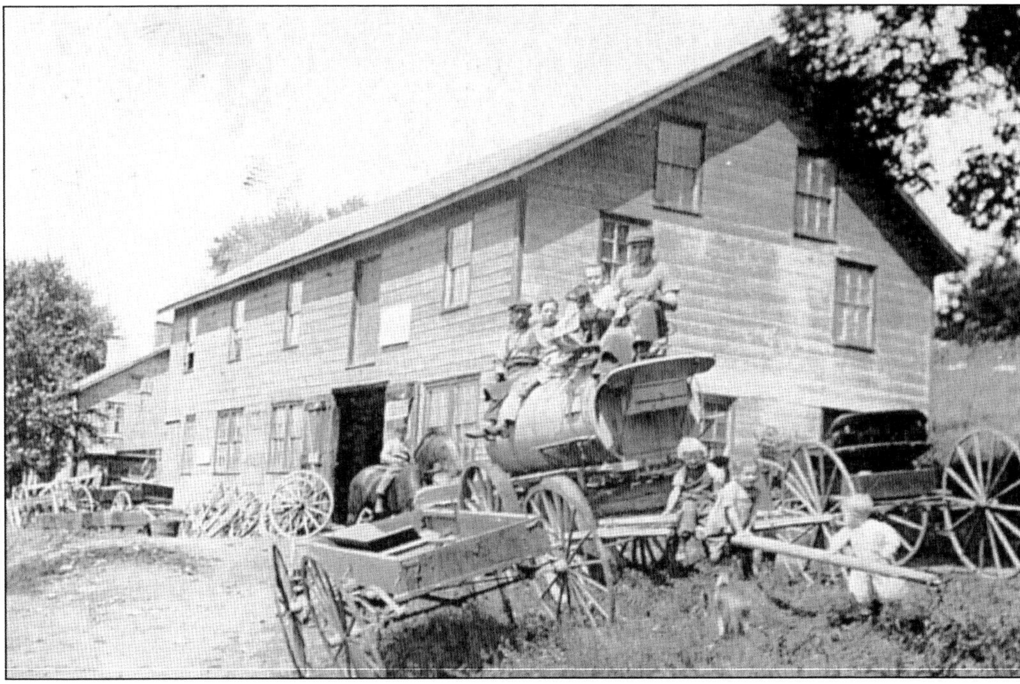

This is a photograph of the blacksmith shop operated by Mike Hausch, which shows a wood stave, waterwagon, as well as various buggies and wagons with wheels awaiting iron work at his Mill Lane forge. (Photograph courtesy of Mary Hausch Sixt.)

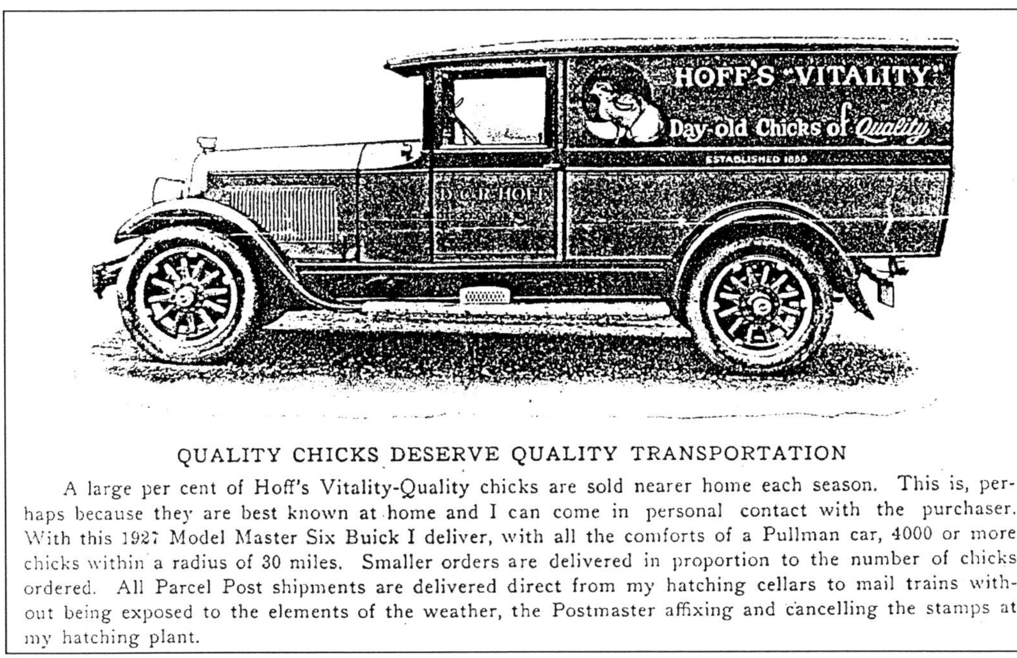

Shown here is an advertisement for the Hoff chick delivery service. This 1927 Buick Master Six was ordered by a funeral director who was unable to take delivery, so Mr. Hoff bought a deluxe delivery van. (Photograph courtesy of Douglas Hoff III.)

D.C. R. Hoff, one of America's pioneer chick producers, established his business in 1888. This photograph dates back to 1925. (Photograph courtesy of Virginia Hoff.)

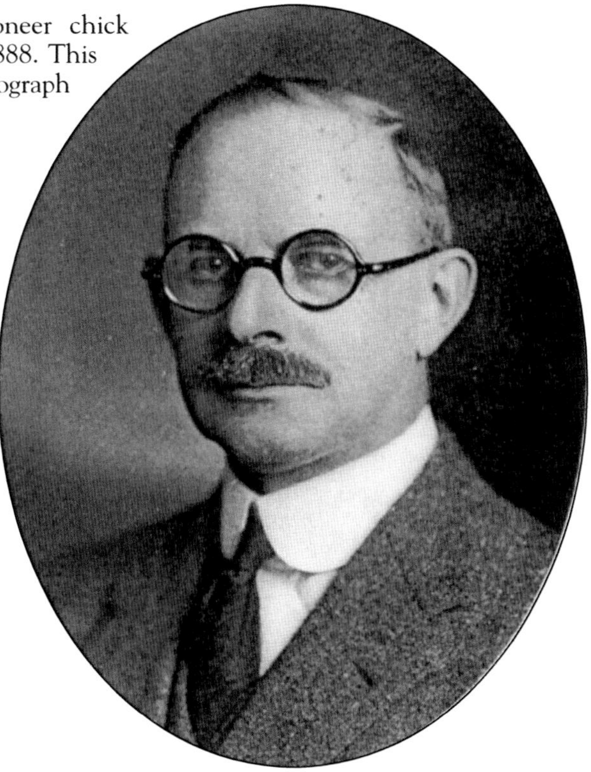

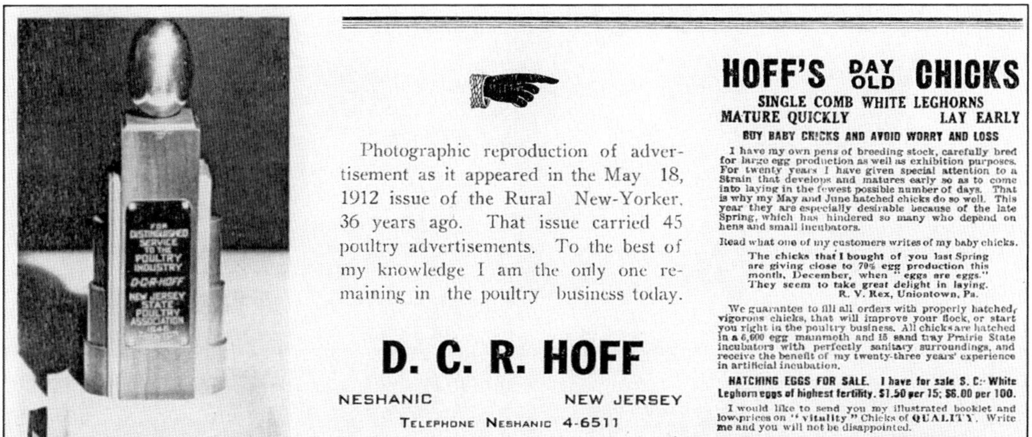

Photographic reproduction of advertisement as it appeared in the May 18, 1912 issue of the Rural New-Yorker, 36 years ago. That issue carried 45 poultry advertisements. To the best of my knowledge I am the only one remaining in the poultry business today.

D. C. R. HOFF

NESHANIC NEW JERSEY

TELEPHONE NESHANIC 4-6511

HOFF'S DAY OLD CHICKS

SINGLE COMB WHITE LEGHORNS

MATURE QUICKLY LAY EARLY

BUY BABY CHICKS AND AVOID WORRY AND LOSS

I have my own pens of breeding stock, carefully bred for large egg production as well as exhibition purposes. For twenty years I have given special attention to a Strain that develops and matures early so as to come into laying in the fewest possible number of days. That is why my May and June hatched chicks do so well. This year they are especially desirable because of the late Spring, which has hindered so many who depend on hens and small incubators.

Read what one of my customers writes of my baby chicks.

> The chicks that I bought of you last Spring are giving close to 70% egg production this month, December, when "eggs are eggs." They seem to take great delight in laying.
> R. V. Rex, Uniontown, Pa.

We guarantee to fill all orders with properly hatched, vigorous chicks, that will improve your flock, or start you right in the poultry business. All chicks are hatched in a 6,600 egg mammoth and 15 sand tray Prairie State incubators with perfectly sanitary surroundings, and receive the benefit of my twenty-three years' experience in artificial incubation.

HATCHING EGGS FOR SALE. **I have for sale S. C. White Leghorn eggs of highest fertility. $1.50 per 15; $6.00 per 100.**

I would like to send you my illustrated booklet and low prices on "vitality" Chicks of QUALITY. Write me and you will not be disappointed.

D. C. R. HOFF, Lock Box 115, NESHANIC STATION, N. J.

Shown here is one of Hoff's day-old chick advertisements, dated May 1912. (Courtesy of Virginia Hoff.)

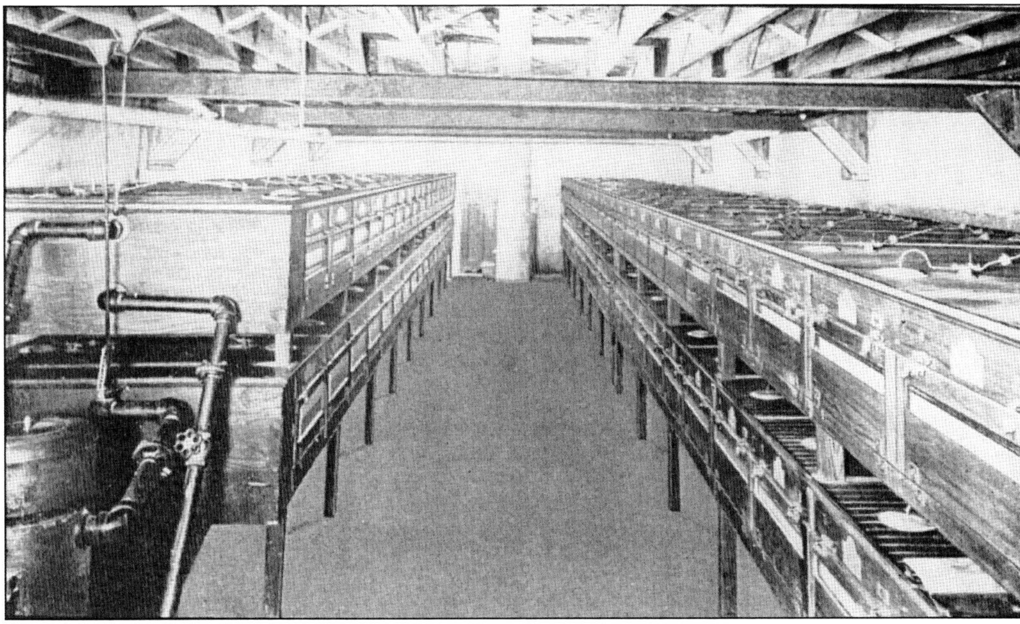
This view shows part of the interior of the incubator cellar located beneath D.C. R. Hoff's home at 420 Olive Street in Neshanic Station. Two incubators had a capacity of over 30,000 eggs. (Photograph courtesy of Douglas Hoff III.)

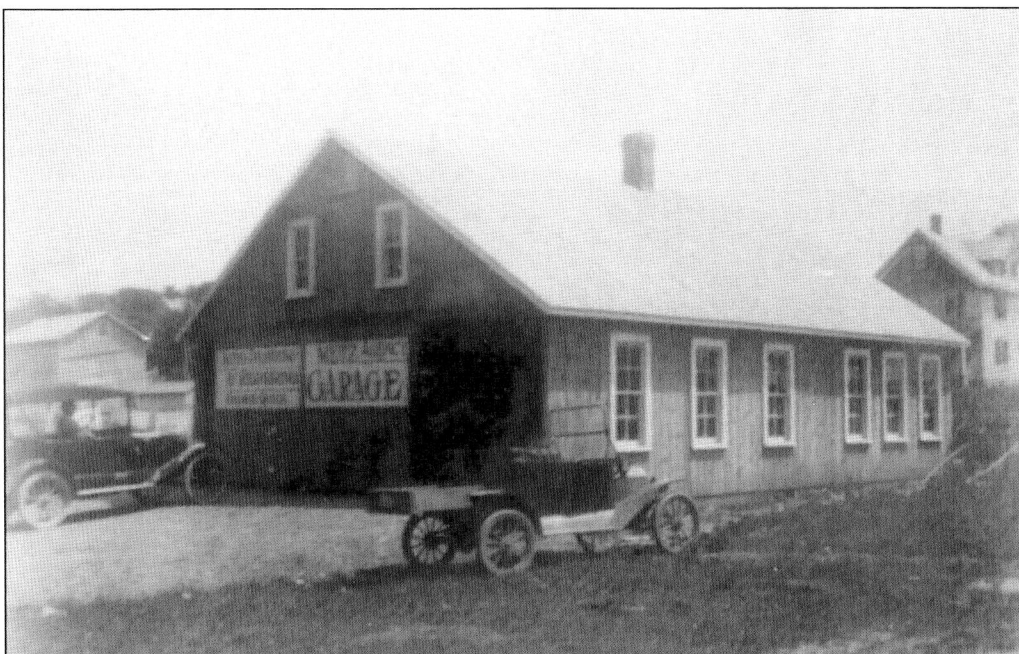

This *c.* 1914 photograph captures the Metz Car Agency operated by George Quick at 416 Olive Street in Neshanic Station. This same building housed D.C. R. Hoff Poultry, the original Hoff's Electrical Service, a bakery, and a firetruck. Today, a barber shop and a residence are located in the building. (Photograph courtesy of Neshanic Station Historical Society.)

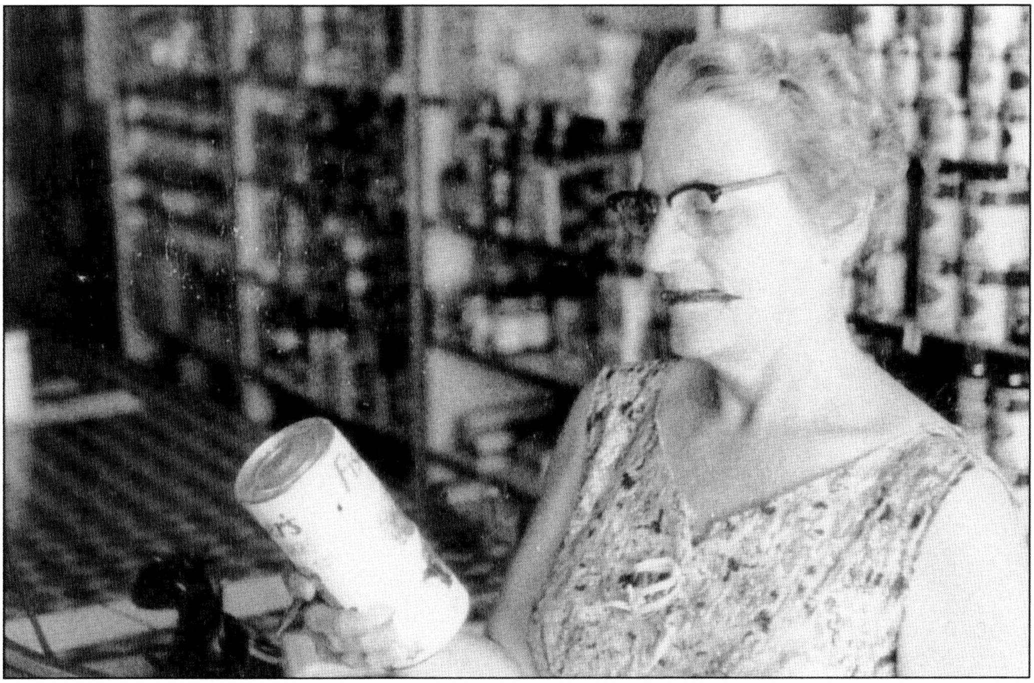

Maude Quick is shown here serving a customer in her general store at 695 Amwell Road in Neshanic, near the two-room school. When Maude started an ice cream and candy store in her home, it became so successful that her husband gave up his business, Metz Garage. They built a new store next door to their home and operated a very successful butcher shop and general store until 1960. (Photograph courtesy of Arthur Saunders.)

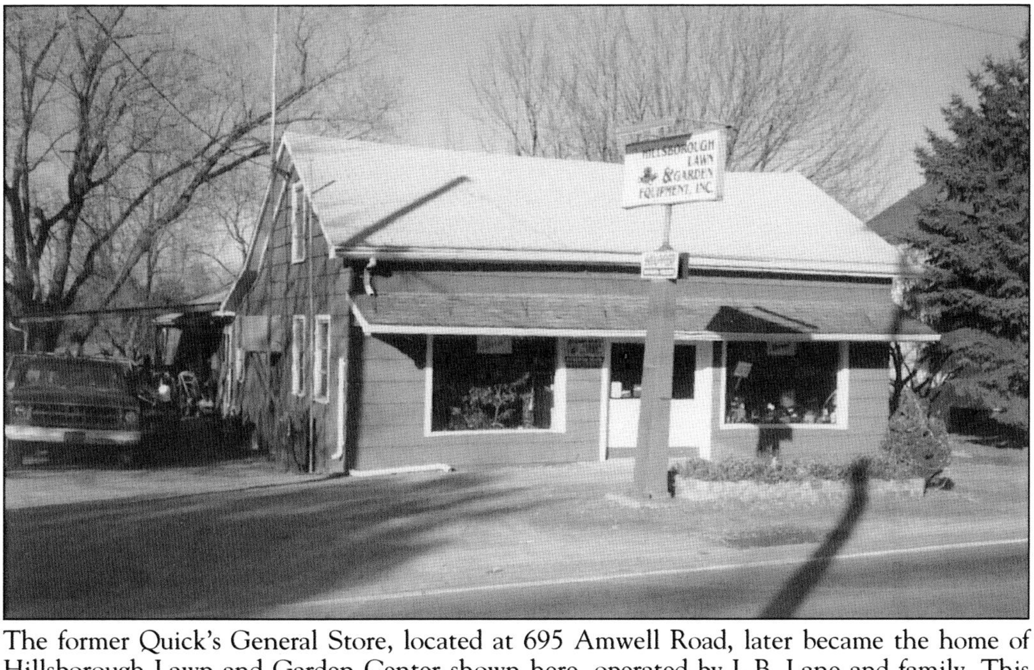

The former Quick's General Store, located at 695 Amwell Road, later became the home of Hillsborough Lawn and Garden Center shown here, operated by L.B. Lane and family. This photograph was taken c. 1970. (Photograph courtesy of L.B. Lane.)

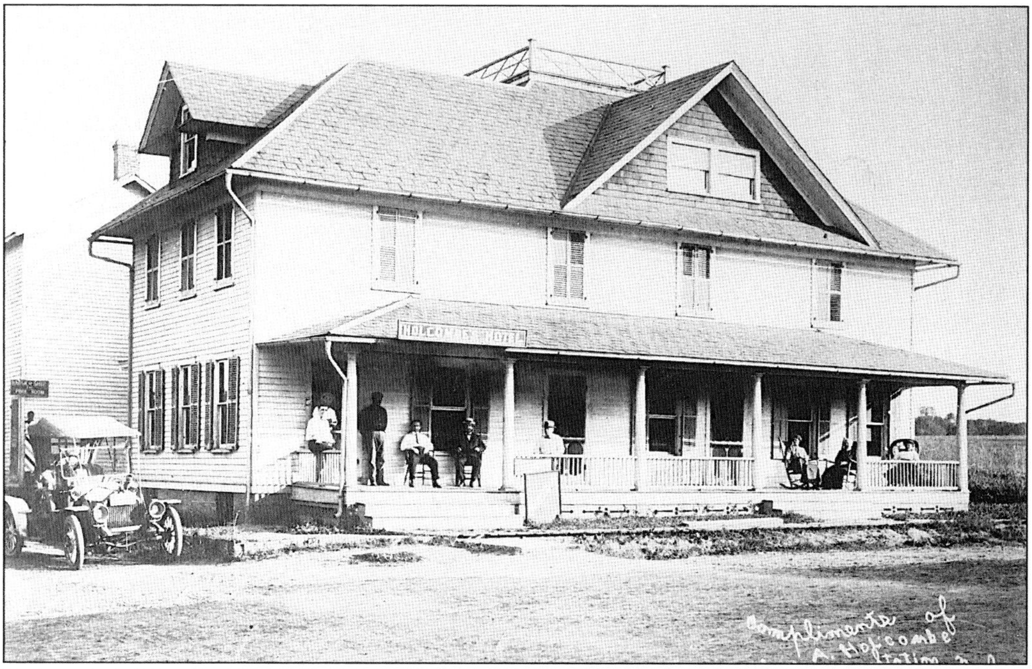

Holcombe's Hotel is shown here after it was rebuilt, following the 1910 fire. The original was built in 1875 after the coming of the Central Railroad of New Jersey. The sign on the rear building shows the location of Harry Barker's barbershop and the poolroom. Note the separate ladies and gents entrances to the hotel. (Photograph courtesy of Neshanic Station Historical Society.)

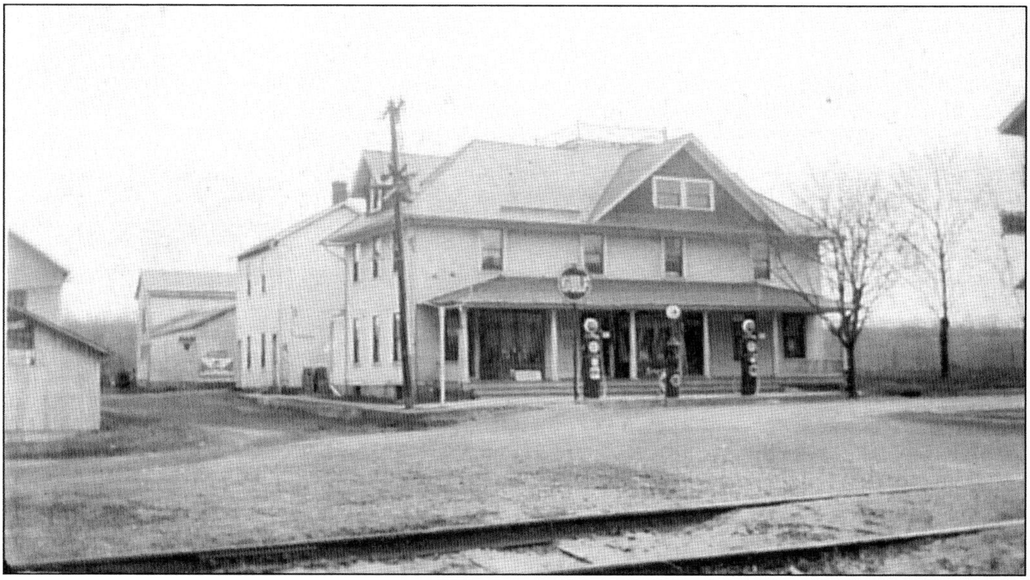

Neshanic Inn, formerly Holcombe's Hotel, was owned in 1930 by A.F. Messig, who sold Gulf gasoline and kerosene at the Riverside Garage. The hotel housed a tavern through the door on the left, a meat market in the center, and a Breyer's Ice Cream shop through the door on the right. The adjacent business, J.S. Amerman Building Material, is also shown. (Photograph courtesy of the Quick Family.)

Shown here is an advertisement for Riverside Garage. (Courtesy of the Quick Family.)

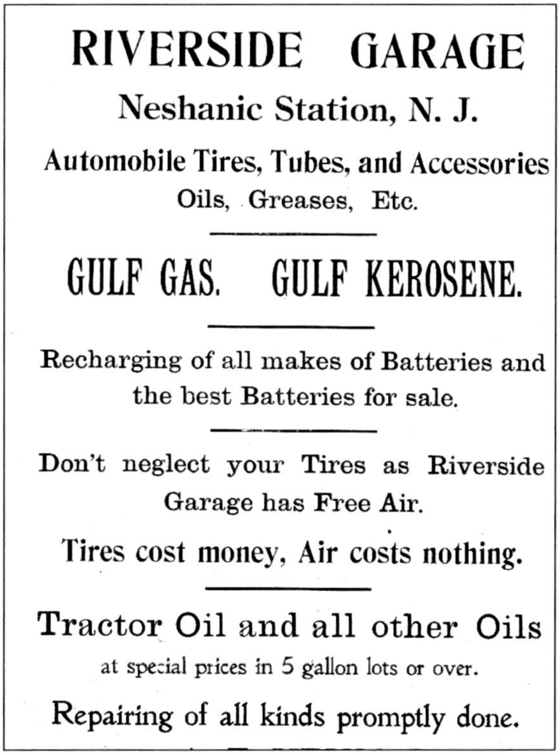

RIVERSIDE GARAGE

Neshanic Station, N. J.

Automobile Tires, Tubes, and Accessories

Oils, Greases, Etc.

GULF GAS. GULF KEROSENE.

Recharging of all makes of Batteries and the best Batteries for sale.

Don't neglect your Tires as Riverside Garage has Free Air.

Tires cost money, Air costs nothing.

Tractor Oil and all other Oils

at special prices in 5 gallon lots or over.

Repairing of all kinds promptly done.

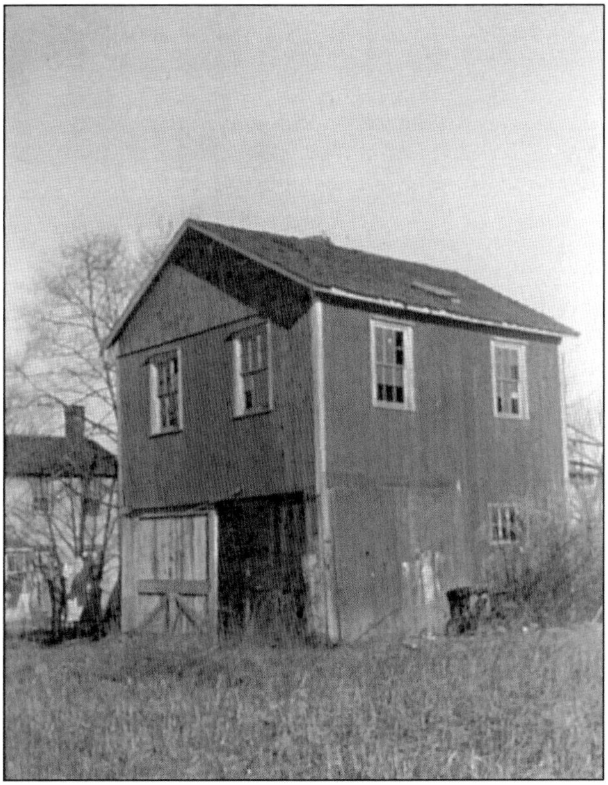

Snell's *History* and some other articles refer to a coffin factory located in Neshanic Station. This *c.* 1900 photograph is the only known picture of the factory, showing it near the driveway entry to the Totten farm, located on Otto Road. (Photograph courtesy of Frank Totten.)

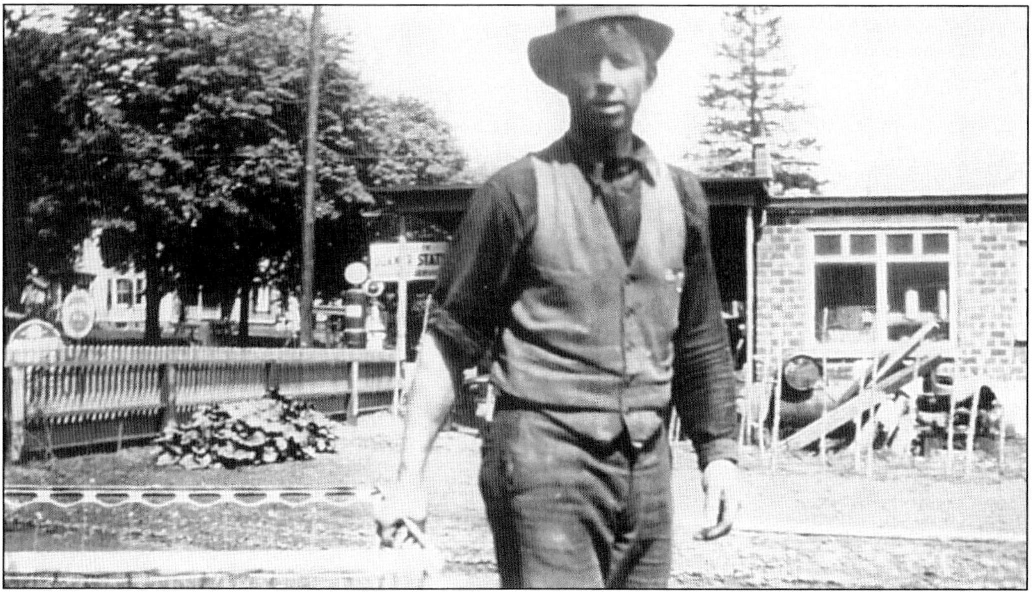

J.S. Covert's Garage building on Pearl Street is shown here in 1923 with Mr. Covert in the foreground. (Photograph courtesy of Jim Covert.)

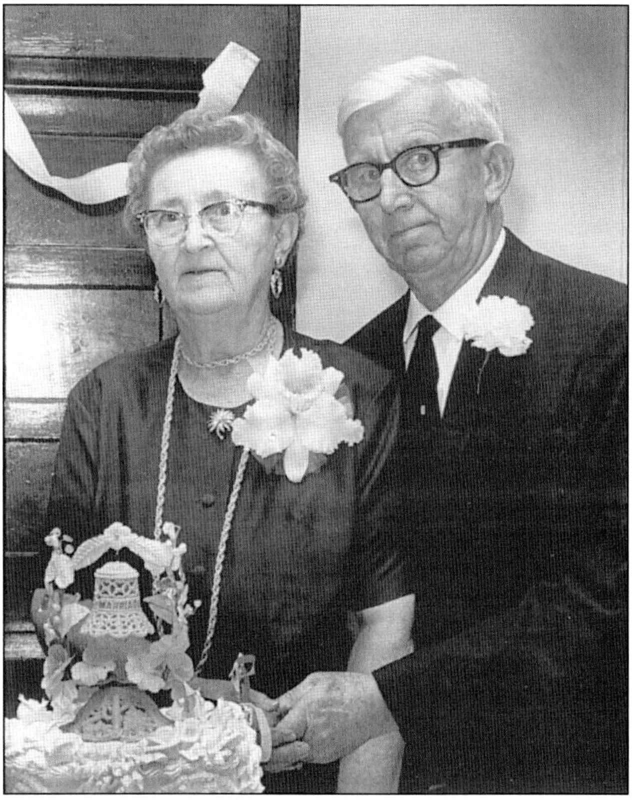

J. Staats Covert and Jeanette Covert are shown here celebrating their 60th wedding anniversary in 1970. Mr. and Mrs. Covert were active in shaping the community. J.S. Covert & Sons was the largest John Deere equipment dealer in New Jersey from 1928 to 1987, and also sold Studebaker cars and trucks from 1937 to 1965. Mrs. Covert started the Bright Buttons 4-H Club in the 1920s. Mr. and Mrs. Covert were instrumental in fund-raising for the creation of the fire company and were charter members. (Photograph courtesy of the Covert Family.)

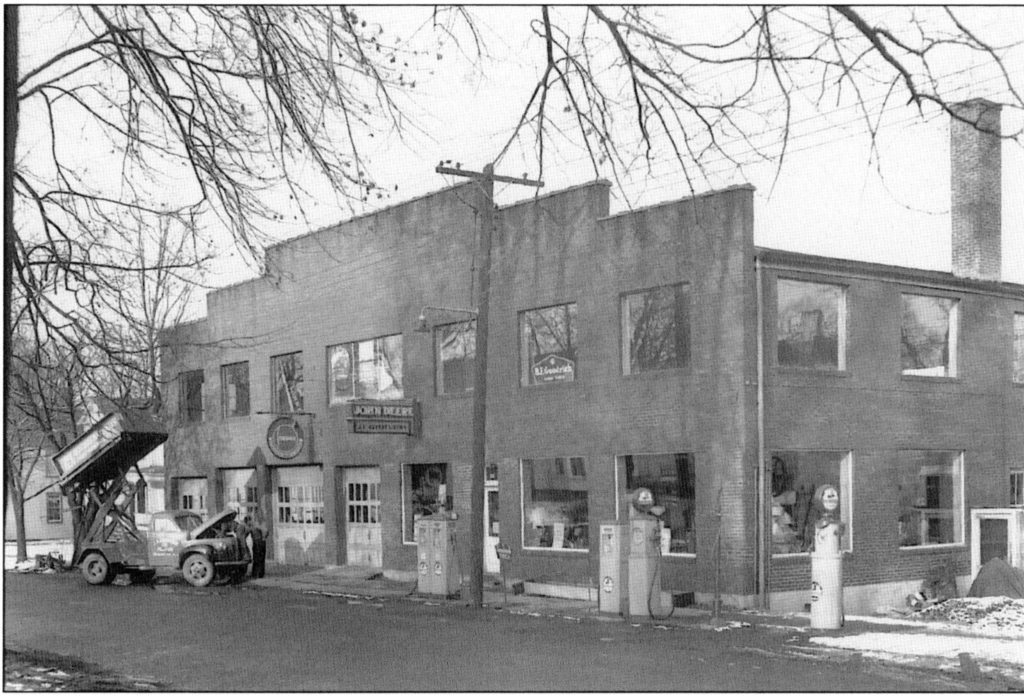

The enlarged J.S. Covert & Sons business is shown here in 1947, with the J.S. Amerman Co., new Studebaker coal truck. (Photograph by A. Schenck Bergen, unpublished work, courtesy of Olivia Cutler.)

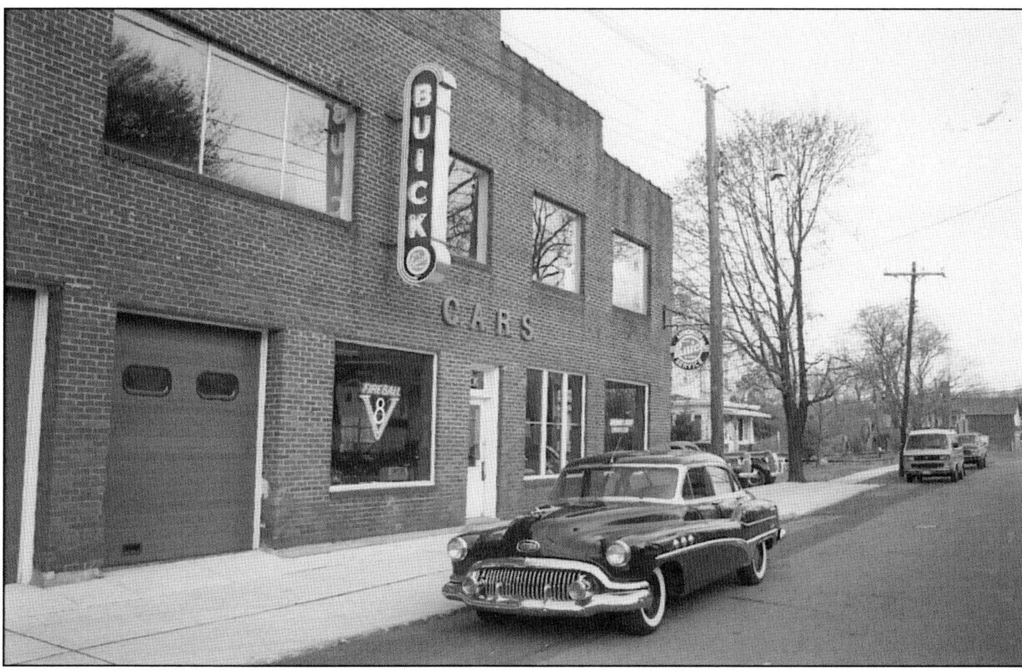

Cars, Inc., owned by Glenn D. Cecchine, took over the former J.S. Covert & Sons location and deals in antique automobiles and parts, specializing in Buick cars. The business started in 1974, and it moved to Neshanic in 1987. (Photograph courtesy of Glenn Cecchine.)

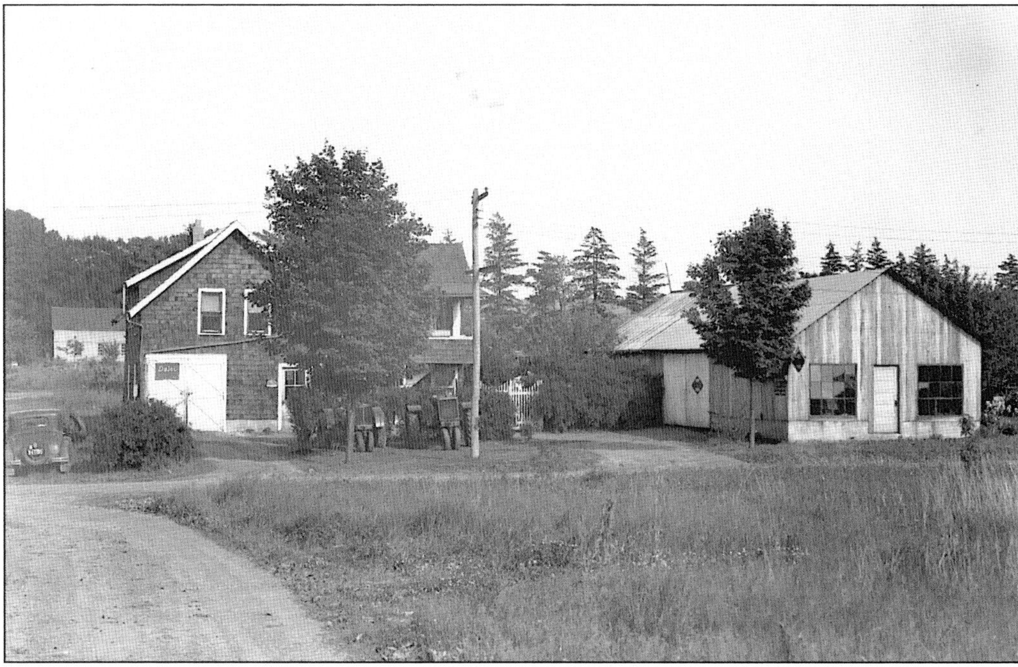

The A. Schenck Bergen home and business are shown here in 1930, at 606 Marshall Street in Neshanic Station. Mr. Bergen sold Allis Chalmers tractors and machinery, as well as Surge milking machines. This is the present location of Don's Service Center. (Photograph by A. Schenck Bergen, unpublished work, courtesy of Olivia Cutler.)

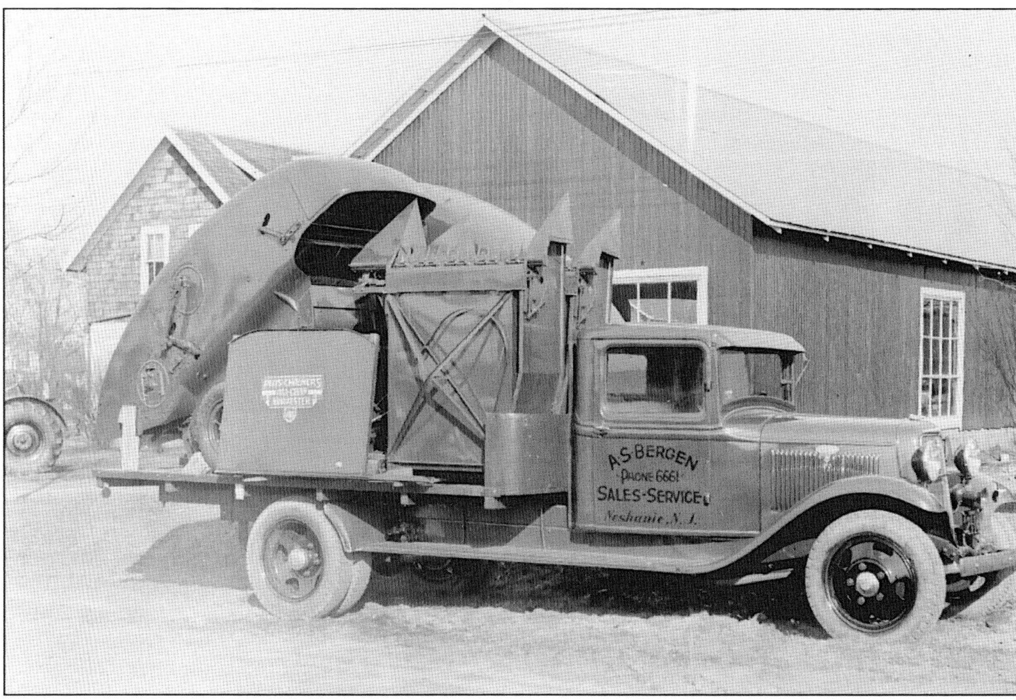

A.S. Bergen's Ford truck is shown here with a new, early model Allis Chalmers combine. (Photograph by A. Schenck Bergen, unpublished work, courtesy of Olivia Cutler.)

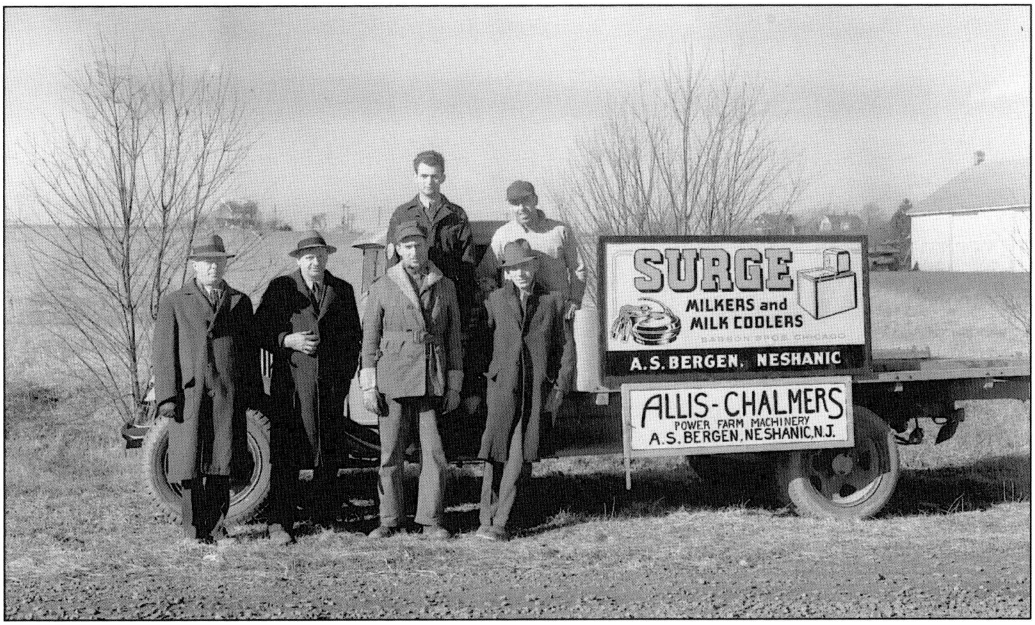

A.S. Bergen employees are shown in the early 1930s, from left to right, as follows: (front row) Perry Packer, William E. Favier, John M. Agans Jr., and A.S. Bergen; (back row) an unknown person and Herbert Ireland. Somerset County Road Department barn is also shown here, in right rear. (Photograph by A. Schenck Bergen, unpublished work, courtesy of Olivia Cutler.)

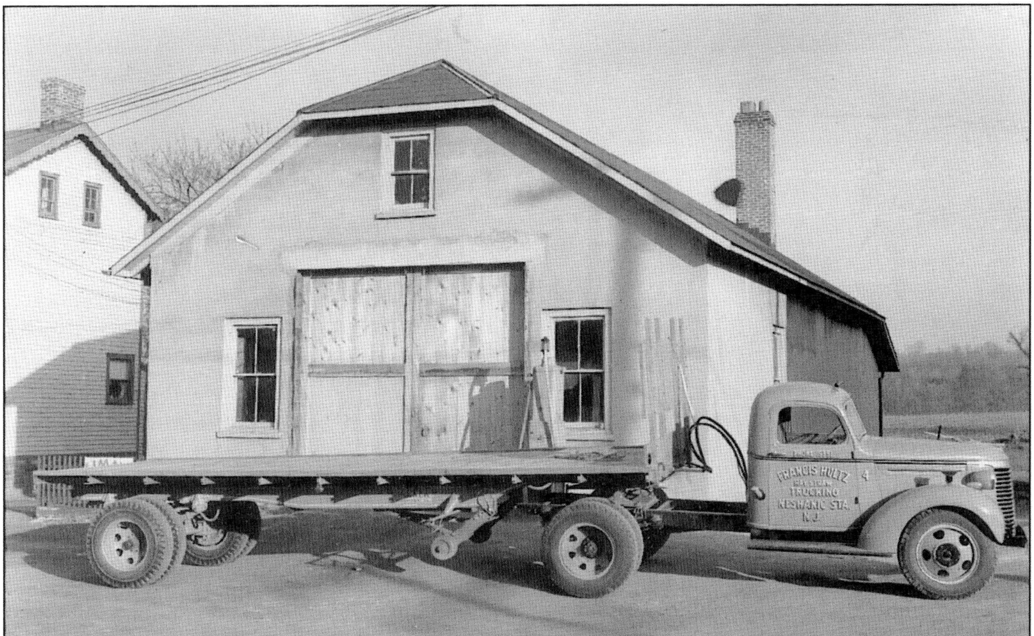

Francis Hultz's truck is shown in this 1930s photograph on Woodfern Road, near the former Gerola Brothers bakery, which was then used as his truck garage. Francis and Lewis Hultz hauled hay and straw from this area to Long Island, as well as delivering coal from Pennsylvania mines to local users. (Photograph by A. Schenck Bergen, unpublished work, courtesy of Olivia Cutler.)

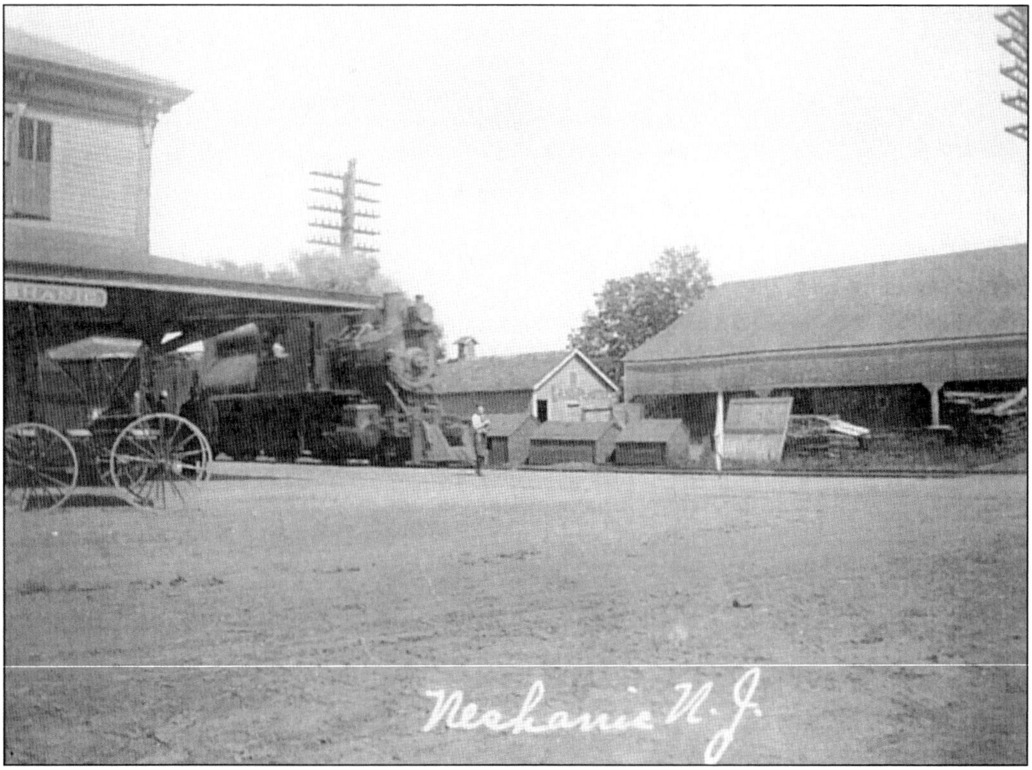

The J.S. Amerman Co. Lumber, Coal, and Feed business is seen here on Woodfern Road, opposite the Central Railroad Station. This photo postcard from 1908 shows the creamery building (with cupola) where the 1910 fire originated. (Photograph courtesy of Robert Yuell.)

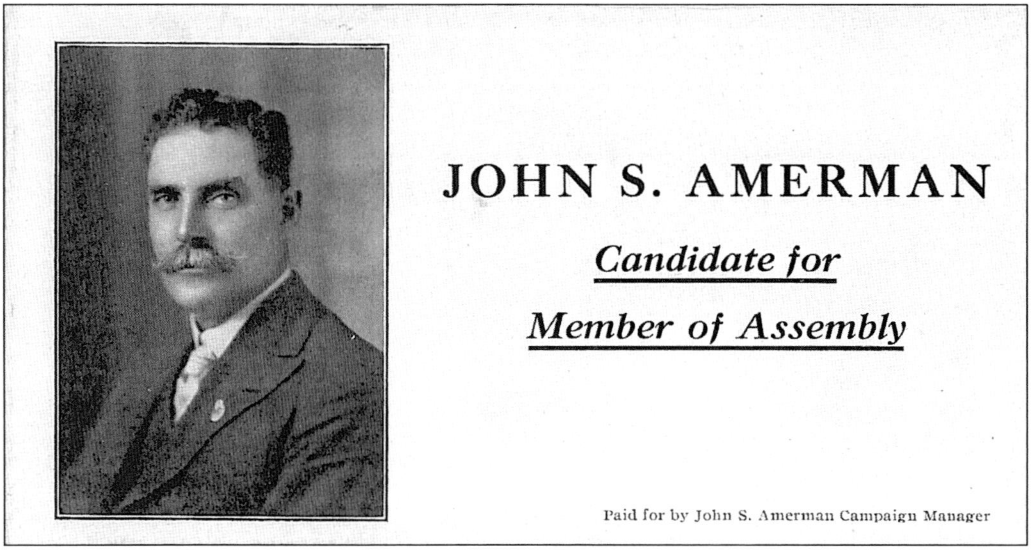

John S. Amerman, candidate for the New Jersey Assembly, was proprietor of the lumberyard from 1906 to 1931. He was a member of the New Jersey Assembly from 1917 to 1919. (Photograph courtesy of J.S. Amerman Co. Collection.)

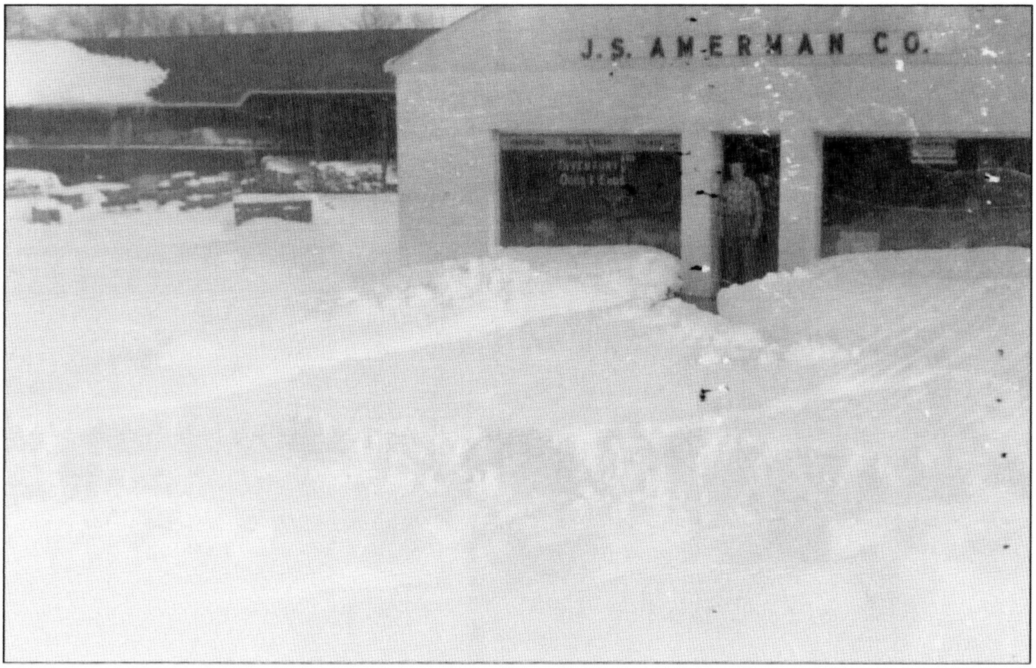

A snow storm was captured in this image on March 19, 1956. George W. Amerman Sr., second generation owner of J.S. Amerman Co., stands in the doorway on what appears to be a very slow business day. (Photograph courtesy of J.S. Amerman Co. Collection.)

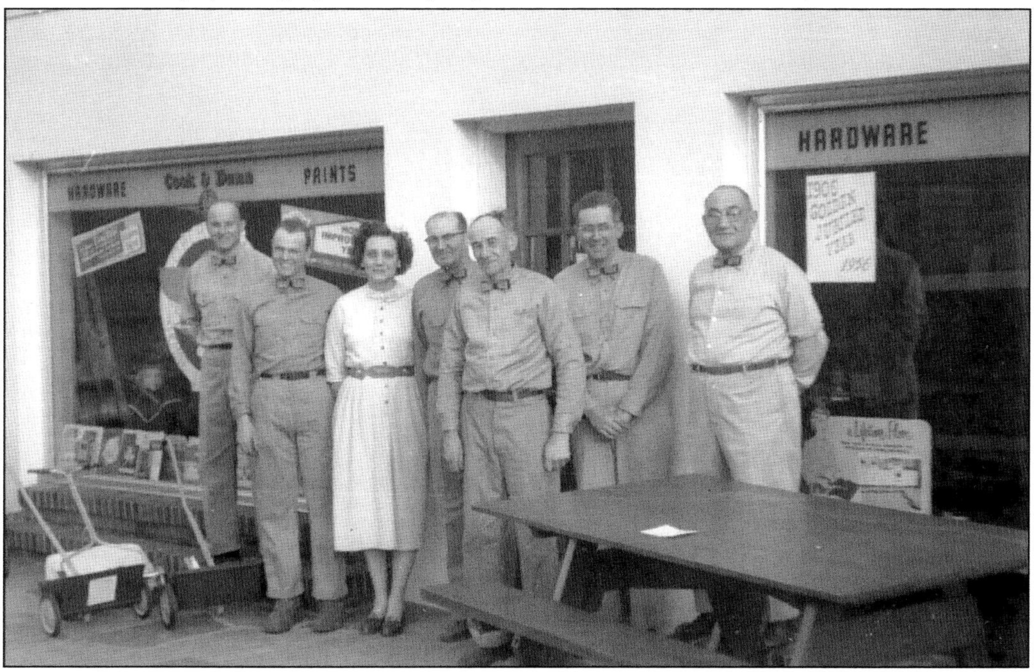

The 50th anniversary of J.S. Amerman Co. (100 Woodfern Road) took place in 1956. Employees, shown here, are G.W. Amerman Jr., Alan Melick, Mae Ten Eyck, President G.W. Amerman Sr., William B. Spratt, Fred Boyd, and Ted Miller. (Photograph courtesy of J.S. Amerman Co. Collection.)

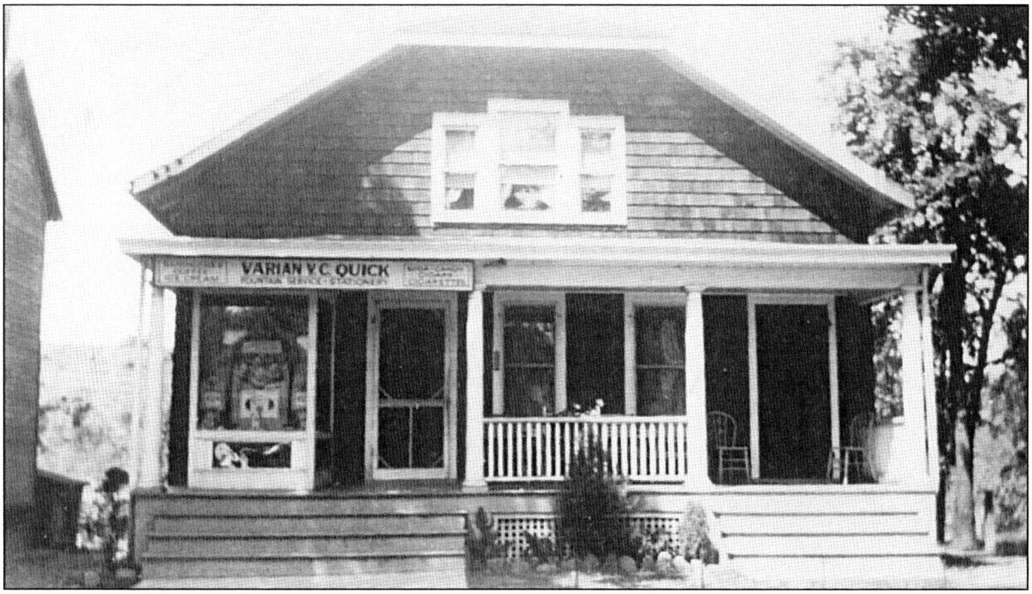

Pictured here is Varian V.C. Quick Sr. Ice Cream and Stationery Store at 409 Olive Street, Neshanic Station, c. 1934. The store at this location was operated by several owners and is now a residence. (Photograph courtesy of Alma Quick Deak.)

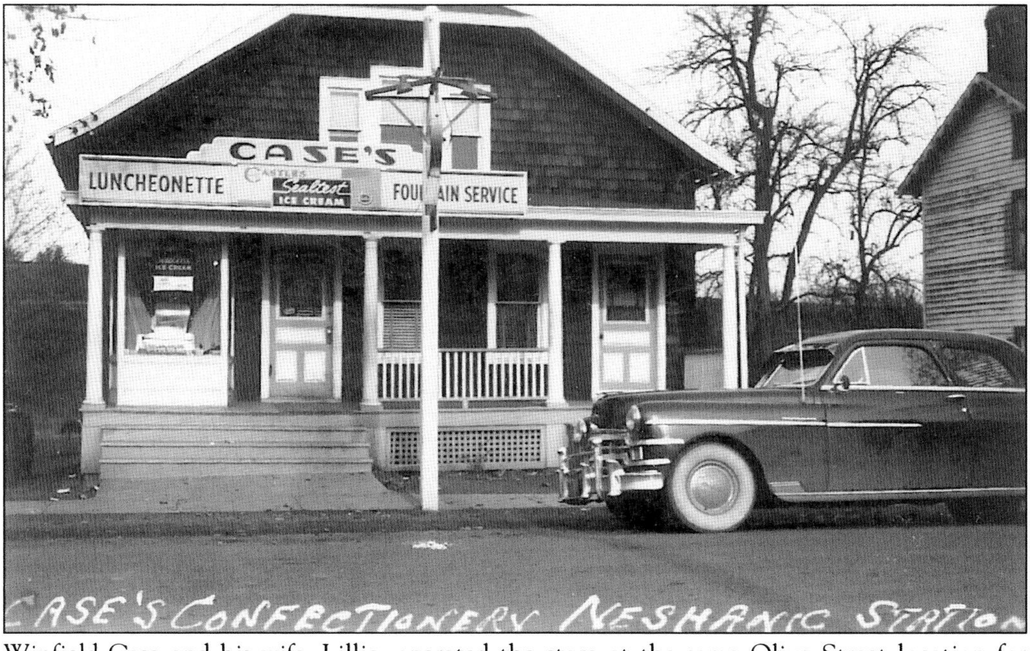

Winfield Case and his wife, Lillie, operated the store at the same Olive Street location for 17 years. (Photo postcard courtesy of Gwen Jamele.)

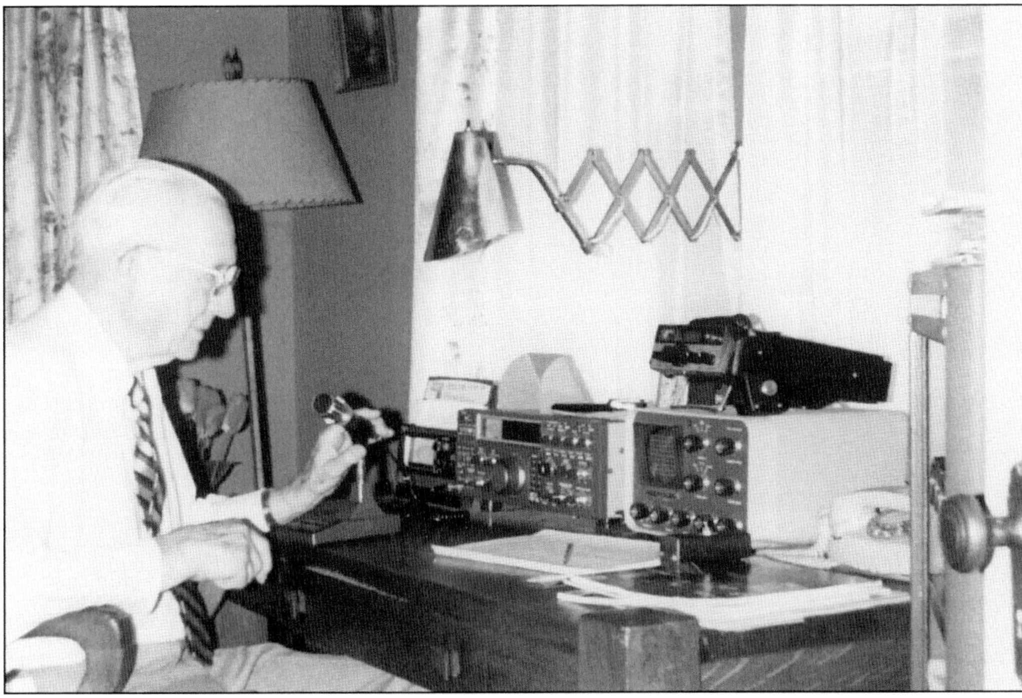

Horace Brokaw started business in 1922, building wireless radio sets for friends. He is seen here in 1972, talking on his Ham radio, celebrating 50 years in business. Mr. Brokaw served as president of the Branchburg Board of Education for 18 years. (Photograph courtesy of H.R. Brokaw.)

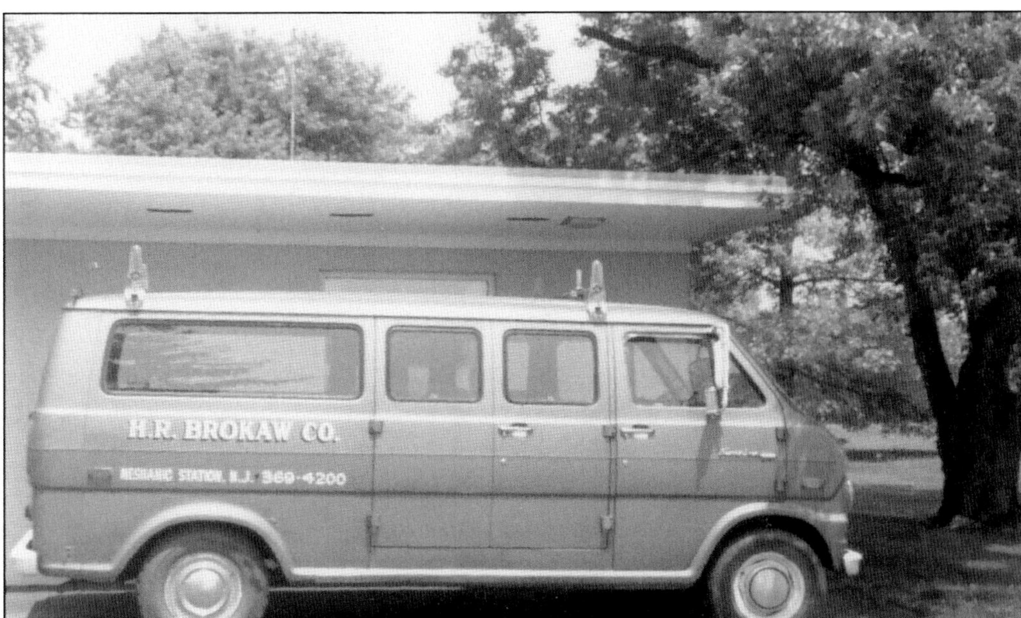

An H.R. Brokaw Co. service truck is shown here in front of a new showroom and shop at 688 Case Road, which was used from 1962 until he retired in 1984. (Photograph courtesy of H.R. Brokaw.)

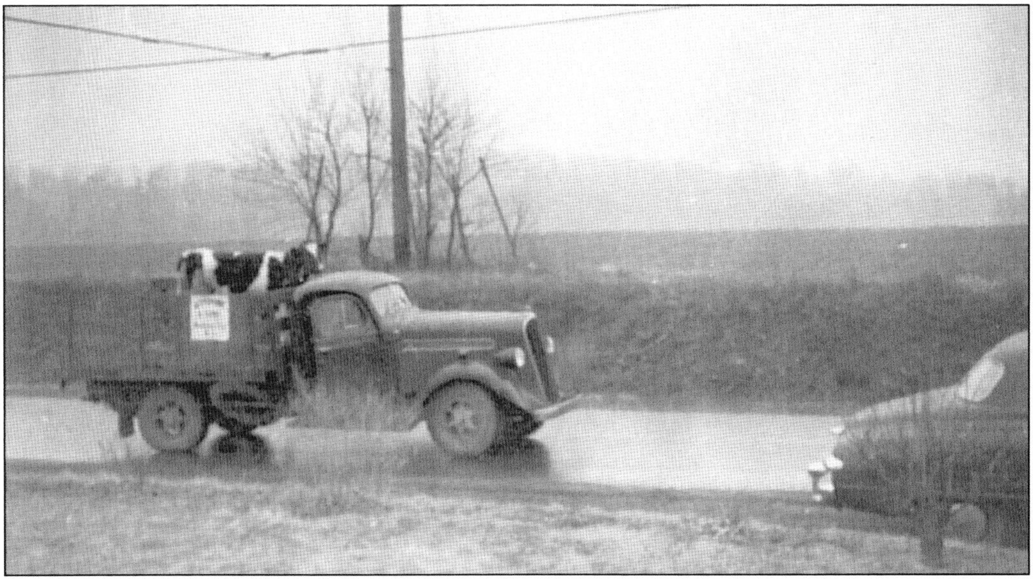

The wide use of Studebakers in the Neshanic area, sold by J.S. Covert & Sons, is illustrated here. A farmer is transporting a heifer from one farm to another on a mid-1930s truck, and a 1950 Studebaker car is waiting to join him. (Photograph courtesy of the Toles family.)

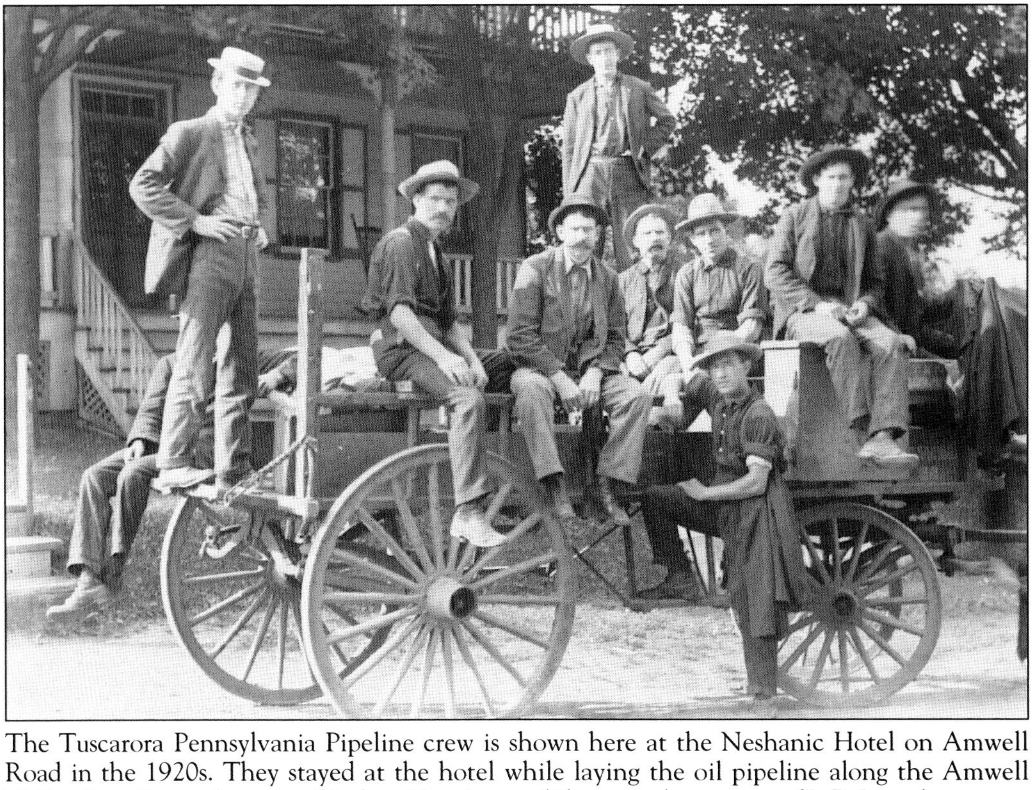

The Tuscarora Pennsylvania Pipeline crew is shown here at the Neshanic Hotel on Amwell Road in the 1920s. They stayed at the hotel while laying the oil pipeline along the Amwell Valley from Pennsylvania to Linden, New Jersey. (Photograph courtesy of L.B. Lane.)

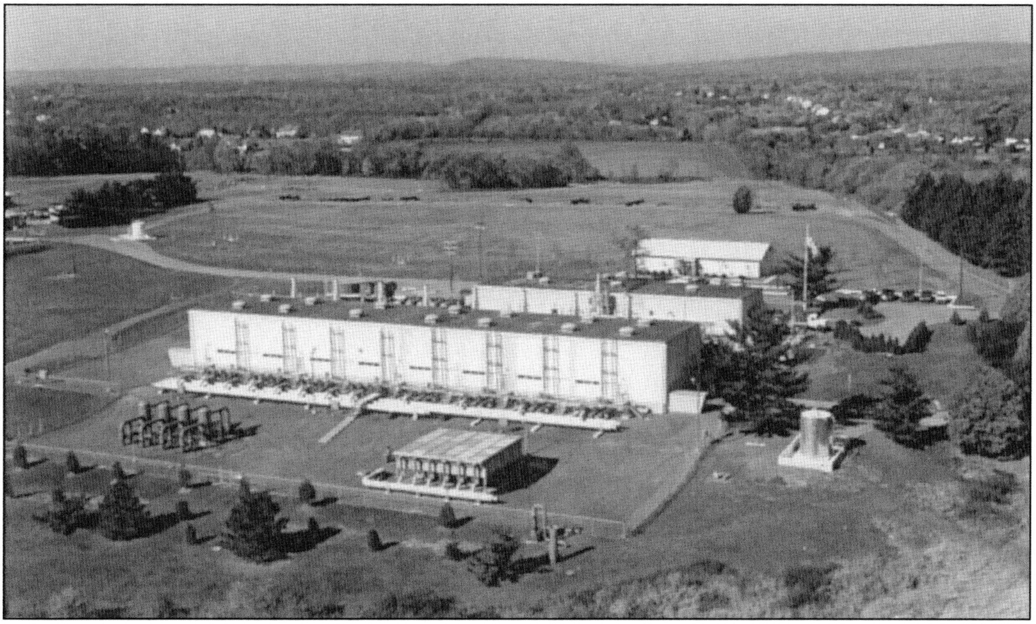

This is an aerial view of the Williams Corp. Transco Gas Line, along South Branch Road, in Branchburg Township. This pipeline compression station entered the area in the early 1960s with a 30-inch and a 36-inch natural gas line. It is being redistributed here for storage in Pennsylvania and final usage in the New York metropolitan area. (Photograph courtesy of the Williams Corp.)

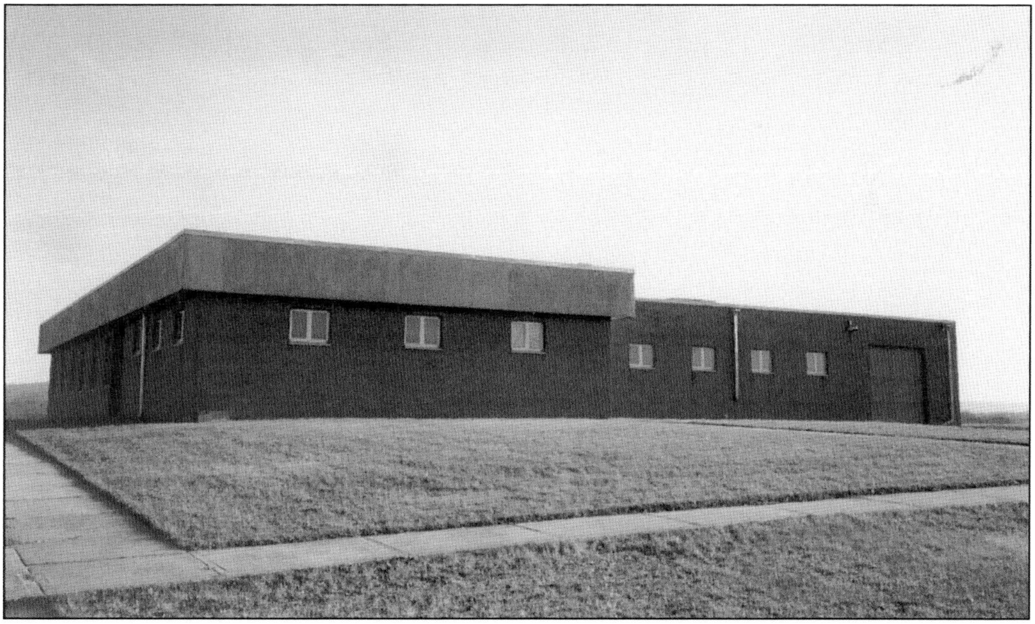

T.M. Long Co., Inc., located on Pleasant Run Road in Neshanic Station, was started in 1967. This firm supplies proprietary laboratory research instruments to firms around the world. About 50 percent of the products goes to U.S. corporations such as DuPont, Eastman, Exxon, Shell, etc. Thirty percent goes to Japan, and the remainder goes to Europe. (Photograph by G.W. Amerman.)

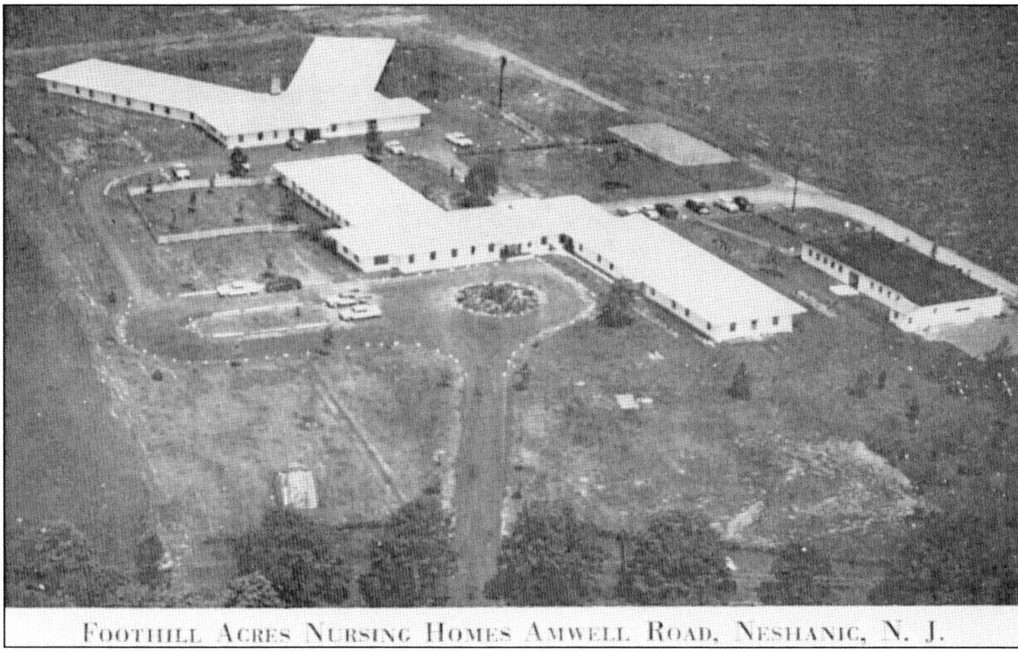

Foothill Acres Nursing Home, on Amwell Road in Neshanic, was started in 1954 by Dr. Samuel H. Husted. This aerial view shows the facility in the early 1960s, before the third building and main office were built. (Photograph courtesy of Foothill Acres Nursing Home.)

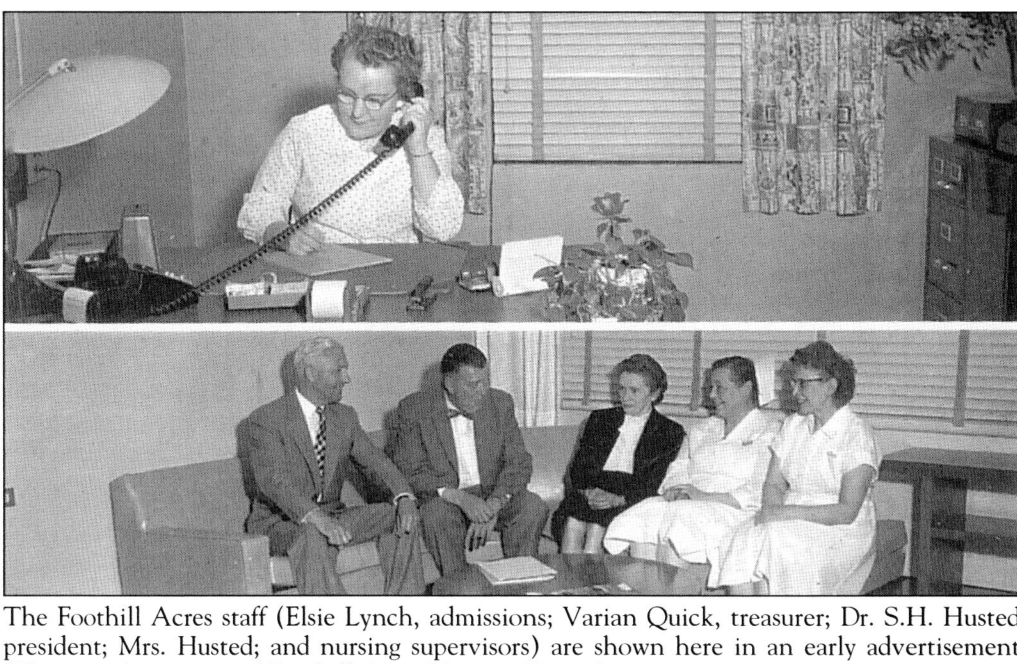

The Foothill Acres staff (Elsie Lynch, admissions; Varian Quick, treasurer; Dr. S.H. Husted, president; Mrs. Husted; and nursing supervisors) are shown here in an early advertisement. (Photograph courtesy of Foothill Acres Nursing Home.)

S.H. Husted, M.D., who was the medical director of Foothill Acres, is shown here. He once said, "I do not concur with the idea that life begins at eighty, but I do believe that an interesting and enjoyable life can be maintained after eighty in proper surroundings in spite of physical handicaps, which are sometimes concurrent with age." (Photograph courtesy of Foothill Acres.)

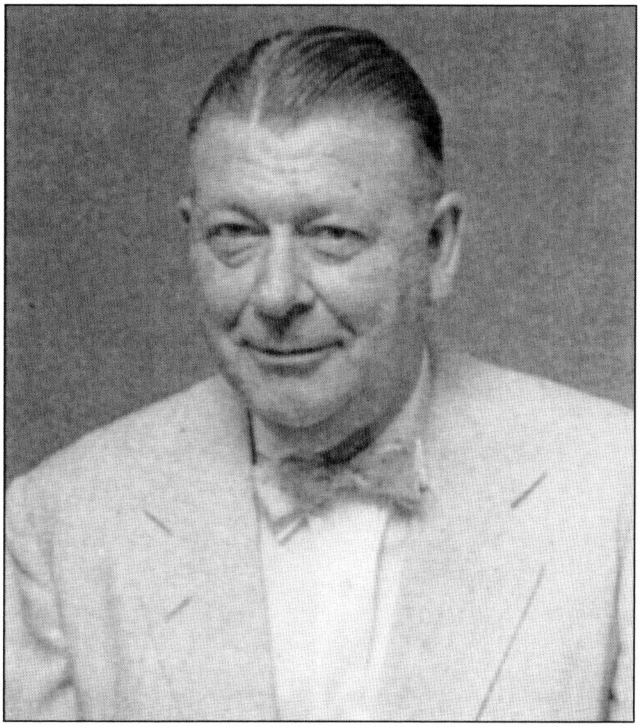

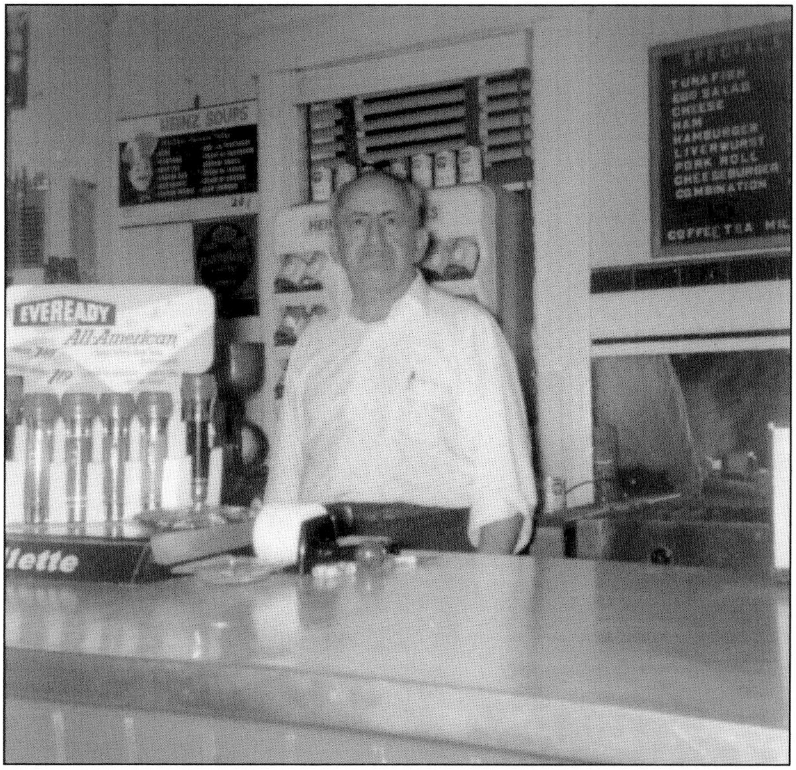

Winfield Case is shown here behind his soda fountain and grill counter located at 409 Olive Street. Mr.Casealsooperated the general store at 211 Pearl Street prior to it becoming the post office. (Photograph courtesy of Gwen Jamele.)

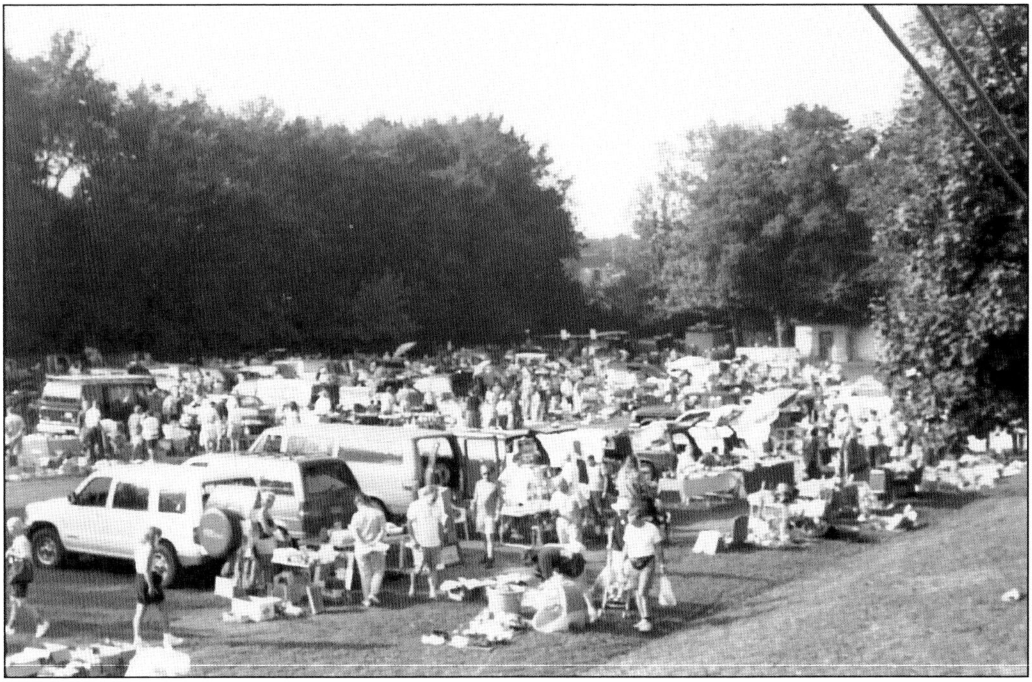

This is a view of the Neshanic Flea Market from the Elm Street Bridge. Started in 1969, the market celebrates its 30th anniversary in 1999. (Photograph by G.W. Amerman.)

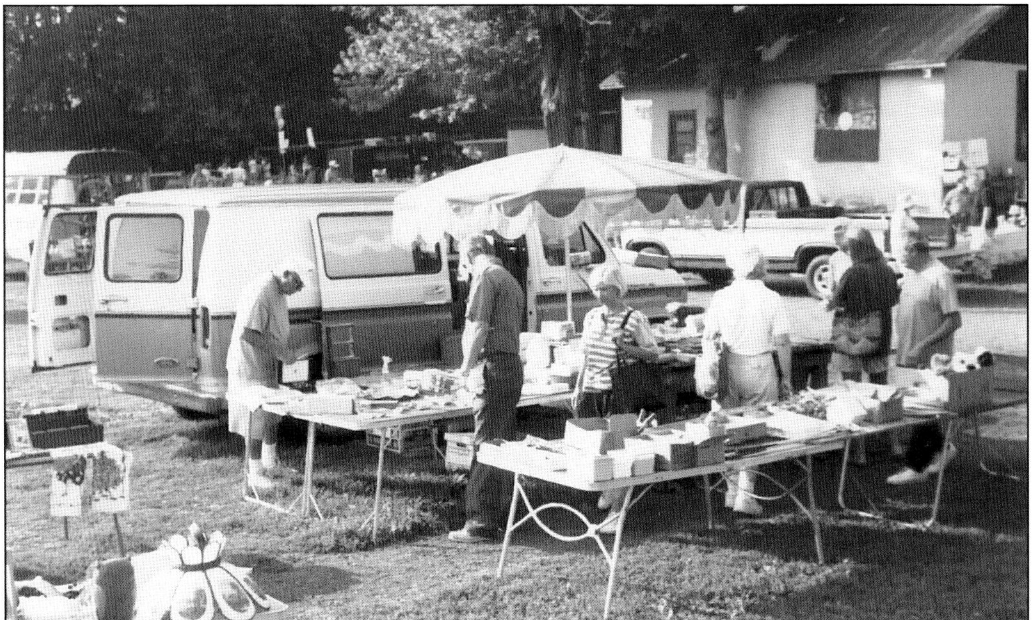

Carmen Panarello, a vendor at Neshanic Flea Market, has attended every week since the market started, traveling from Pennsauken, New Jersey. (Photograph by G.W. Amerman.)

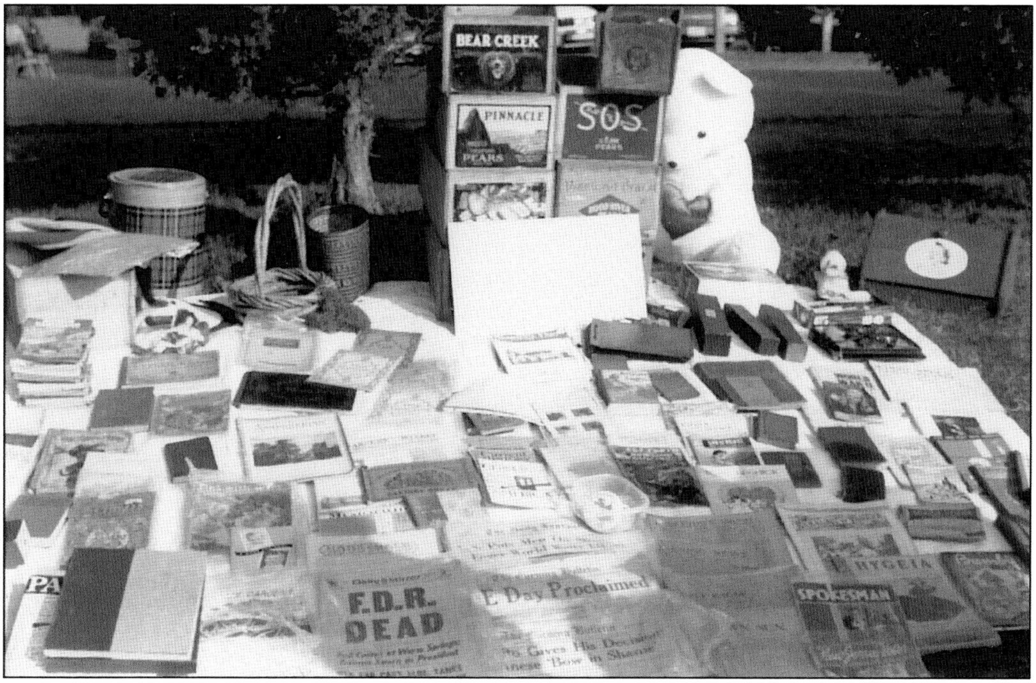

Flea market vendors are shown here with a representative display of memorabilia, always a crowd favorite. (Photograph by G.W. Amerman.)

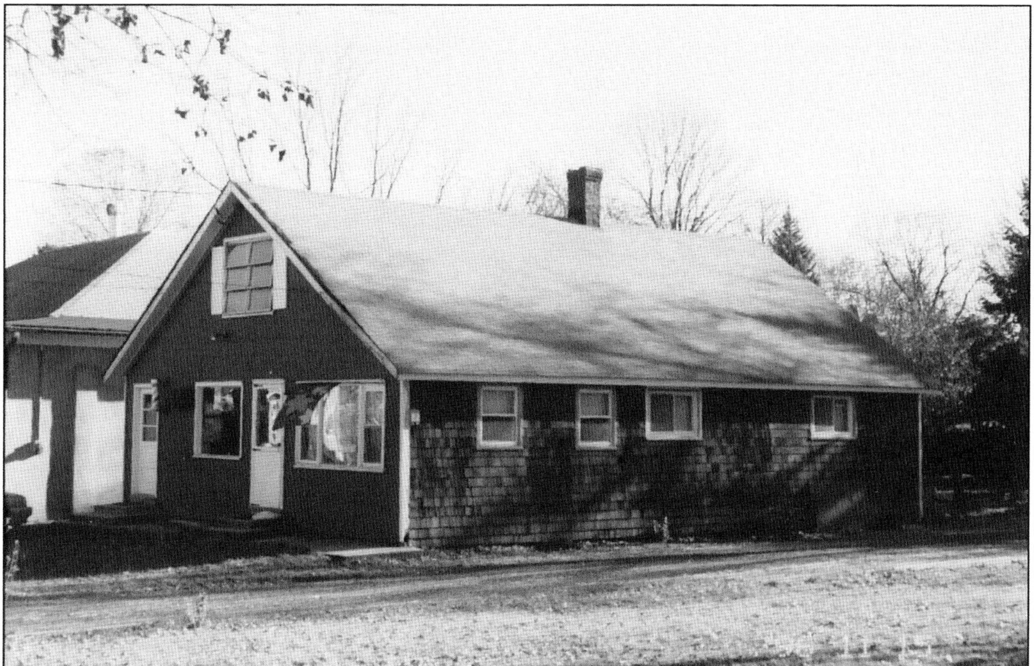

This is a local barbershop, located at 416 Olive Street. This building, shown on page 94 as a Metz Auto Agency, has been used as a poultry house, a radio and TV repair shop, a bakery, a firehouse for the 1929 Pirsch, a barber shop, and as a dwelling. (Photograph by G.W. Amerman.)

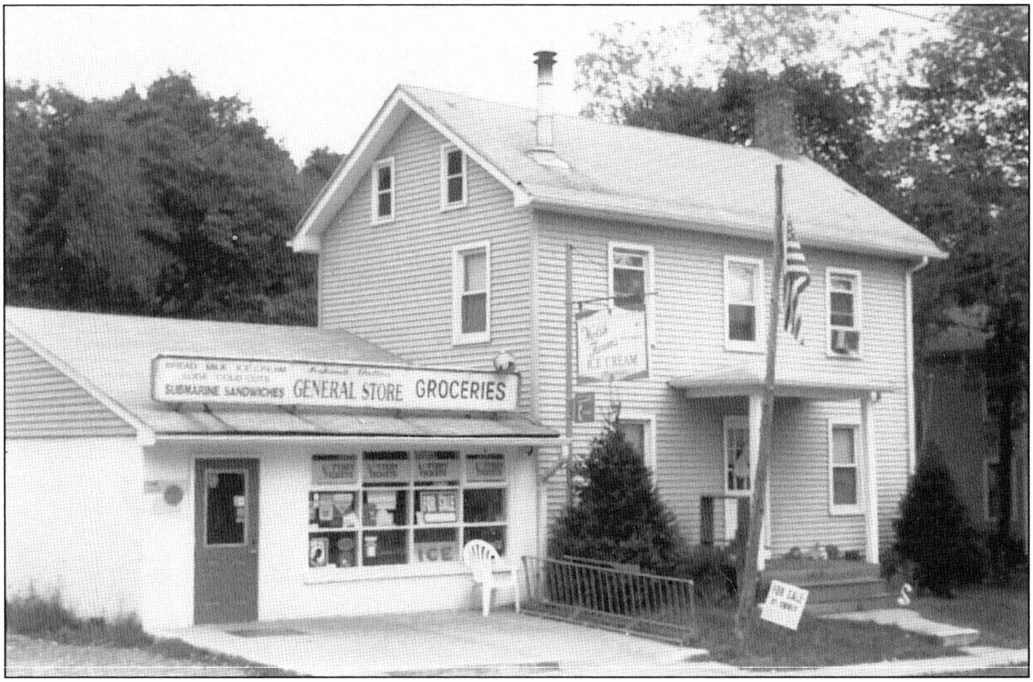

The last active general store, located at 419 Olive Street, was built by George Moser as an addition to his home. It is now owned and operated by Sal and Darlene Della Ventura, who purchased it in 1985. (Photograph by G.W. Amerman.)

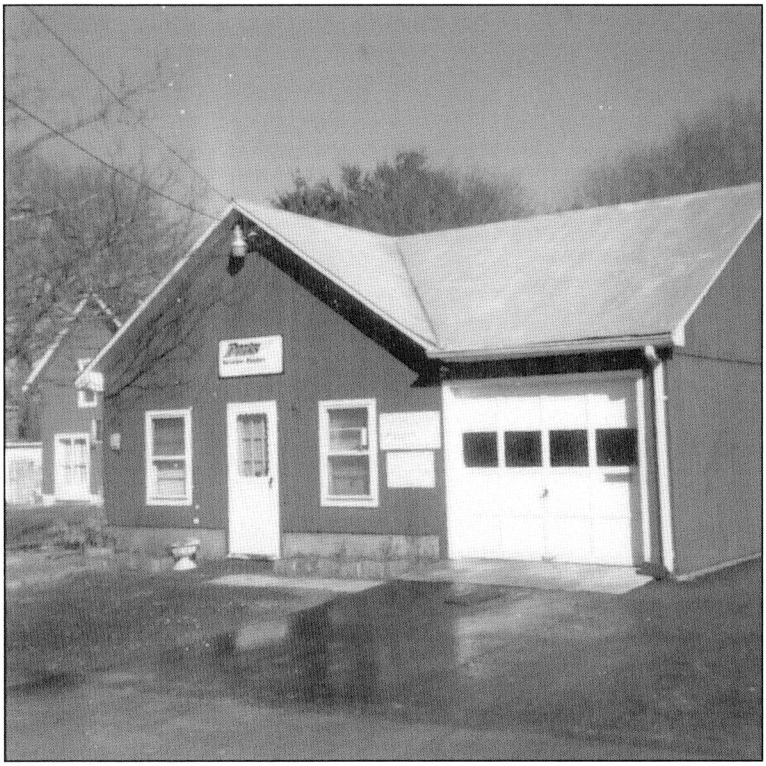

Don's Service Center, shown in this photograph, is located at 606 Marshall Street. This business, started in 1963, has been operated as a repair and repainting service by Don Crane Sr. and Don Crane Jr. for the last 36 years. It is shown on page 100 as the A. Schenck Bergen Allis Chalmers Machinery Agency. It was also operated by John Agans as a repair shop, and as N & T Repair by Simon Nevius and Raymond Toles. (Photograph by Don Crane Jr.)

Eight

Recreation, Leisure, and Community Activities

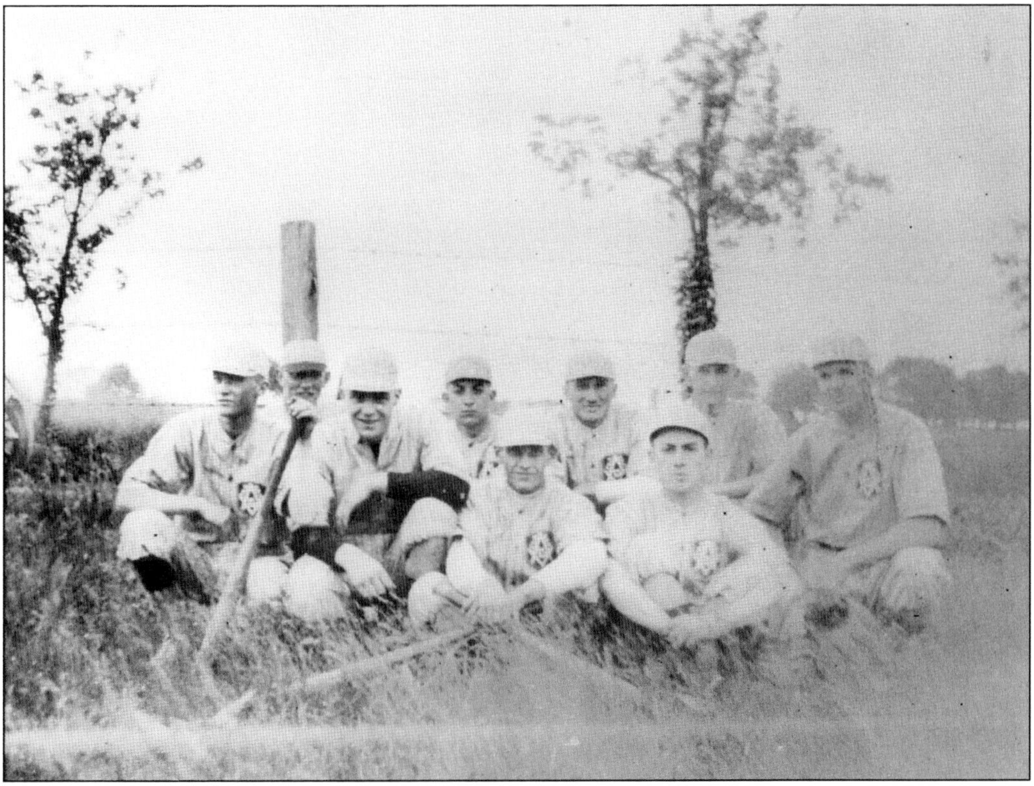

Baseball was always a featured sporting event in the rural towns of America before WW II, and for a few years after, until travel and industry changed the character and lifestyle of these communities. Neshanic was no exception. The earliest team photograph was of the 1920 Local Lodge players. The players are shown here as follows: Russell Edgar, Russell Cray, Wes Horner, Fred Allegar, Doug Hoff, George Amerman, Lester Gulick, Maurice Griscom, and David Amerman. (Photograph courtesy of Neshanic Station Historical Society.)

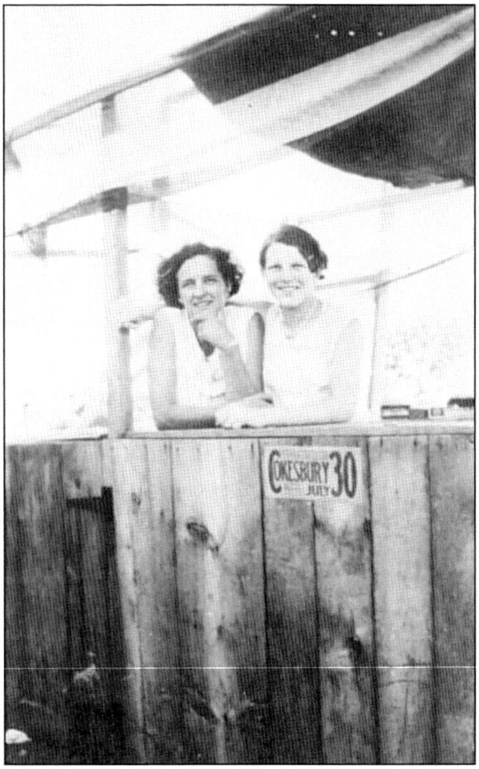

Anne Hausch Thompson and Mary Hausch Sixt are seen here working the ice cream stand at the Neshanic Baseball Field in October 1931. (Photograph courtesy of Mary Hausch Sixt.)

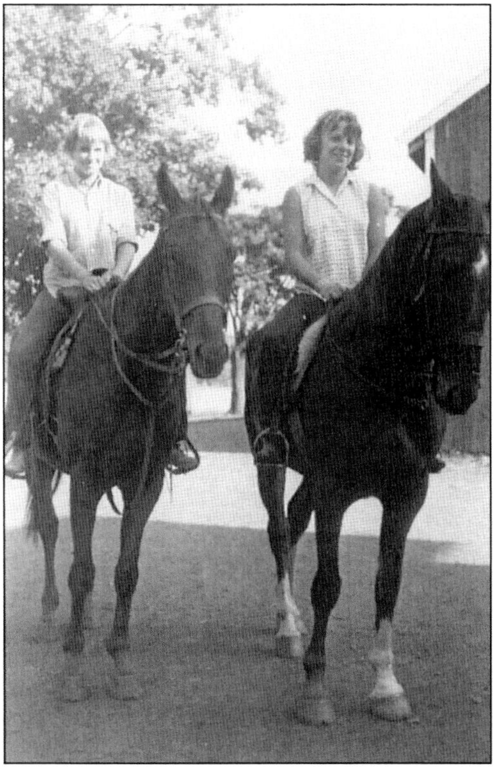

In the days of the dairy farm and the dirt road, horseback riding was another pleasure. Shown here in 1959 are Heidi Schlatter and Stacy Smith mounted on Sham and Pan at the River Edge Stock Farm on River Road. (Photograph courtesy of Heidi Schlatter Saunders.)

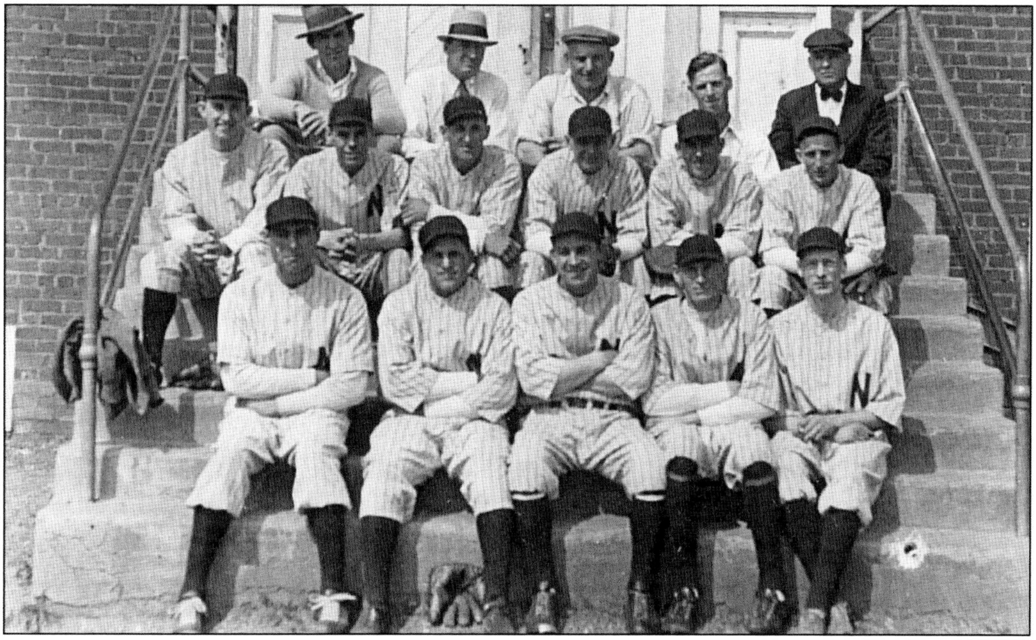

The Farmers' Baseball Neshanic Team is seen here seated on the rear steps of the Fairview School (by Marshall Street) in 1934. The players are, from left to right, as follows: (bottom row) Bill Kip, Pete Hausch, George Howiler, Hal McBride, and Herb Thompson; (middle row) Harold Neubeck, PeeWee Austin, Stan Hall, Doug Hoff, Earl Vlerebone, and Junior Hall; (top row) Bob May, George Amerman, Mike Hausch (manager), Harold Docherty, and Vin Savage (umpire). (Photograph courtesy of Mary Hausch Sixt.)

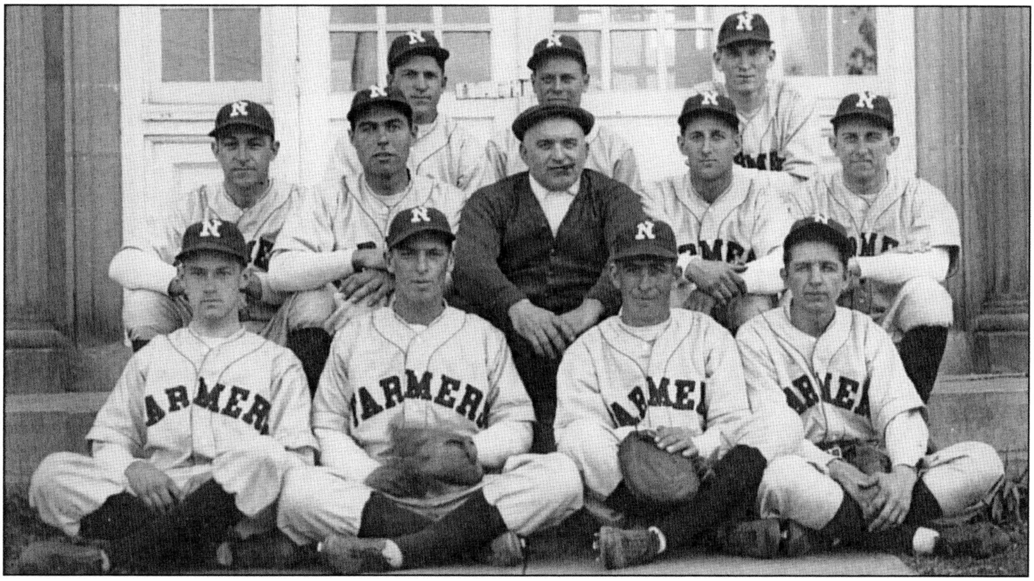

Farmers' Baseball Neshanic Team is shown here in 1935, in new uniforms on the front steps of the Fairview School. The players are, from left to right, as follows: (front row) Harold O'Brien, Harold Docherty, Earl Vlerebone, and Walt Kulaski; (middle row) George Howiler, Bill Kip, Mike Hausch (manager), Stan Hall, and Harold Nedbeck; (back row) Pete Hausch, John Wirzman, and Hal McBride. (Photograph courtesy of Mary Hausch Sixt.)

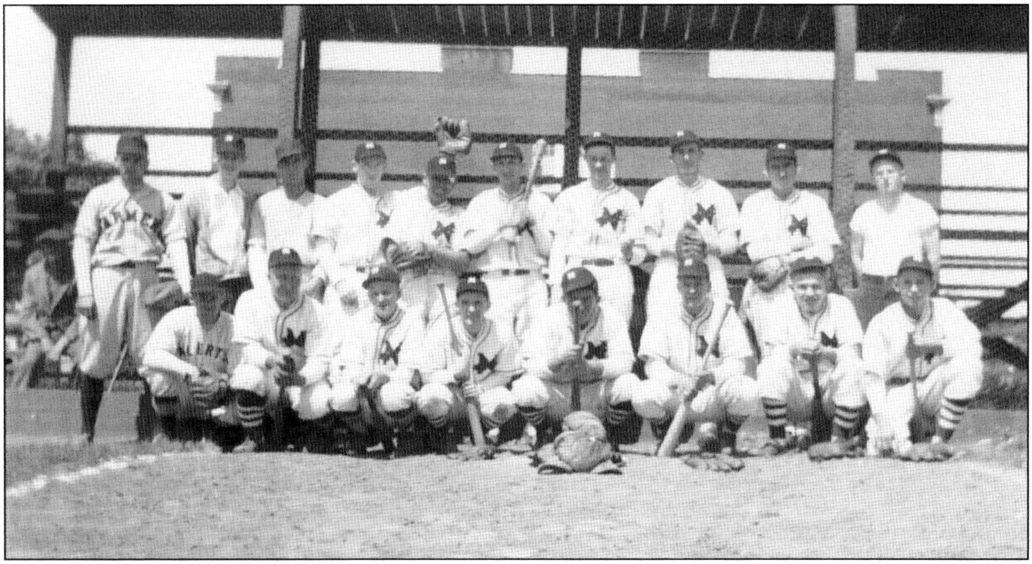

The Neshanic Social Club Team of 1938 is shown here in front of the grandstand, behind the Fairview School. The players are, from left to right, as follows: (front row) Jack Kalpin, Frank Czech, Adam Kalpin, Ernest Snyder, Alan Cray, Art Beers, William Connett, and Frank Kinney; (back row) Donald Hoff, Cliff Hall, Harold Docherty, Duncan O'Brien, Gus Kowalski, Varian Quick, Harold O'Brien, Fred Peabody, Clarence Runyon, and Art Saunders (manager). (Photograph courtesy of Arthur Saunders.)

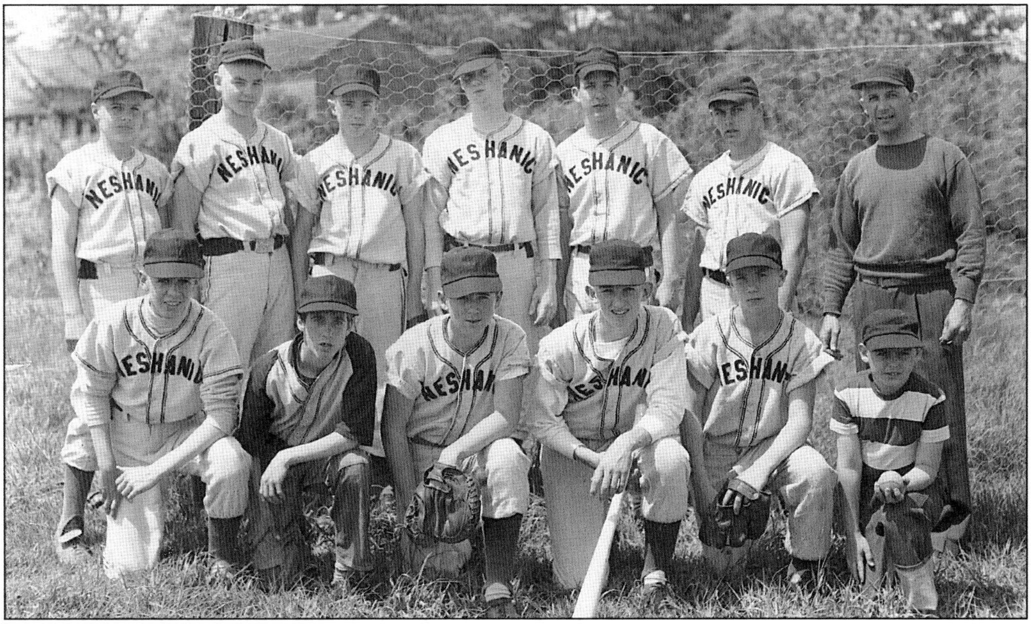

Neshanic Little Bigger League Team are shown here playing at Saunders Field, on Woodfern Road, in 1956. The players are, from left to right, as follows: (front row) Don Quick, Tom Tharp, Brud Emery (catcher), Taylor Quick (pitcher), Dennis Peterson, and Jim Covert (batboy); (back row) Bucky Covert, Ken Koteles, Mik Peterson, Jim Bowman, Ted Saunders, Fritz Maier, and Varian Quick (manager). (Players not shown are Reid Saunders, Kevin Morton, Bill Tepper, and Chuck Conover.) (Photograph courtesy of the Quick family.)

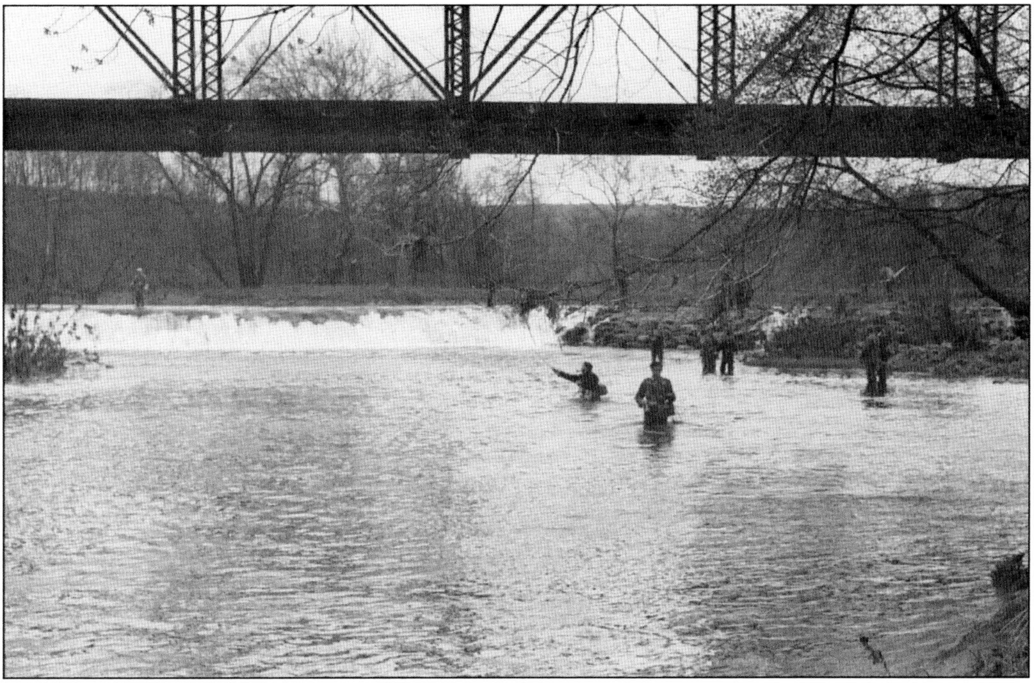

This view shows a few anglers trying their luck near the Neshanic dam in 1955. The first day of trout season is always busy on the south branch of the Raritan River. The Neshanic Fire Company Ladies Auxiliary often ran a food stand in the Firemen's Field for the first few weekends of the season. (Photograph courtesy of Walter Kostro.)

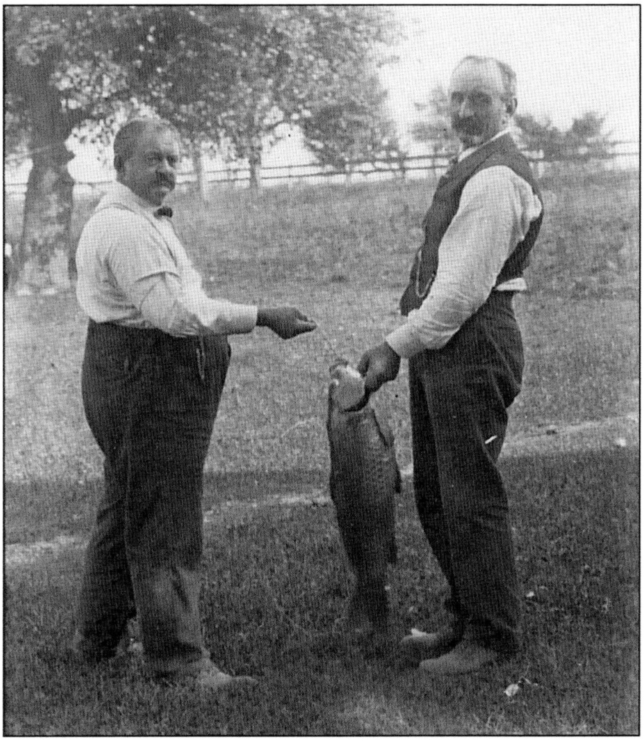

Early carp fishing on the south branch of the Raritan River produced this Sunday catch for Chance Titman and his brother Henry, who operated the Neshanic Hotel on Amwell Road at the turn of the century. (Photograph courtesy of L.B. Lane.)

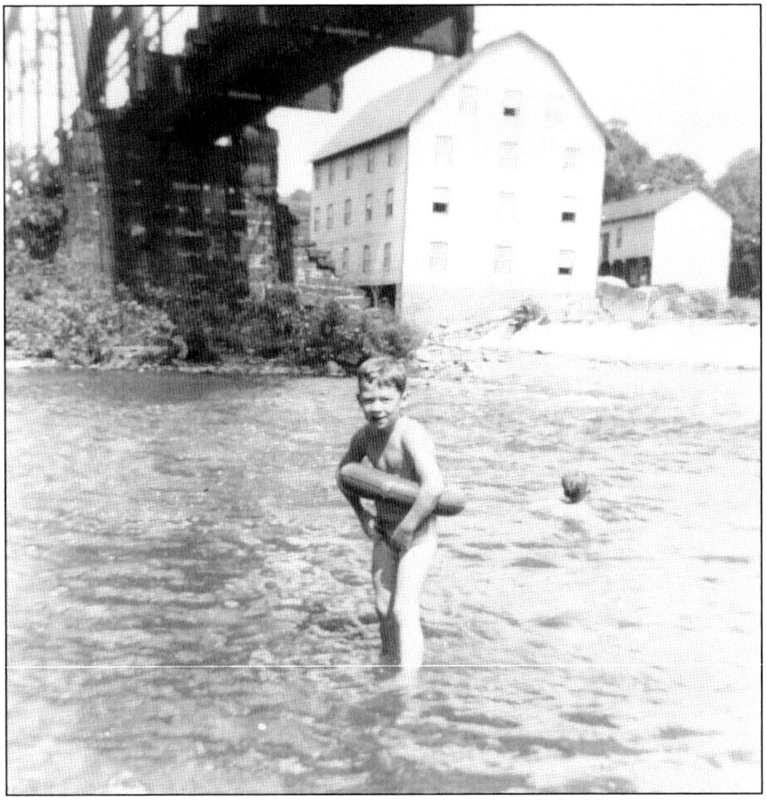

Swimming by the Neshanic dam has long been a pastime for area residents. Prior to the demolition of the dam, the favorite swimming hole was above the dam where leaping off rocks into a 12-foot pool provided endless entertainment on sultry summer days. Those less daring were happily cooled in the more shallow waters below the dam, as seen in this 1948 picture of Daniel Schlatter and a friend. (Photograph courtesy of Heidi Schlatter Saunders.)

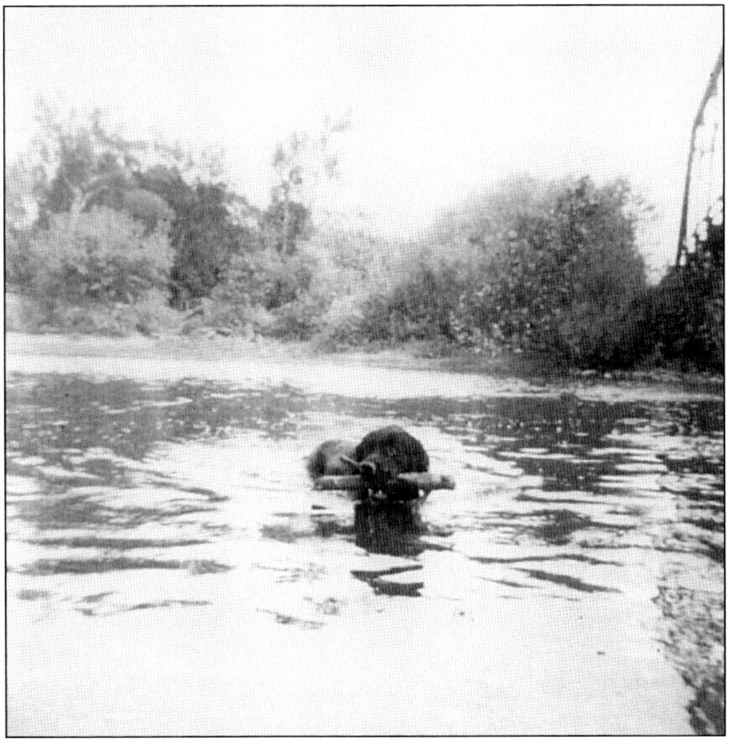

Even pets were not beyond taking the plunge! (Photograph courtesy of Heidi Schlatter Saunders.)

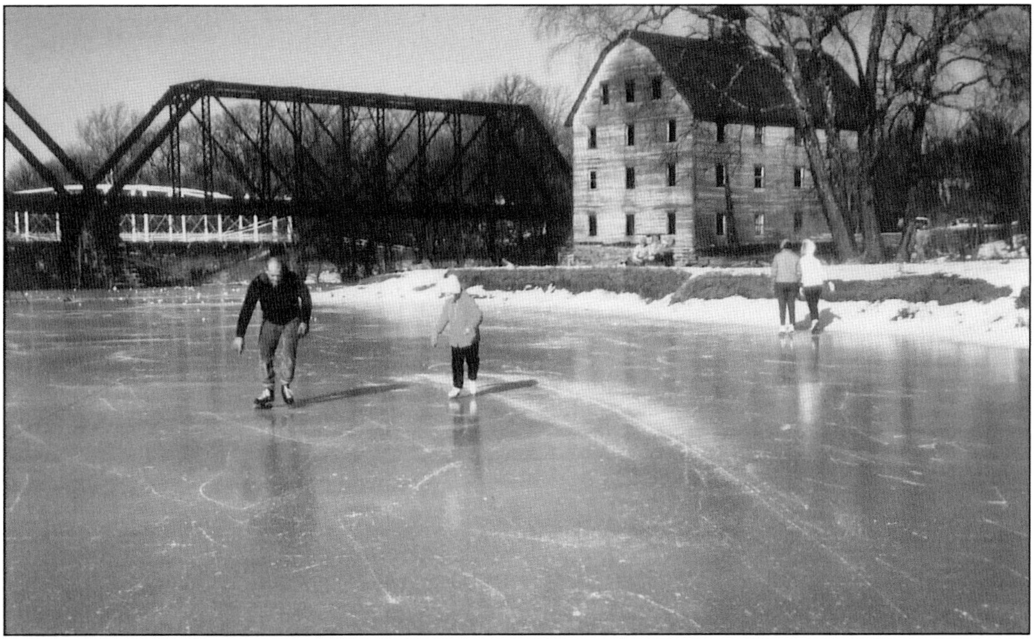

Ice-skating was another popular river sport. Shown here in 1965, William Toman shows Carol Amerman the basics. Notice the moms, busy talking their way downstream. (Photograph courtesy of G.W. Amerman.)

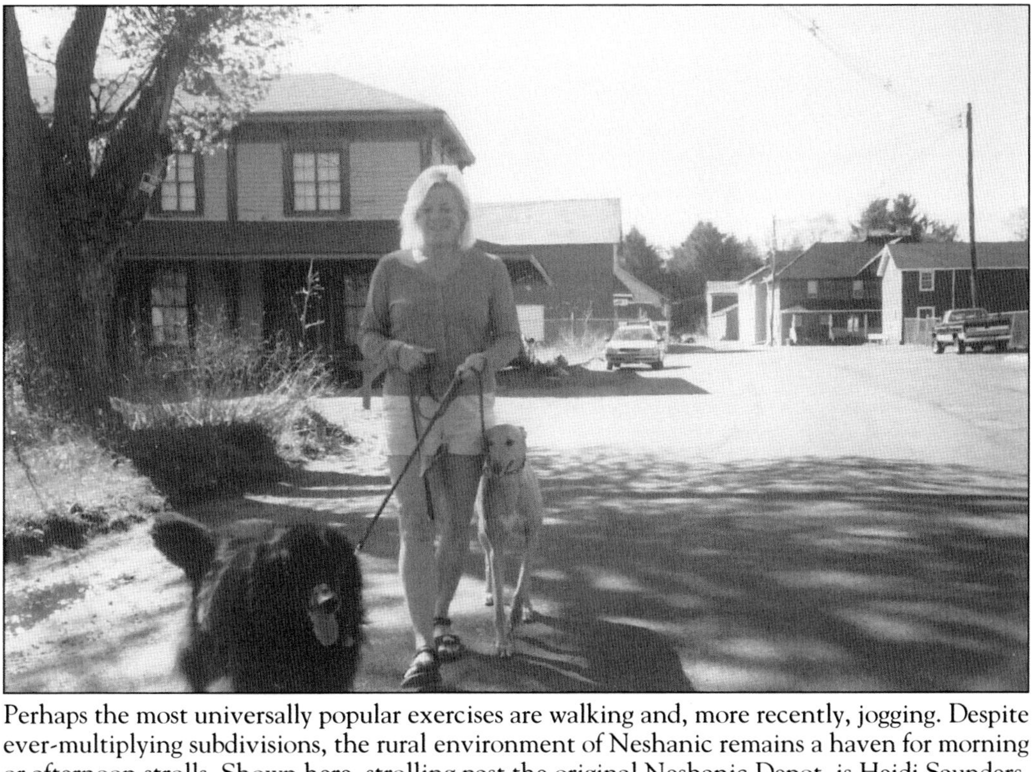

Perhaps the most universally popular exercises are walking and, more recently, jogging. Despite ever-multiplying subdivisions, the rural environment of Neshanic remains a haven for morning or afternoon strolls. Shown here, strolling past the original Neshanic Depot, is Heidi Saunders. (Photograph courtesy of Ted Saunders.)

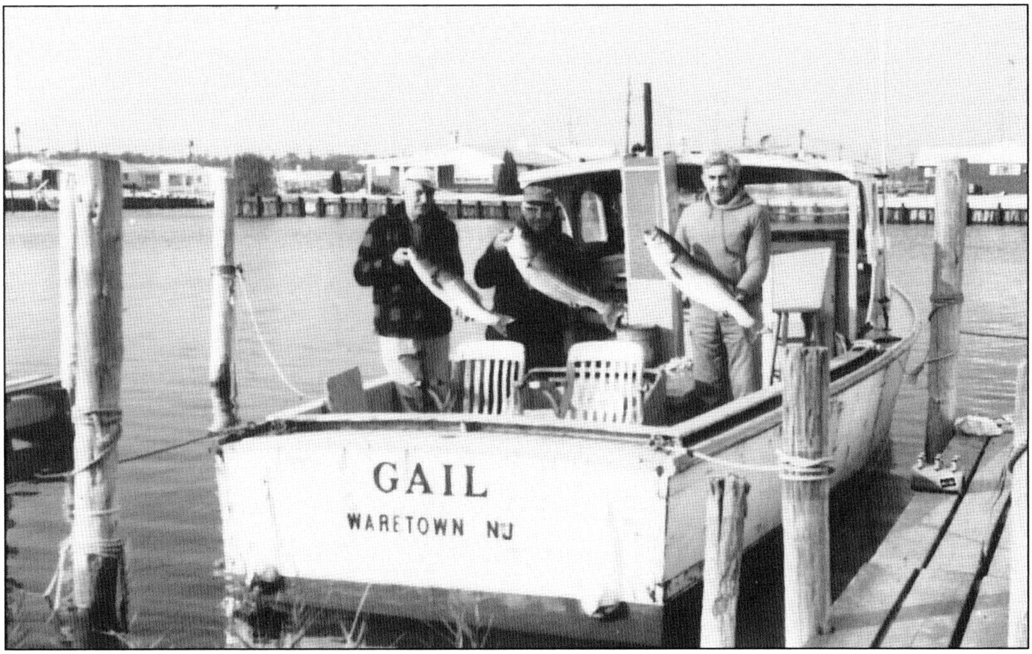

Neshanic firemen have long enjoyed saltwater fishing on the Jersey shore. John O'Brien, Captain Percy Giddes of Waretown, and Larry Lane show off a portion of the day's catch of striped bass. Captain Giddes sailed his wood garvey from 1947 until 1994, and Neshanic men fished with him most of those years. (Photograph courtesy of G.W. Amerman.)

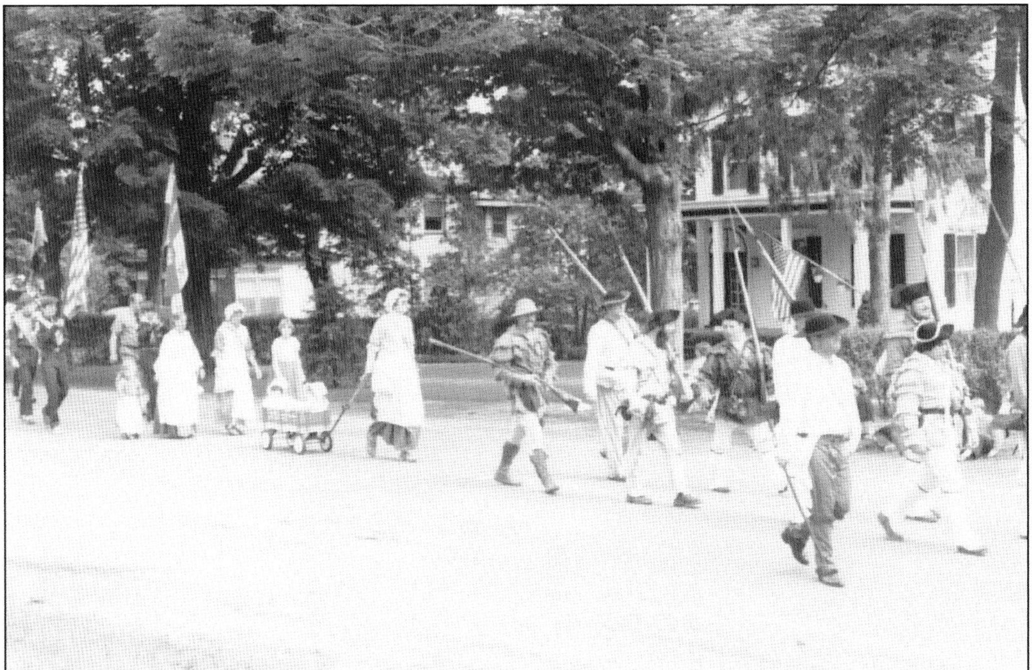

Boy Scout Troop 1776, sponsored by the Neshanic Reformed Church, is seen here marching in colonial attire in the 1979 Memorial Day Parade. (Photograph courtesy of G.W. Amerman.)

Shown here are announcements for dances in the early 1900s. Holcombe's Pavilion is now Murphy's Crocodile Inn (formerly the Neshanic Inn). (Courtesy of Dan Bassuk.)

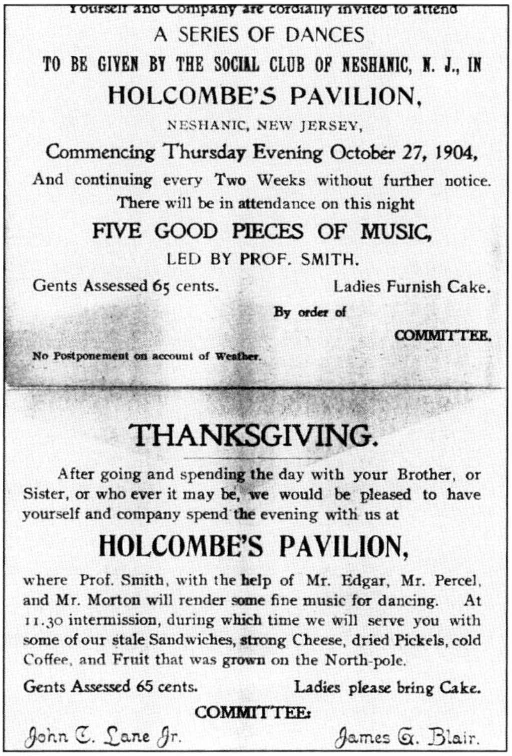

Yourself and Company are cordially invited to attend

A SERIES OF DANCES

TO BE GIVEN BY THE SOCIAL CLUB OF NESHANIC, N. J., IN

HOLCOMBE'S PAVILION,

NESHANIC, NEW JERSEY,

Commencing Thursday Evening October 27, 1904,

And continuing every Two Weeks without further notice.

There will be in attendance on this night

FIVE GOOD PIECES OF MUSIC,

LED BY PROF. SMITH.

Gents Assessed 65 cents. Ladies Furnish Cake.

By order of

COMMITTEE.

No Postponement on account of Weather.

THANKSGIVING.

After going and spending the day with your Brother, or Sister, or who ever it may be, we would be pleased to have yourself and company spend the evening with us at

HOLCOMBE'S PAVILION,

where Prof. Smith, with the help of Mr. Edgar, Mr. Percel, and Mr. Morton will render some fine music for dancing. At 11.30 intermission, during which time we will serve you with some of our stale Sandwiches, strong Cheese, dried Pickels, cold Coffee, and Fruit that was grown on the North-pole.

Gents Assessed 65 cents. Ladies please bring Cake.

COMMITTEE:

John C. Lane Jr. James G. Blair.

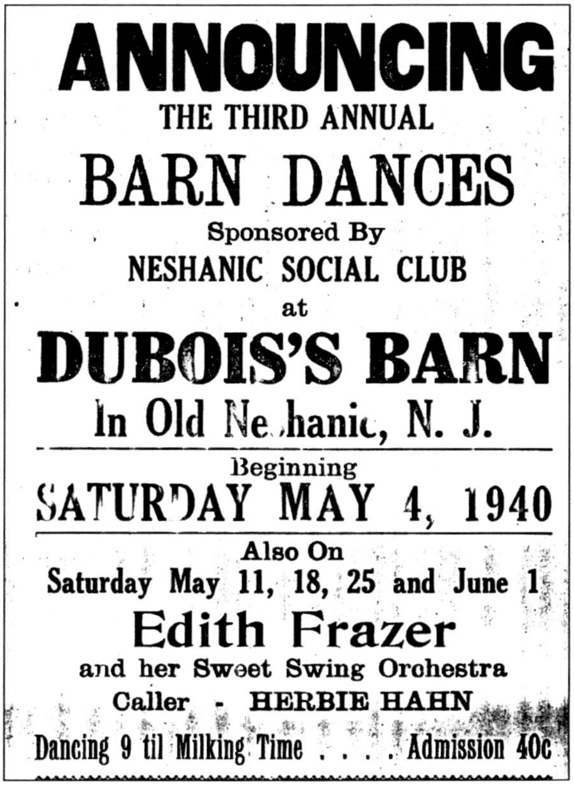

ANNOUNCING

THE THIRD ANNUAL

BARN DANCES

Sponsored By

NESHANIC SOCIAL CLUB

at

DUBOIS'S BARN

In Old Neshanic, N. J.

Beginning

SATURDAY MAY 4, 1940

Also On

Saturday May 11, 18, 25 and June 1

Edith Frazer

and her Sweet Swing Orchestra

Caller - HERBIE HAHN

Dancing 9 til Milking Time . . . . Admission 40c

Neshanic Social Club dances were an annual event at the DuBois barn. (Courtesy of Dan Bassuk.)

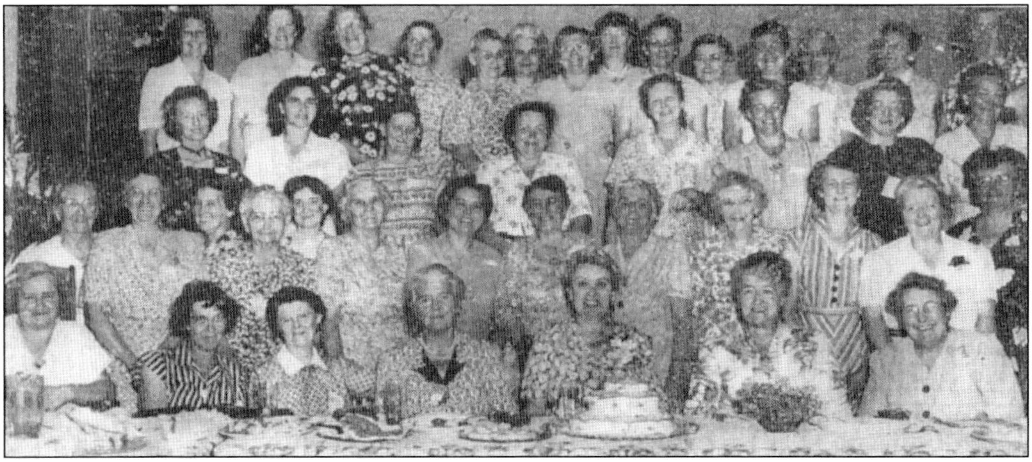

Members of the Neshanic Garden Club are seen here celebrating the club's 20th anniversary in July 1948. In the caption that appeared with this photograph in the *Plainfield Courier News*, it was noted that 48 of the club's 57 members attended this luncheon at the firehouse. Mrs. Anne Griscom, a charter member, was among those in attendance. The Neshanic Garden Club is still active today. (Photograph courtesy of E. Saums.)

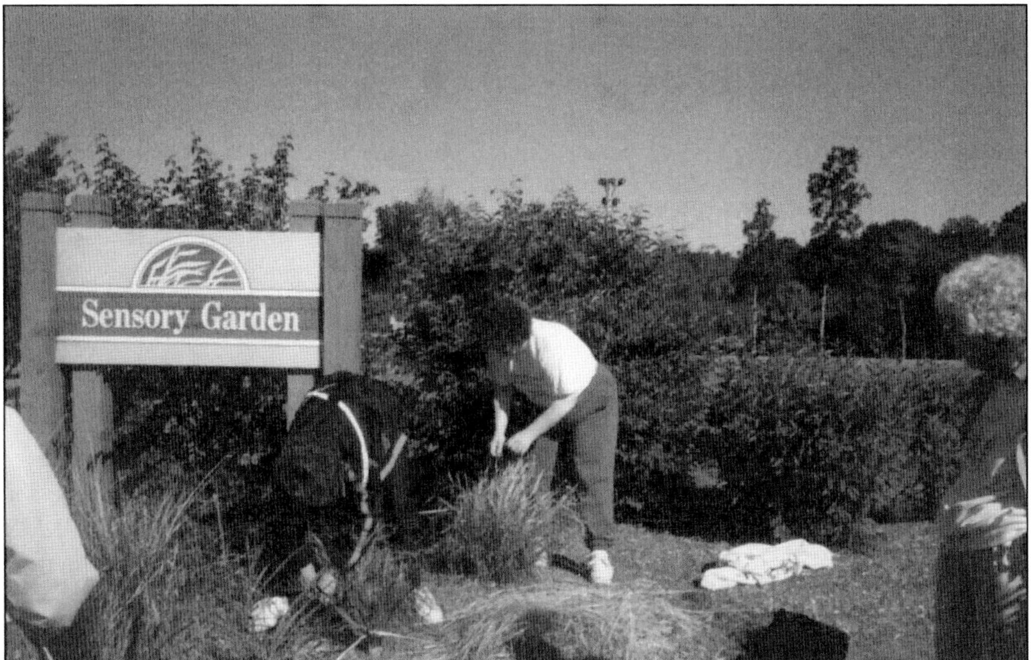

Neshanic Garden Club members are seen here completing work at the sensory garden, which they built in Hillsborough at the Anne Van Middlesworth Park. (Photograph courtesy of Joan Raymond.)

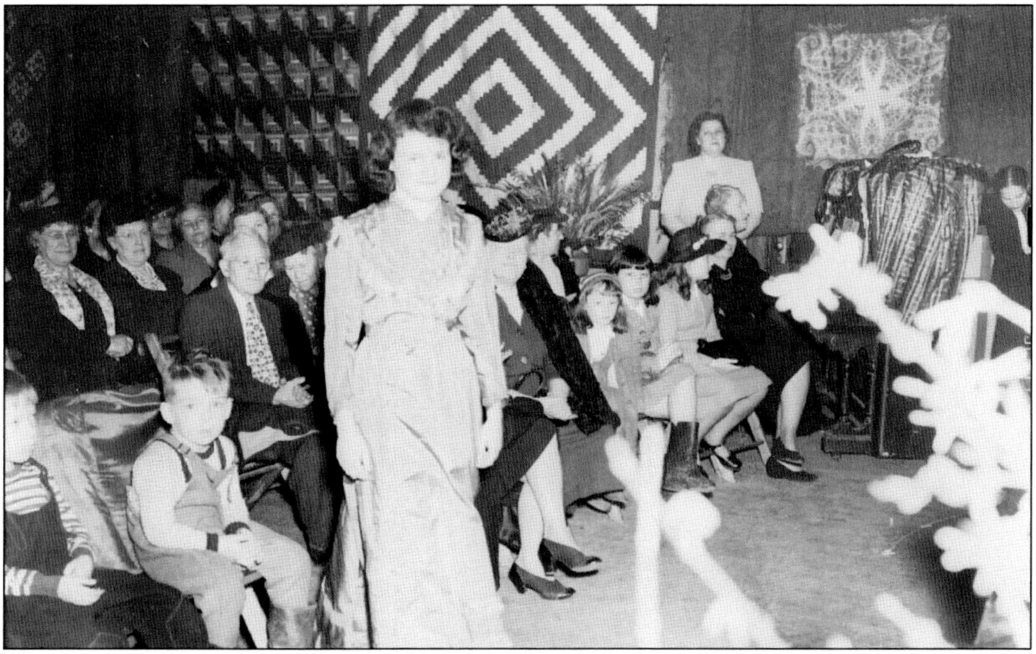

This photograph illustrates the Neshanic Garden Club "Parade of Brides." Many local groups, as well as commercial firms, used the Neshanic Firemen's Hall for a variety of affairs. Before the days of television, the local halls were filled with social activities, including dances, card parties, plays, minstrel shows, and fashion shows. (Photograph courtesy of Phyllis Amerman Polenz.)

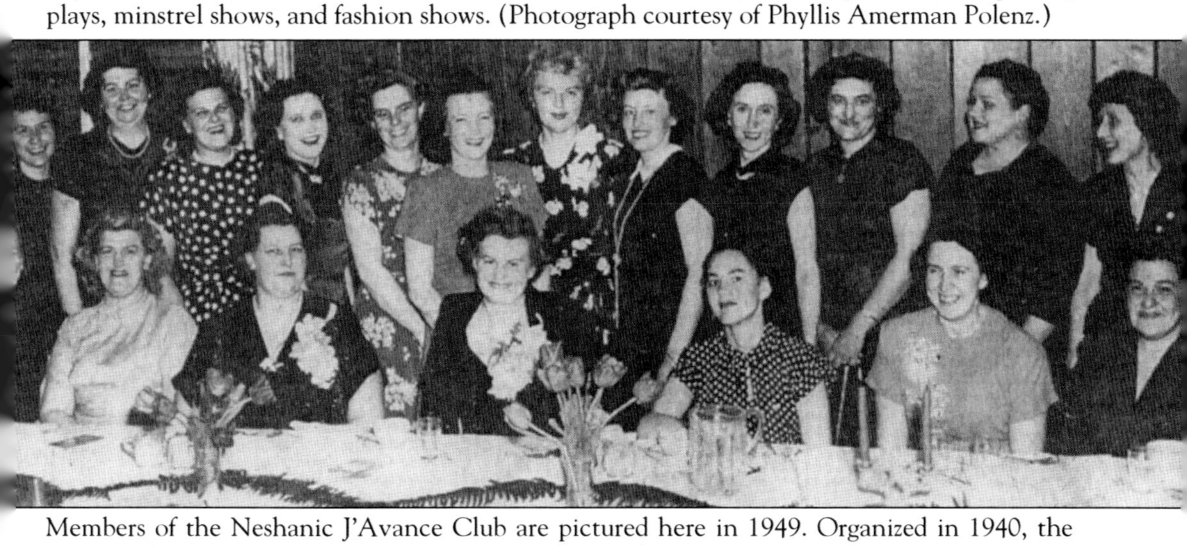

Members of the Neshanic J'Avance Club are pictured here in 1949. Organized in 1940, the club was limited to 20 members and met in the members' homes. One program meeting and one recreational evening were held each month. The members also participated in community service and fund-raising activities to benefit local organizations. Members pictured here, from left to right, are as follows: (front row) Miss Myrtle Connet, Mrs. William Campbell, Mrs. Harold Amerman, Miss Virginia Hoff, Mrs. Charles A. Zulauf, Mrs. John Schenck, and Mrs. John Merrill; (back row) Mrs. William Kip, Miss Alice Hoagland, Mrs. Michael Kowalski, Miss Elsie Campbell, Mrs. Gilberta Napolitan, Mrs. Edward Stryker, Miss Mary Hastings, Mrs. Gerald Doran, Mrs. Alice McCaleb, Mrs. William Sheppard, Mrs. Richard Tippett, and Mrs. Herman Thompson. (Photograph courtesy of E. Saums.)

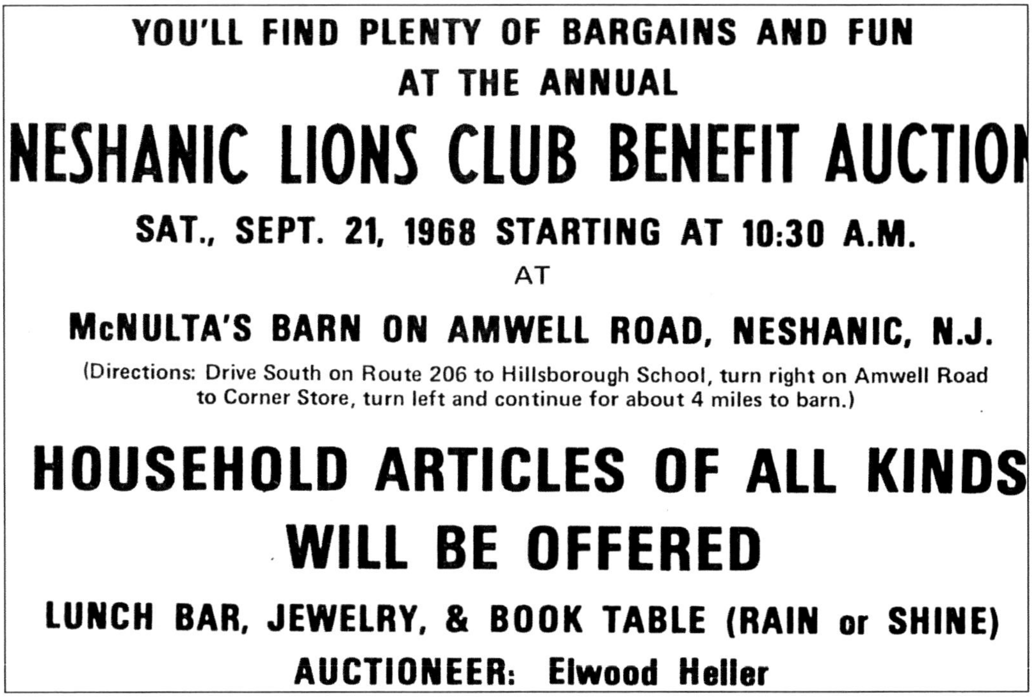
YOU'LL FIND PLENTY OF BARGAINS AND FUN
AT THE ANNUAL
NESHANIC LIONS CLUB BENEFIT AUCTION
SAT., SEPT. 21, 1968 STARTING AT 10:30 A.M.
AT
McNULTA'S BARN ON AMWELL ROAD, NESHANIC, N.J.
(Directions: Drive South on Route 206 to Hillsborough School, turn right on Amwell Road to Corner Store, turn left and continue for about 4 miles to barn.)
HOUSEHOLD ARTICLES OF ALL KINDS
WILL BE OFFERED
LUNCH BAR, JEWELRY, & BOOK TABLE (RAIN or SHINE)
AUCTIONEER: Elwood Heller

Shown here is an announcement for a September 1968 Neshanic Lions Club Benefit Auction at McNulta's Barn, 789 Amwell Road. (Photograph courtesy of Neshanic Lions Club.)

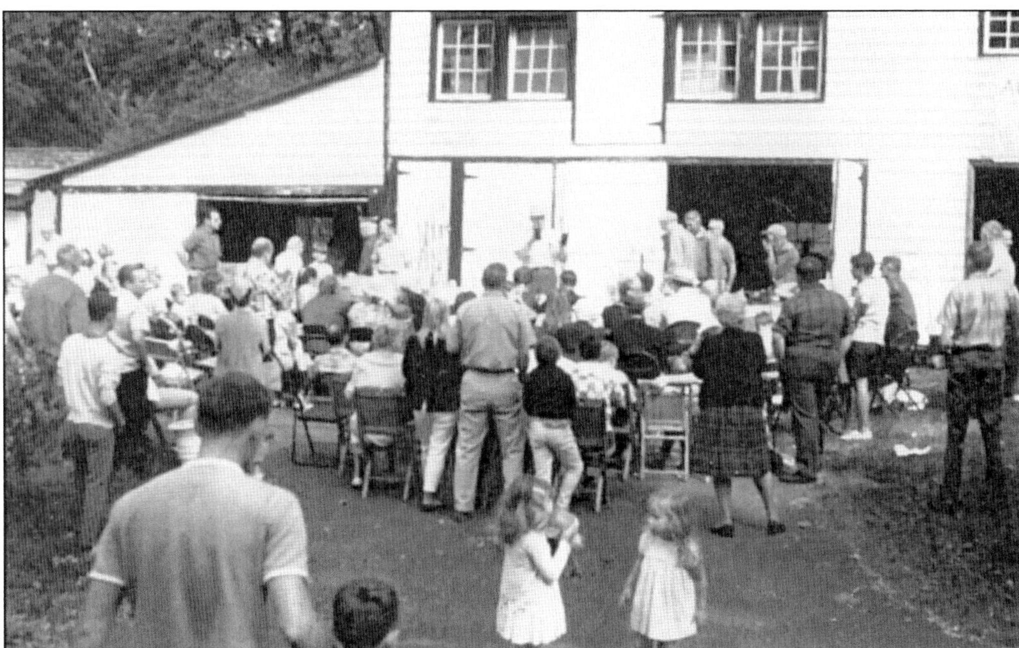

The actual Neshanic Lions Club Benefit Auction is represented in this photograph. (Photograph courtesy of the Neshanic Lions Club.)

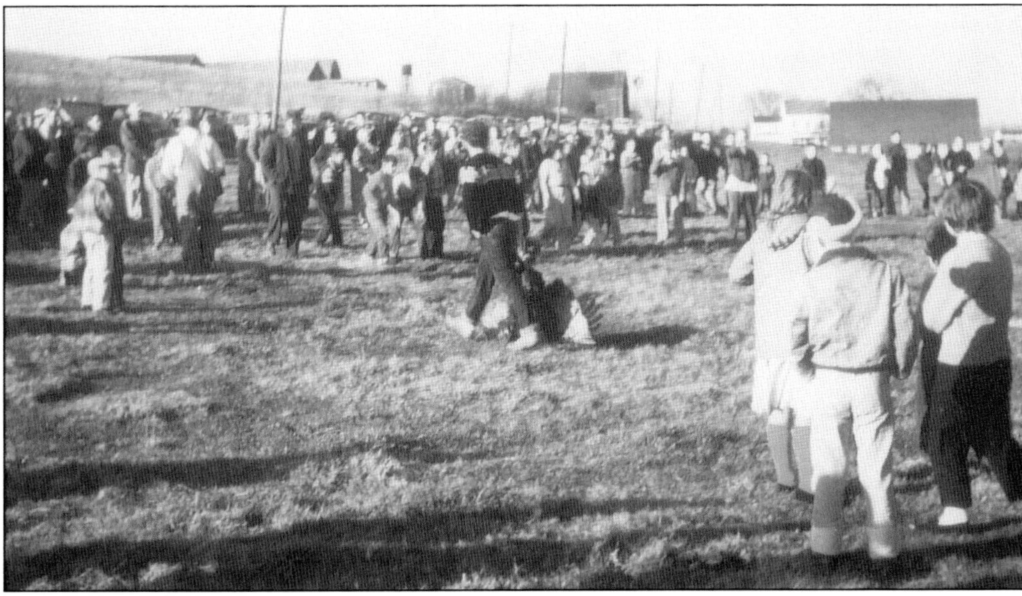

This photograph illustrates a c. 1955 Greased Pig and Guinea Chase. From the mid-1930s to the mid-1950s, the Greased Pig and Guinea Chase provided an opportunity for local farmers to make donations for the support of the fire company, as well as providing fun for local residents. Farmers donated guinea hens, pigs, and turkeys while participants paid to run in a race for a chance to catch the prize. (Photograph courtesy of the Toles family.)

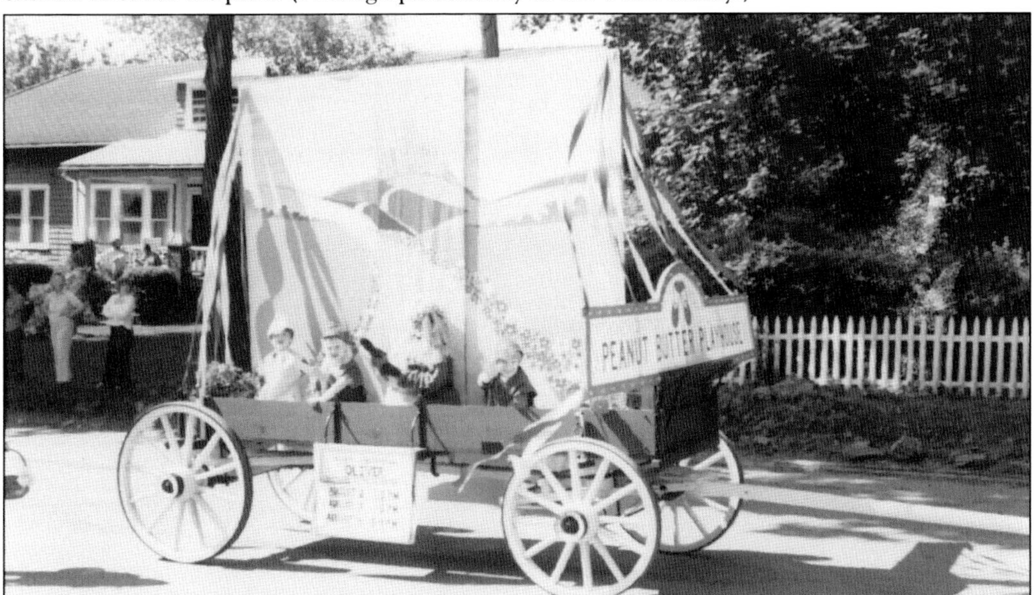

The Peanut Butter Playhouse, described as "a theater by children for people of all ages," opened in the old firehouse, on Olive Street, in 1978. The float pictured here appeared at the Memorial Day parade of that year. The playhouse was started by four local couples and produced musicals between 1978 and 1982. Auditions attracted hundreds of young performers aged eight to 18 years from across the state, and performances were usually sold out. (Photograph courtesy of Robert Guterl.)

Program and Cast

Stumpville Sewin' Circle,

Neshanic Station M. E. Church,

Friday Evening, November 19, 1909.

H. D. AGANS & CO.,

NESHANIC STATION, N. J.

A Clean Store with a Clean Stock.

Your money's worth or your money back without question.

Highest cash price paid for Fresh Eggs.

Orders taken and delivered free of charge.

Agents for the

Celebrated Bridgeport Standard Paint

GIVE US A TRIAL.

This is the cover of the program for *Stumpville Sewin' Circle*. (Courtesy of Harold Van Fleet.)

AUNT JULIA'S PEARLS

A Hope Moulton Comedy

Presented by

NESHANIC EPWORTH LEAGUERS

(CHARACTERS)

Mr. Richard Hunter, *a successful business man*..............Schenck Bergen

Mrs. Margaret Hunter, *his wife who has lost all interest in her appearance* Marie Runke

Betty, *Their daughter who isn't backward about speaking her mind* Ada Smith

Jim. *Their son, who wastes a lot of time tinkering with the family fliver* Donald Hoff

Claire Nelson, *Jim's fiancee, who has clever ideas*..............Grace Doyle

Marmaduke Waldron, a *foppish young man, who appears harmless but isn't*,..............Verian Quick

Aunt Julia, *an elderly relative just arrived from India, who isn't all she seems to be*,..............William Kip

Mr. William Somers, *Her New York lawyer, who has an observing eye* Robert May

Time — *The Present*

Place — *Any small suburb.*

Synopsis

Act I—*Hunters living room, morning*

Act II—*Same, a week later.*

Act III—*Same, early evening two days later.*

This is the cover of the program for *Aunt Julia's Pearls*. (Courtesy of Harold Van Fleet.)

Shown here is the flyer for *St. Patrick's Dance*. (Courtesy of Harold Van Fleet.)

St. Patrick's Dance

at the

Neshanic Firemen's Hall

Neshanic Station, New Jersey

FRIDAY EVENING MARCH 25, 1938

Music by

Hi - De - Ho Boy's of Elizabeth

Sponsored By

NESHANIC SOCIAL CLUB

YOU'RE A SWEETHEART

Chorus

You're a sweetheart if there ever was one,
If there ever was one it's you.
Life without you was an incomplete dream,
You are ev'ry sweet dream come true:
My search was such a blind one and I was all at sea,
I never thought I'd find one quite so perfect for me.
You're a sweetheart if there ever was one.
If there ever was one it's you.

I SEE YOUR FACE BEFORE ME

I see your face before me
Crowding my ev'ry dream
This is your face before me
You are my only Theme
It doesn't matter where you are
I can see how fair you are
I close my eyes and there you are always
If you could share the magic
If you could see me too
There would be nothing tragic
In all my dreams of you
Would that my love could haunt you so
Knowing I want you so
I can't erase your beautiful
Face before me.

Door Prizes :-: Refreshments

DANCING 9 to 1 - ADMISSION 40c

"CIVIL SERVICE"

or

"OLD R. F. D."

An American Drama in Three Acts.

PRESENTED BY THE
NESHANIC REFORMED CHURCH PLAYERS

CAST OF CHARACTERS:-
(In the order of their appearance)

The Mailing Clerk, Simpson Peavy.....William Ackerman
The Post Master's Daughter, Octavia Reynolds.....Mrs. Geo. B. Scholten
The Young Money-Order Clerk, Steve Audaine.....John Bittle
The Post Master, J. L. Reynolds.....George Quick
Old R. F. D., A Mystery.....Herbert Bingham
The Country Boy, Goldie Wex.....Tom Bray
A Collector, Miss Goldstein.....Mrs. George Quick
A Lady of Importance, Mrs. T. R. Jeffs.....Mrs. Herbert Bingham
The Plucky Little Stamp-Clerk, Kate Kenyon.....Dorothy Van Liew
A Hired Girl, Birdie Bivins,.....Elizabeth Rue
The Inspector, B. J. Cochran.....John C. Lane

Time — The Present.

Place — A Small City in the Middle West.

Act I— The Work-Room of a Postoffice. The Saturday after Christmas The Thief.

Act II— Same as Act I. A Week Later. ..... The Trial.

Act III— Same as Acts I and II The Next Morning. ..... The New Life

Shown here is the program for *Civil Service*. (Courtesy of Harold Van Fleet.)

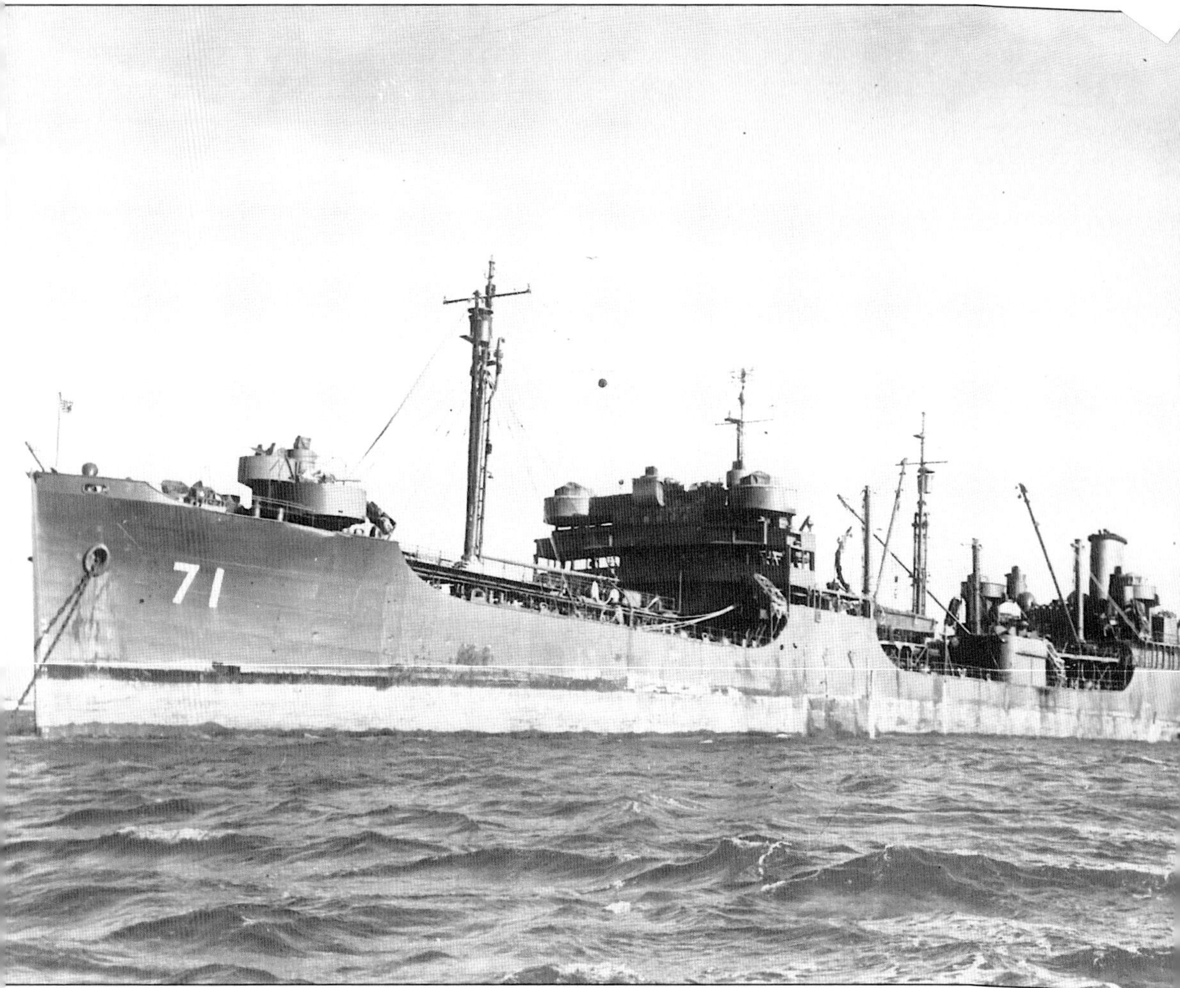

An auxiliary oiler named for the Neshanic River, the USS *Neshanic* was launched at Sparrows Point, Maryland, by Bethlehem Steel. Following shakedown, she sailed from Hampton Roads. (During WW II, auxiliary ships were named for rivers.) In convoy in April 1943, she steamed with a full cargo of petroleum for the Pacific islands. She served in the Solomons, Tarawa, Hawaii, and the Aleutian Islands. Off Saipan, she was hit on deck with a bomb, which injured 33 of her damage control party. Later, she served in Tokyo Bay. On her return to Norfolk, Virginia, she was decommissioned on December 19, 1945, having been awarded nine battle stars during WW II. She was sold to Gulf Oil Corp., and after serving in the Great Lakes, she was eventually scrapped. (Photograph and records from the Office of Chief of Naval Operations, Volume V, 1970. Courtesy of Thomas E. Tisza, who served in the Pacific as chief executive officer aboard Landing Ships.)